Register for Free Membership to

solutions@syngress.com

Over the last few years, Syngress has published many best-selling and critically acclaimed books, including Tom Shinder's *Configuring ISA Server 2000*, Brian Caswell and Jay Beale's *Snort 2.1 Intrusion Detection*, and Angela Orebaugh and Gilbert Ramirez's *Ethereal Packet Sniffing*. One of the reasons for the success of these books has been our unique **solutions@syngress.com** program. Through this site, we've been able to provide readers a real time extension to the printed book.

As a registered owner of this book, you will qualify for free access to our members-only solutions@syngress.com program. Once you have registered, you will enjoy several benefits, including:

- Four downloadable e-booklets on topics related to the book. Each booklet is approximately 20-30 pages in Adobe PDF format. They have been selected by our editors from other best-selling Syngress books as providing topic coverage that is directly related to the coverage in this book.

- A comprehensive FAQ page that consolidates all of the key points of this book into an easy-to-search web page, providing you with the concise, easy-to-access data you need to perform your job.

- A "From the Author" Forum that allows the authors of this book to post timely updates, links to related sites, or additional topic coverage that may have been requested by readers.

Just visit us at **www.syngress.com/solutions** and follow the simple registration process. You will need to have this book with you when you register.

Thank you for giving us the opportunity to serve your needs. And be sure to let us know if ~~~~~ anything else we can do to make your job easier.

D1383313

SYNGRESS®

Sarbanes-Oxley
IT Compliance Using
COBIT and Open Source Tools

Christian B. Lahti

Roderick Peterson

KEY	SERIAL NUMBER
001	HJIRTCV764
002	PO9873D5FG
003	829KM8NJH2
004	GHJ87DRPL4
005	CVPLQ6WQ23
006	VBP965T5T5
007	HJJJ863WD3E
008	2987GVTWMK
009	629MP5SDJT
010	IMWQ295T6T

PUBLISHED BY
Syngress Publishing, Inc.
800 Hingham Street
Rockland, MA 02370

Sarbanes-Oxley IT Compliance Using COBIT and Open Source Tools

Publisher: Andrew Williams   Page Layout and Art: Patricia Lupien
Acquisitions Editor: Gary Byrne   Copy Editors: Beth Roberts and Judy Eby
Cover Designer: Michael Kavish   Indexer: J. Edmund Rush

Distributed by O'Reilly Media, Inc. in the United States and Canada.
For information on rights, translations, and bulk purchases, contact Matt Pedersen, Director of Sales and Rights, at Syngress Publishing; email matt@syngress.com or fax to 781-681-3585.

Acknowledgments

Syngress would like to acknowledge the following people for their kindness and support in making this book possible.

Syngress books are now distributed in the United States and Canada by O'Reilly Media, Inc. The enthusiasm and work ethic at O'Reilly are incredible, and we would like to thank everyone there for their time and efforts to bring Syngress books to market: Tim O'Reilly, Laura Baldwin, Mark Brokering, Mike Leonard, Donna Selenko, Bonnie Sheehan, Cindy Davis, Grant Kikkert, Opol Matsutaro, Steve Hazelwood, Mark Wilson, Rick Brown, Leslie Becker, Jill Lothrop, Tim Hinton, Kyle Hart, Sara Winge, C. J. Rayhill, Peter Pardo, Leslie Crandell, Regina Aggio, Pascal Honscher, Preston Paull, Susan Thompson, Bruce Stewart, Laura Schmier, Sue Willing, Mark Jacobsen, Betsy Waliszewski, Dawn Mann, Kathryn Barrett, John Chodacki, Rob Bullington, and Aileen Berg.

The incredibly hardworking team at Elsevier Science, including Jonathan Bunkell, Ian Seager, Duncan Enright, David Burton, Rosanna Ramacciotti, Robert Fairbrother, Miguel Sanchez, Klaus Beran, Emma Wyatt, Chris Hossack, Krista Leppiko, Marcel Koppes, Judy Chappell, Radek Janousek, and Chris Reinders for making certain that our vision remains worldwide in scope.

David Buckland, Marie Chieng, Lucy Chong, Leslie Lim, Audrey Gan, Pang Ai Hua, Joseph Chan, and Siti Zuraidah Ahmad of STP Distributors for the enthusiasm with which they receive our books.

David Scott, Tricia Wilden, Marilla Burgess, Annette Scott, Andrew Swaffer, Stephen O'Donoghue, Bec Lowe, Mark Langley, and Anyo Geddes of Woodslane for distributing our books throughout Australia, New Zealand, Papua New Guinea, Fiji, Tonga, Solomon Islands, and the Cook Islands.

Authors

Christian Lahti is a computer services consultant with more than 15 years' experience in the IT industry. He is an expert in security, systems, and networking, having developed and implemented global IT infrastructures with a focus on Linux and open source, as well as providing consulting expertise for successful cross-platform integrations and interoperability. In addition, he is also skilled in database design and Web development. Christian is a speaker and tutorial presenter at both LinuxWorld and O'Reilly's OSCON. He was a technical editor and contributing author to *Windows to Linux Migration Toolkit* (Syngress Publishing, ISBN: 1-931836-39-6).

Roderick Peterson is currently employed at NeoMagic as Information Technology Director. He has more than 20 years' experience in the IT industry. His diverse background includes knowledge of mainframe operations, LAN, Internet, IT infrastructure, business applications, and the integration of emerging technologies. He has successfully led the development and deployment of major applications at several global companies. He also successfully owned and operated an IT consulting business for more than five years.

Contributors

Steve Lanza has more than 20 years of business experience ranging from Fortune 500 to small private and public companies. He has held positions responsible for Global Business Operations, Sales, Marketing, Manufacturing, Finance, Administration, Business Development, and Engineering along with being a Public and Private Company Chief Financial Officer. His current position is Executive Vice President, Operations and Business Development, Chief Financial Officer responsible for Sales, Operations, Marketing, Finance, and Administration of a private technology company. He has a Bachelor of Science Degree in Finance from Cal Poly in San Luis Obispo, an MBA from GGU, and a Certificate in Engineering Management from Cal Tech (IRC). He also is a Certified Management Accountant (CMA).

Chris Riccomini is currently enrolled as a computer science major at Santa Clara University. He takes an active interest in computers and is currently employed part-time at a tech company in Silicon Valley. In addition to work on eGroupWare's workflow application, he has been instrumental in various other projects involving PHP and MySQL.

Author Acknowledgments

When you sit down to write a book, it is often true that you believe the process will be a relatively straightforward undertaking. Unfortunately, this is sometimes not the case, as the effort required to complete the task can be easily underestimated. It is with this admission that I wish to sincerely thank my wife, Patricia, who graciously suffered through the pregnancy of our first child, shielding me from her personal needs in order to allow me the time to finish this book among other projects. For being supportive, even in the time when I should have been more so in return, I am grateful. I would also like to thank Chris Riccomini. Without his efforts in molding our ideas into workflows, we would have been far worse off in our compliance efforts, and this book would have been less than it is. I wish him success in his endeavors beyond school and out into the wild beyond.

—*Christian B. Lahti*

I was once told there are only two tragedies in life, not getting what you want and getting what you want. As with most quotes, this quote is frequently paraphrased. The actual quote is from George Bernard Shaw: "Life contains but two tragedies. One is not to get your heart's desire; the other is to get it." I fully agree with George Bernard Shaw. Life truly has a circuitous way of teaching us lessons. Up until writing this book I would read the acknowledgments of other books with cynicism and for amusement. Having to write during every free moment in order to complete this book, I often found myself saying to friends and loved ones, "I would like to, but I really need to work on the book." I now realize why writers often acknowledge so many people, because the time you spend writing is not just your time; it is family's and friends' time as well. So, with that said, I would like to acknowledge Theresa Peterson, my wife of 24 years, for her patience with me during this project and all the many projects I have had during our 24 years together. Thank you! I would like to say thank-you to my children, Tiffiny Peterson, Trinity (Bud) Peterson, and Byron Austin, for their understanding. I also want to acknowledge various family members: my mother, Daisy Peterson, for keeping me focused during the writing of the book; my aunt, Thelma Williams; and my sisters Beverly Kennedy, Debbie Bass, Cynthia Peterson, and Yolanda Peterson for endeavoring to read my material. I would like to thank my colleague Giri Uppuganti for the many conversations we had that I drew upon for inspiration when I needed a subject for the book.

Although he is no longer with us, lastly, I would like to thank my uncle, Elbert Charles Peterson, who spent many a late night listening to me and giving me his insights into life. Those conversations and his impact on my life enabled me to persevere while writing this book.

—*Roderick W. Peterson*

Contents

Chapter 1 Overview: The Goals of This Book **1**

The Audit Experience: An Introduction 2

   What This Book Is 4

   What This Book Is Not 5

      Disclaimer 5

The Audit Experience: An Introduction 2

Who Should Read This Book? 6

The Live CD Concept 8

   Running the CD 9

   Retaining Changes You've Made 10

   Installing to Your Hard Drive .11

The Portals 16

   SiteManager 17

      Main 17

      Launch Pad 18

      Reference 18

   Home 19

   Admin 19

   Email 20

   Calendar 20

   Address Book 20

   InfoLog 20

   Fud Forum 21

   Projects 21

   Wiki 21

      Wiki Page Header 22

      Wiki Page Footer 22

   Bookmarks 23

   News Admin 23

   Knowledge Base 23

Workflow 24
Summary 25
Solutions Fast Track 26
Frequently Asked Questions .28

Chapter 2 SOX and COBIT Defined 31
SOX Overview 32
What Will SOX Accomplish? 32
Section 302 33
Section 404 33
SOX: Not Just a Dark Cloud 33
Why IT COBIT? 34
The Six COBIT Components 35
Entity Level Controls versus Control Objectives 36
What Are the Four COBIT Domains? 37
Planning and Organization 37
Acquisition and Implementation 37
Delivery and Support 37
Monitoring 37
Are the Developers of COBIT Controls Crazy? Is This
Practical? 38
What Controls Should I Use? 45
Server Room 45
Desktops 45
Outsourced Services 46
Outsourced Services 46
Planning and Organization 47
Acquire and Implement 48
Delivery and Support 48
Monitor and Evaluate .49
Sustainability Is the Key 50
Summary 53
Solutions Fast Track 53
Frequently Asked Questions .57

Chapter 3 The Cost of Compliance 59

Overview 60
  Section 404 60
Why Comply? 61
Tools and Applications .62
  What's Out There? 64
    Security 64
    Monitoring 66
    Change Management 68
    Logical Access 69
    Kerberos 69
    PAM 69
The Human Factor 69
Walk the Walk 72
BuiltRight Construction Company 73
  Information Technology 73
    1.0 Overview 73
    2.0 Purpose 74
    3.0 Scope 74
    4.0 Policy 74
    4.1 General 74
    4.2 Guidelines 74
    4.2.1 General Password Construction Guidelines 74
    4.2.2 Password Protection Standards 75
    4.3 System Policy 75
    5.0 Review 76
    6.0 Enforcement 76
Summary 77
Solutions Fast Track 78
Frequently Asked Questions 80

Chapter 4 Why Open Source? 81

The Open Source Model .82
Closed Source Application Development 83
  Application Requirements 84
  System Design and Application Development 85
  Debugging and Regression Testing 86

Customer Beta Testing and Application Release 86

Bug Fixes and Support Cycle 86

Open Source Application Development 87

Application Requirements 88

System Design and Application Development 89

Application Release, Debugging, and Bug Fixes 90

The Business Case for Open Source 91

Free ! = No Cost 91

Distribution Vendors 92

Project Developers 92

In-House 92

Does It Really Save Money? 93

Get Off the Merry-Go-Round 94

Platform-Agnostic Architecture 94

Open Source and Windows 94

Mixed Platforms 95

Migration: a Work in Progress 95

Assessing Your Infrastructure 96

Open Source for IT Systems 97

Open Source to Support Proprietary Systems 98

Case Studies: Introduction to the Sample Companies 98

BuiltRight Construction Company 99

IT Infrastructure 99

Server Room 99

Desktops 100

Network Topology 100

NuStuff Electronics, Inc. 101

IT Infrastructure 101

Server Room (General, Sales, Support, and Executive) 101

Server Room (Engineering and Design) 102

Desktops (Sales, Support, and Executive) 102

Desktops (Engineering and Design) 102

Network Topology 102

Summary 105

Solutions Fast Track 106

Frequently Asked Questions 109

Chapter 5 Domain I: Planning and Organization 111

Overview 112
The Work Starts Here 112
What Work? 113
What Do Planning and Organization Mean? 114
    1. Define a Strategic IT Plan 115
    2. Define the Information Architecture 115
    3. Determine Technological Direction 116
    4. Define the IT Organization and Relationships . . .116
    5. Manage the IT Investment 117
    6. Communicate Management Aims and Direction . .117
    7. Manage Human Resources 118
    8. Ensure Compliance with External Requirements .118
    9. Assess Risks 118
    10. Manage Projects 118
    11. Manage Quality 119
Working the List 120
NuStuff Electronics Inc. 121
    Information Technology .121
        Single-Page Strategy 121
        Financial Summary 122
FastTrack CD 125
    The Players 125
Policy Management 127
    BuiltRight Corporate Policy Documents 128
    NuStuff Corporate Policy Documents 130
    Defining Your Own Policies 132
    Policy Approval Workflow 133
        Workflow Roles .134
        Workflow Activities 135
    Defining Your Own Policy Approval Workflows 135
Summary 137
Solutions Fast Track 137
Frequently Asked Questions 139

Chapter 6 Domain II: Acquisition and Implementation 141

Overview 142
Evaluating In-House Expertise .142
    Deployment and Support Proficiency Considerations 143
    Addressing Deficiencies .145
Automation Is the Name of the Game 146
What Do Acquisition and Implementation Mean? 147
    1. Identify Automated Solutions 148
        1.1 Definition of Information Requirements
        (Repositioning) 148
        1.10 Audit Trails Design (SOX) 148
        1.15 Third-Party Software Maintenance
        (Repositioning) 149
    2. Acquire and Maintain Application Software 149
        2.2 Major Changes to Existing Systems (SOX and
        Repositioning) 149
        2.8 Definition of Interfaces (SOX) 149
        2.14 IT Integrity Provisions in Application Program
        Software (SOX) 149
        2.15 Definition of Interfaces (SOX) 150
    3. Acquire and Maintain Technology Infrastructure 150
        3.3 System Software Security (SOX) 150
        3.5 System Software Maintenance (SOX and
        Repositioning) 150
        3.6 System Software Change Controls (SOX) 150
        3.7 Use and Monitoring of System Utilities (SOX) .150
    4. Develop and Maintain Procedures 150
        4.1 Operational Requirements and Service Levels . .151
        4.3 Operations Manual .151
    5. Install and Accredit Systems 151
    6. Manage Changes 151
        6.1 Change Request Initiation and Control (SOX and
        Repositioning) 152
        6.2 Impact Assessment (Repositioning) 152
        6.3 Control of Changes (SOX and Repositioning) . .152
        6.4 Emergency Changes (SOX and Repositioning) .152

6.5 Documentation and Procedures (SOX and
Repositioning) 152
6.6 Authorized Maintenance (SOX) 152
Working the List 153
FastTrack CD 154
Automation and Workflow 154
BuiltRight Construction Example
Implementation: Web Server Migration 155
NuStuff Electronics Example Implementation:
Intrusion Detection System 156
Infrastructure Change Request Workflow 157
Workflow Roles 158
Workflow Activities 159
Implementation Planning 160
BuiltRight Construction Web Server Migration 160
NuStuff Electronics Snort IDS 161
Implementation 163
Documentation 164
Other Change Management Workflow Examples 165
Firewall Change Request 165
Oracle Change Request .166
Summary 169
Solutions Fast Track 170
Frequently Asked Questions 172

Chapter 7 Domain III: Delivery and Support 175
Overview 176
What Do Delivery and Support Mean? 177
1. Define and Manage Service Level Agreements 178
1.2 Aspects of SLAs (SOX and Repositioning) 178
1.3 Monitoring and Reporting (Repositioning) 178
1.4 Review of SLAs and Contracts (Repositioning) 178
2. Manage Third-Party Services 178
2.4 Third-Party Qualifications (SOX and
Repositioning) 178
2.7 Security Relationships (SOX) 179
2.8 Monitoring (Repositioning) 179

3. Manage Performance and Capacity 179
    3.2 Availability Plan (Repositioning) 179
    3.3 Monitoring and Reporting (SOX and
    Repositioning) 179
    3.4 Proactive Performance Management (SOX and
    Repositioning) 179
    3.8 Resources Availability (SOX and Repositioning) 179
4. Ensure Continuous Service 180
    4.12 Off-Site Backup Storage (SOX) 180
5. Ensure Systems Security 180
    5.2 Identification, Authentication, and Access (SOX) 180
    5.3 Security of Online Access to Data (SOX) 180
    5.4 User Account Management (SOX) 180
    5.5 Management Review of User Accounts (SOX)   180
    5.8 Data Classification (SOX) 180
    5.9 Central Identification and Access Rights
    Management 181
    5.10 Violation and Security Activity Reports (SOX) 181
    5.19 Malicious Software Prevention, Detection, and
    Correction (SOX) 181
    5.20 Firewall Architectures and Connections with
    Public Networks (SOX) 181
6. Identify and Allocate Costs .181
7. Educate and Train Users 181
    7.3 Security Principles and Awareness Training (SOX) 182
8. Assist and Advise Customers 182
    8.2 Registration of Customer Queries (SOX
    and Repositioning) 182
    8.3 Customer Query Escalation 182
    8.4 Monitoring of Clearance (SOX
    and Repositioning) 182
    8.5 Trend Analysis and Reporting (SOX and
    Repositioning) 182
9. Manage the Configuration .182
    9.4 Configuration Control 183
    9.5 Unauthorized Software (SOX) 183

9.7 Configuration Management Procedures 183
10. Manage Problems and Incidents 183
10.1 Problem Management System (SOX) 183
10.2 Problem Escalation (SOX) 183
11. Manage Data 183
11.23 Backup and Restoration (SOX) 183
11.24 Backup Jobs (SOX) 184
12. Manage Facilities 184
12.1 Physical Security (SOX) 184
12.3 Visitor Escort (SOX) 184
12.5 Protection Against Environmental Factors 184
12.6 Uninterruptible Power Supply (SOX) 184
13. Manage Operations 184
13.6 Operations Logs 185
13.8 Remote Operations (SOX) 185
Working the List 185
Performance, Capacity, and SLAs 186
SLAs 186
What Is an SLA? 187
Key SLA Elements 187
Template: Internal SLA 188
Fault Tolerance 189
High Availability 192
Load Balancing 194
System and Application Security 197
Network Security 197
Enterprise Identity Management 198
Security 199
Transparency 199
Reliability 199
Scalability 199
Authentication Systems .199
Data and Storage 201
Systems and Applications .203
Account Management 203
Password Policy Enforcement 204

Administrator Roles 206
Configuration and Data Management 206
Systems and Network Devices 207
Application Data and Backups 207
FastTrack CD 208
SLAs 208
Webmin 209
Security and Operations Workflows 210
Account Activation Request 210
Account Termination Request 211
Oracle Account Activation Request 211
Oracle Account Termination Request 212
Data Access Request 212
Data Restoration Request 213
Report a Virus or Spyware 213
Virtual Private Network Access Request 214
Sample Configurations 214
Authentication Cluster (NuStuff Electronics) 215
Web Server (BuiltRight Construction) 215
Summary 216
Solutions Fast Track 217
Frequently Asked Questions .220

Chapter 8 Domain IV: Monitoring 223
Overview 224
What Does Monitoring Mean? 224
Deming's PDCA Cycle 225
1. Monitor the Processes 226
1.2. Assessing Performance (SOX and Repositioning) 226
1.3. Assessing Customer Satisfaction (SOX and
Repositioning) 227
2. Assess Internal Control Adequacy 227
Working the List 228
Monitoring in Practice 228
Monitoring with Nagios 229
Architecture 229
Nagios Monitor Targets .229

Nagios Plugins 231
Nagios Escalations 232
Configuration Monitoring 233
Syslog 233
Tripwire and Advanced Intrusion Detection
Environment (AIDE) 233
Kiwi CatTools 234
Compliance Monitoring 234
FastTrack CD 234
Nagios by Example 234
Nagios Configuration 235
Nagios Monitoring of Windows Hosts 236
Nagios Integration with syslog 237
Compliance Workflows 238
Annual Oracle Admin Review 238
Bi-annual IT Policy Review 238
Monthly Data Restoration Test 239
Monthly Off-site Backup 239
Monthly Oracle Active User Review 239
Quarterly AV Inventory Report 240
Quarterly File Permissions Review 240
Quarterly Infrastructure Change Review 241
Quarterly Oracle DBA Review 241
Quarterly Oracle System Defaults Review 242
Quarterly Security and Monitoring Review 242
Quarterly VPN Access Review 242
Gluing Nagios and Workflow Together 243
Rolling Your Own Workflows .245
Workflow Configuration 245
Basic Workflow Example: General IT Request 245
Creating the Process 246
Creating Roles 247
Creating Activities 248
Code and Templates 250
Request IT Help 250
Handle IT Request 252

    Close IT Request 253
    End 254
  Testing 255
  Advanced Topics 256
    Switches 256
    File Uploading 257
    Wiki Integration 258
    Schedule Processes (CRON) 258
  Summary 259
  Solutions Fast Track .259
  Frequently Asked Questions 261

Chapter 9 Putting It All Together **263**
  Overview 264
  Organization—Repositioning 265
  Policies, Processes, and Service Level Agreements (SLAs) . . .266
    SOX Process Flow 267
  Control Matrices, Test Plan, and Components 268
    Control Matrix 268
    Gap and Remediation 270
    Test Plan 272
    What Makes a Good Test Plan 274
  Return on Investment (ROI) 275
  Summary 278
  Solutions Fast Track .278
  Frequently Asked Questions 280

Appendix A COBIT Control Objectives **281**
  Planning and Organization 282
    1. Define a Strategic IT Plan 282
    2. Define the Information Architecture 282
    3. Determine Technological Direction 282
    4. Define the IT Organization and Relationships 283
    5. Manage the IT Investment 283
    6. Communicate Management Aims and Direction 283
    7. Manage Human Resources 284
    8. Ensure Compliance with External Requirements . . .284

9. Assess Risks 285
10. Manage Projects 285
11. Manage Quality 285
Acquisition and Implementation .286
1. Identify Automated Solutions 286
2. Acquire and Maintain Application Software 287
3. Acquire and Maintain Technology Infrastructure 288
4. Develop and Maintain Procedures 288
5. Install and Accredit Systems 288
6. Manage Changes 289
Delivery and Support 289
1. Define and Manage Service Levels 289
2. Manage Third-Party Services 290
3. Manage Performance and Capacity 290
4. Ensure Continuous Service 290
5. Ensure Systems Security .291
6. Identify and Allocate Costs 292
7. Educate and Train Users .292
8. Assist and Advise Customers 292
9. Manage the Configuration 292
10. Manage Problems and Incidents 293
11. Manage Data 293
12. Manage Facilities 294
13. Manage Operations 294
Monitoring 295
1. Monitor the Processes 295
2. Assess Internal Control Adequacy 295
3. Obtain Independent Assurance 295
4. Provide for Independent Audit 296

Appendix B KNOPPIX Live CD Parameters 297
Cheat Codes 298
lang=bg|be|ch|cn|cs|cz|da|de|dk|es|fi|fr|ie|it
|ja|nl|pl|ru|sk|tr|tw|uk|us 298
keyboard=us 298
xkeyboard=us 298
atapicd 298

screen=1280x1024 298

xvrefresh=60 or vsync=60 298

xhrefresh=80 or hsync=80 298

xserver=XFree86 | XF86_SVGA 298

xmodule=ati | radeon | fbdev | vesa | savage | s3 | nv | i810
| mga | svga | tseng 298

2 299

myconfig=scan | floppyconfig | floppyconf 299

myconf=/dev/sda1 299

myconf=scan (or config=scan) 299

noapic noagp noapm nodma nomce nofirewire nopcmcia
noscsi noswap nousb nosmp noaudio 299

pci=irqmask=0x0e98 299

ide2=0x180 nopcmia 300

pci=biosirq 300

mem=128M 300

noeject 300

noprompt 300

nodhcp 300

splash 300

modules-disk 301

toram 301

tohd 301

fromhd 301

bootfrom=/dev/hda1 301

bootfrom=/dev/hda1/KNX.iso 301

gmt | uce 302

vga=normal 302

vga=ext 302

dma 302

home=scan 302

blind 302

brltty=type,port,table 302

alsa 302

alsa=es1938 302

testcd 303

pnpbios=off 303
acpi=off 303
pci=bios 303
knoppix_dir=KNOPPIX 303
knoppix_name=KNOPPIX .303
Kernels 303
knoppix or linux 303
knoppix26 or linux26 303
knoppix26 acpi=off or linux26 acpi=off 304
knoppix-txt 304
fb1280x1024 or fb1024x768 or fb800x600 304
failsafe 304
expert 304
expert26 304
knoppix –b 304
memtest 304

Appendix C The GNU General Public License 305
Version 2, June 1991 305
Preamble 306
Terms and Conditions for Copying, Distribution and
Modification 307

Appendix D CD Contents at a Glance 315
Main Toolbar 316
BuiltRight Construction Site Index 317
Main 317
Home Page 317
Portal 317
Launch Pad 317
The Other Side 317
Webmin Admin 317
Nagios Monitoring 317
Reference 318
Bookmarks and Links 318
Knowledge Base 318
Sample Configurations .318

NuStuff Electronics Site Index 319

    Main 320

        Home Page 320

        Portal 320

    Launch Pad 320

        The Other Side 320

        Webmin Admin 320

        Nagios Monitoring 320

    Reference 320

        Bookmarks and Links 320

        Knowledge Base 320

        Sample Configurations 320

Index. **325**

Chapter 1

Overview: The Goals of This Book

Solutions in this chapter:

- The Audit Experience: An Introduction
- What This Book Is
- What This Book Is Not
- Who Should Read This Book
- The "Live" CD Concept
- The Portals

☑ Summary

☑ Solutions Fast Track

☑ Frequently Asked Questions

The Audit Experience: An Introduction

Imagine yourself as Bob, the busy IT manager of a moderately sized company. You are trying to stay on top of the daily problems of the environment—user needs, new systems to deploy, the normal. You have noticed a few unfamiliar faces, provided access to the guest network and perhaps a phone extension for them in the Accounting department while they are busy humming away, bustling back and forth between the CIO and the Controller's office muttering something about a big audit coming up. "Big deal, we always have an annual audit," you say to yourself as you toil away at the operational tasks to be done. While chatting in the office kitchen with Beth the accounts payables clerk about the activity in her department, you notice she looks a bit harried as she mutters something about having to produce yet another set of reports for the auditors. "Well, the IT department is involved in the annual audit every year, and we haven't had any major problems so far," you comment, giving her a consoling pat on the shoulder as you walk away. Thinking about the audit, the auditors seem to ask the same set of questions from the same set of papers, and your response pages must be rote to them. Oh well, business as usual, until…

Your phone rings, and you are called into a meeting with the CEO, CIO, and Controller to discuss this "SOX" thing. The expected crowd is there along with a couple of those slightly familiar faces you have seen around the office. "Bob, this is Bill and Jane from WeHelpU Consulting, and they have been spending the past couple of months helping us to prepare for our Sarbanes-Oxley audit," says the CIO. The consultants go on to explain that they are there to help Finance analyze their business processes and reporting structures for the financial chain, and after a few minutes your eyes begin to glaze over so you decide to read your e-mail; after all, meetings are the best time to catch up on this sort of thing. You nod a few times when your name is mentioned, catching phrases here and there such as "control objectives" and "material weakness"…say that doesn't sound too good. Wait a minute! You suddenly realize these people have been here for *several months* and you are just now getting dragged into something that you instantly know you really don't want any part of, but it is becoming apparent that unfortunately you will have no choice in the matter. Moreover, these people are all acting as if you have been clued in from day one! "Ok, no problem" you say after listening to them intently, "we will just revamp the old audit material from last year and add to it what we need." Everyone agrees that it sounds like a reasonable place to start, and the meeting is adjourned, but somewhere in the back of your mind, something tells you this is going to be anything but the ordinary run-of-the-mill audit. It would be unwise for you to ignore that feeling, because it happens to be true.

Whether this story has any shred of similarity to your introduction to the seemingly long road to Sarbanes-Oxley compliance, the fact is that as an IT professional, whether you are a system administrator or a CIO, at some point this will become a major blip on your radar screen if you work for a publicly held company.

NOTE

Even if you are not an IT professional, we hope you will continue to read this book, as there are many reasons why you might need to understand how IT relates to SOX compliance, and more importantly, how open source fits into the discussion. Whether you are an auditor or finance professional, we attempt to put into perspective some of the items covered that would be of interest to you later in this chapter.

So, what exactly is this Sarbanes-Oxley, and why do I care? You might ask this question, and in Chapter 2, "SOX and COBIT Defined," we delve into this subject in (probably) excruciating detail, so we won't spoil you with details just yet. When we set out to write this book, we thought is was important to give you an idea of what this book is really about, and the audience for whom it is intended. First, a few facts and figures from some annotated sources:

- U.S. public companies are spending $4.36 million each, on average, to comply with Section 404 of Sarbanes-Oxley (March 2005 survey conducted by Financial Executives International).

- Sun Microsystems' CEO, Scott McNealy, calls the new law aimed at preventing future Enrons and other corporate bad behavior a disaster. It's so time consuming and laden with red tape that it's like throwing "buckets of sand into the gears of the market economy." (*USA Today*, August 2003).

- In a poll of 190 companies on SOX compliance activities, nearly 50 percent indicated that they would conduct more than 5,000 discrete control activities in 2005 (*Business Finance Magazine*, March 2005).

- Many companies are now planning to invest in technology to ensure they can sustain compliance. Thirty-six percent plan to increase spending, while 52 percent plan to maintain current levels. (*AMR Research* survey, March 2005)

So what does this mean? You might surmise from the figures cited in the previous list that Sarbanes-Oxley compliance is proving to be an expensive, resource-intensive undertaking and that IT plays an integral role in that process.

The Transparency Test...

The CFO Perspective

"Today's managers have a tremendous number of areas clamoring for their attention. Unfortunately, to remain a public company, or become one if you are private, Sarbanes-Oxley is dominating the priorities. While there is no debating the detrimental impact the Enrons and TYCOs have had on the investor community, and that corporate governance and control did need to increase, it is not at all clear that the monies and time spent on Sarbanes-Oxley are merited. Hopefully, approaches such as those included here will begin to streamline the process and the time and cost involved with being certified, and thus allow top management to return their focus to market share, profitability and growth." — *Steve Lanza*

What This Book Is

This book is essentially a technical book, with as much applicable content as we could muster by way of open source technologies and how they fit into the Sarbanes-Oxley sphere of influence. That being said, by reading Chapter 2 and perhaps Chapter 3, "The Cost of Compliance," you might get the feeling that this book has very little to do with *implementing* open source, since the subject matter seems geared toward explaining the business side of the equation.

We apologize.

The Sarbanes-Oxley affair will inevitably permeate your organization, making it a requirement that IT staff—from the CIO to the network engineer and desktop support personnel—have a certain level of understanding of what Sarbanes-Oxley means, some of the hows and whys of business processes, and the impact this will have on their day-to-day jobs. In fact, Sarbanes-Oxley is so far reaching that virtually every person in your organization will be affected to some degree. Therefore, as a reader, one could view this as two books in one. On one hand, we delve into the business processes and organizational considerations surrounding SOX and open source, and in the next breath we talk about specific tools and implementation strategies on how best to exploit the applicable open source technologies. We will endeavor to keep the former at a level so that it serves as a frame of reference for the more technological discussions. If you happen to get anything remotely related to satisfaction reading either aspects, or both, we have served our purpose.

By way of analogy, we like to compare the SOX audit experience with becoming pregnant. During your term, you can choose to not change your daily routine, and ignore the impending reality of birth by eating the wrong foods and not exercising. That is certainly your right; however, once labor begins, those extra 20 pounds and the shortness of breath after 10 minutes of effort are going to make for a very long and unpleasant experience. Alternatively, you could do the opposite and prepare yourself as much as possible by eating healthy foods, attending breathing classes, and practicing yoga for instance. As with anything in life, these activities are no guarantee that you will have an easy and cheery birthing experience, but most assuredly you *are* guaranteeing an unpleasant if not terrible encounter if you do not adequately prepare. We hope this serves as a guide, to be your coach and show you a few things to help you survive with your sanity intact, and perhaps save a buck or two.

What This Book Is Not

It would be impossible to write a book on "how to pass your SOX Audit." Every business is different in operation and philosophical approach, and we could not begin to write a do–this, do–that, and viola, somehow the auditors magically accept your IT infrastructure at face value and give you three gold stars. Speaking of IT, if you are looking for advice on anything remotely related to your finances, this is also not the book for you. This is a book written by geeks for geeks, even those at heart, and we make absolutely no attempt to embellish this with nuggets of wisdom on any other topic, including financial reporting. We do hope there are nuggets to be gleaned, but they are apt to be along the lines of "configure X to ensure the certificate can be used by both cluster nodes" for example, and it is important that we establish this up front. That being said, we need to get a little piece of subject matter out of the way.

Disclaimer

The authors of this book and Syngress Publishing do not assert that the use of this book or technologies presented herein will affect your Sarbanes-Oxley compliance efforts positively or negatively, and the contributors make no representation or warranties that the use of principles in this text will by its nature influence the outcome of an audit. Although many examples of IT controls, policies, procedures, and tests are presented, they are merely examples of what your controls might look like. However, since every business is different, readers should apply appropriate judgment to the specific control circumstances presented by their unique environment. This book has not received any endorsement from the SEC or any other standards-setting organization, and as such, companies should seek specific advice regarding SOX compliance from their respective auditors.

This book is intended to give the readers an understanding of how open source technology and tools might be applied to their individual requirements. However, without specific knowledge of your environment and business practices, it would be impossible for the authors to make specific recommendations in a work intended for general consumption.

Who Should Read This Book?

There are two main focuses on open source as it relates to the Sarbanes-Oxley discussion:

- If you have deployed or are considering the deployment of open source technologies in your IT organization, you might have concern on where or whether they fit in the compliant IT environment. We discuss various open source applications and then demonstrate—some by example and others by technical reference—a few of the example configurations that have passed a compliance audit.

- Regardless of what your IT landscape may be, there are many opportunities to make your life easier and even reduce the amount your audit may cost in terms of resources and money by employing open source technologies to help in the monitoring, process, and documentation of the various items that come under the SOX microscope.

Although there are many books and reference materials on the financial and business side of SOX compliance, very little material is available that directly addresses the information technology considerations, even less so on how open source software fits into that dialogue. This book, therefore, encompasses a wide range of readers who might find this useful, as the scope of Sarbanes-Oxley compliance includes all publicly traded companies in the United States regardless of their size or annual revenue. Here we attempt to illustrate what this book might mean to different individuals, namely:

- **CFO, VP, director of finance** Since the Sarbanes-Oxley act is squarely aimed at responsible financial controls and reporting, the executive finance team of any company should be interested in the ways open source can reduce their cost of compliance. Every chapter in the book begins with the management perspective of compliance as it relates to the subject material contained within. Even though you may not be in the IT department directly, you will have an over-arching understanding of how open source software can help.

- **CIO, VP, director of IT** This book focuses on the IT aspects of compliance, in both the use of open source software as the infrastructure components that make up the core IT footprint within the enterprise, and the use of open source software to assist and automate the task of documenting and tracking compliance and internal controls, independent of whether they are derived from proprietary or open source systems.

- **IT operations management, administration** Although the book deals with many of the management considerations in the deployment of open source software, the latter chapters deal with technical examples included in the book and on the accompanying Live CD. These tools and configurations provide a base of technical information that IT professionals can directly employ to streamline their compliance processes.

- **IT consultants** Since Sarbanes-Oxley compliance can be a daunting task, many organizations are choosing to outsource all or portions of their compliance preparation to third parties to leverage best-known methods and the success of other client audits to ensure their audit goes smoothly. This being the case, this book will arm the consultant with a powerful toolset in which to quickly and efficiently streamline the preparation process while avoiding the cost of proprietary software solutions. Consequently, they may be able to reduce their fees and win more business.

- **CEO, VP, owners of nonpublic companies** The specter of spending time, money, and resources on Sarbanes-Oxley compliance surely factors into the decision for a privately held company to go public. This book will assist those companies in assessing their infrastructure and compliance preparedness while avoiding the major expense involved in a formal audit. Owners and executives can also use some of the technical aspects of this book to lower their IT costs.

Lessons Learned...

Deja Vu All over Again

Back in 2000 when we were re-architecting all of the enterprise data storage, we interviewed the members of each department to find out how they currently stored their files and the typical usage model for access. As we defined what was currently out there, we attempted to reorganize and restructure most of this data to fit our project goals as an IT organization, which were manageability, security, and disaster recovery. During this process, we received considerable resistance to change, especially in the areas of file access and permissions. We ended up with a few compromises that *we* considered less than optimal; however, management did not provide top-down support for the changes we felt were necessary.

Fast forward to 2004. When we were going through our discovery phase for the SOX compliance audit, we again revisited many of the same topics we had previously covered with varying levels of success, including our storage footprint. We again identified changes and refinements that needed to be made for manageability, security, and disaster recovery, and again experienced the same resistance from the users. The main difference this time was the top-down support we received from management to make the necessary changes to meet our goals.

The moral of the story is that in some ways, Sarbanes-Oxley can be used as an enabler of IT initiatives. You can and should take advantage of your newfound backing to help more politically sensitive projects move forward, and although this is not necessarily a license to effect severe change, SOX can be immensely helpful in acquiring resources, financial commitment, and management support for important IT projects.

The Live CD Concept

The Live CD included with this book is a completely self-contained version of Linux and a collection of open source software and tools designed to be a companion to the examples used in Chapters 5 and beyond. You can boot the CD on any computer that can boot from a CD-ROM, which virtually all modern computers can do. The only other requirement is that the computer has at least 256MB of memory, and optionally a storage mechanism if you would like to save changes you make during your session. There is no need to worry about any operating system that might already be installed on the computer, such as Windows, since the CD creates its own file system in memory and will not disturb your existing setup.

This particular Live CD was originally based on the XFLD distribution, which is a derivative of the original Knoppix Live CD project. The main difference between Knoppix and XFLD is the use of the XFCE window manager instead of KDE, which we thought would be better for our purposes since the memory and resource requirements are much less. You should be able to run the Live CD on any x86 computer PII and higher as long as you meet the minimum memory requirements.

Running the CD

To run the CD, simply place the disc in your CD drive and boot the system. You will be automatically logged in as the user "knoppix," and a welcome dialog will appear with some useful options for you to explore. Figure 1.1 shows the default desktop.

TIP

You can pass many parameters to the boot that affect the way the Live CD will behave. For example, if you want to make sure the screen resolution is 1024 by 768, you can specify *xfld screen=1024x786* at the boot prompt. For a complete listing of boot options (Cheat Codes), refer to Appendix B, "Knoppix Live CD Parameters."

Figure 1.1 Live CD Welcome Screen

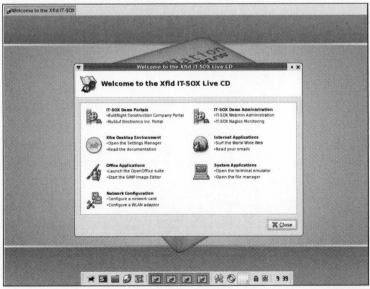

Retaining Changes You've Made

It is important to note that because the CD-ROM creates a virtual file system in memory, any changes made to the system will not be kept upon reboot. If you want to keep your changes, however, there is an option to save your changes to a removable device such as a USB pen drive, ZIP drive, or an available hard drive partition. While you could technically use a floppy disk, this is not a practical option, since the minimum space needed is 256MB. If you do decide to keep your changes, when you boot the CD subsequently, you must specify the following "Cheat Code" parameter at the boot prompt:

```
xfld home=scan
```

This will signal the CD boot manager to look for the pen drive or hard disk partition where you chose to save your changes. To create the initial saved configuration, use the following procedure. Figure 1.2 shows the menu option to initiate the configuration save procedure. Figure 1.3 shows the various options you can select for later retrieval, and Figure 1.4 shows the suitable destinations that have been automatically detected. You will want to make sure the Personal Configuration option is selected, as this will retain changes made to the applications, particularly to the sample company portals that are used in later chapters.

Figure 1.2 Live CD Save Configuration Menu Selection

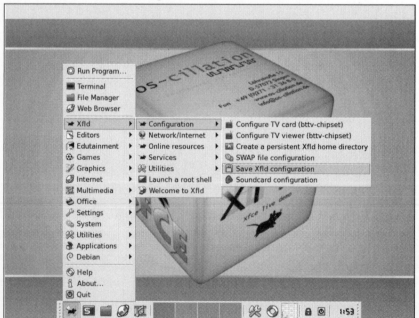

Figure 1.3 Live CD Save Configuration Options

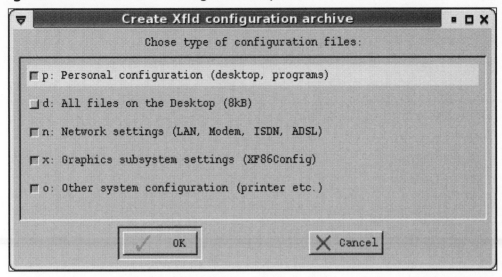

Figure 1.4 Live CD Save Configuration Destination Options

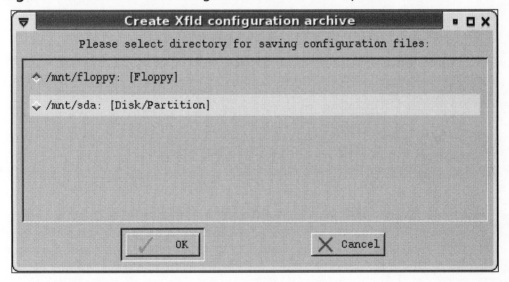

Installing to Your Hard Drive

If you have an available hard drive partition, you might choose to install the Live CD directly to disk. Doing so will enable you to make any changes you wish to the samples, and those changes will automatically be saved upon reboot without any special consideration. You will also enjoy a speed advantage, although the hardware requirements of the CD boot method are not very demanding. If you do opt for this choice, Figure 1.5 shows the menu option to initiate the procedure, followed by Figure 1.6, which shows the standard Knoppix installer dialog.

Figure 1.5 Live CD Install to Hard Disk Menu Option

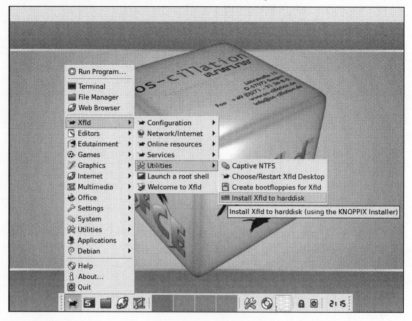

Figure 1.6 Live CD Install to Hard Disk Knoppix Notice

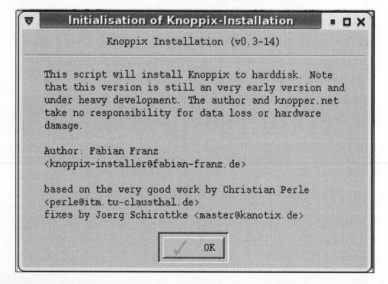

Once you begin the installation process, you might see the warning dialog shown in Figure 1.7. For the Live CD to be installed, you will need to create two Linux partitions on the hard drive: one to contain the actual operating system, and the other to provide a Linux swap file. Selecting the **Partition** option in the dialog box in Figure 1.8 will launch the qtPartd disk partitioning utility shown in Figure 1.9. This utility allows you to create and manage partitions and automatically detects the hard drive(s) installed on your system.

Figure 1.7 Live CD Install to Hard Disk Detection Dialog

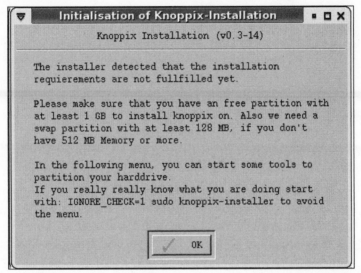

Figure 1.8 Live CD Install to Hard Disk Partitioning Selection Dialog

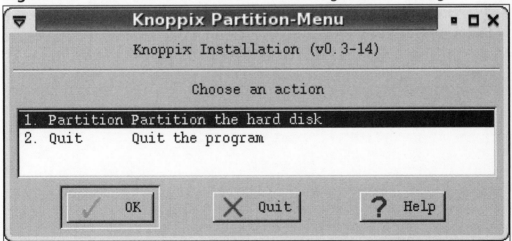

Figure 1.9 Live CD Install qtPartd Hard Drive Partition Utility

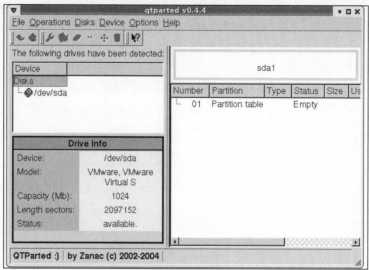

You can use the qtPartd utility to select the partition on the physical drive you want to use. You will need to create a 3GB or larger partition for the main installation target. This partition should be formatted as an ext3 file system. In addition, you will need a partition that is two times the installed system memory formatted as a Linux swap partition. For example, if your system memory is 256MB, the swap partition should be 512MB. After creating the partitions (or if they were already available when you launched the hard disk), the dialog in Figure 1.10 gives you the remaining options to complete the installation. You should choose option number 1 to make the final configuration selections, shown in Figure 1.11. We recommend the Knoppix-style system option, since that is how we set up the Live CD to run properly when installed to hard disk. After making this selection, you will be returned to the previous menu where you can select **Start Installation**. A reboot will be required once the installation has completed, but you should be able to boot from disk without the CD.

Figure 1.10 Live CD Install to Hard Disk Options Menu

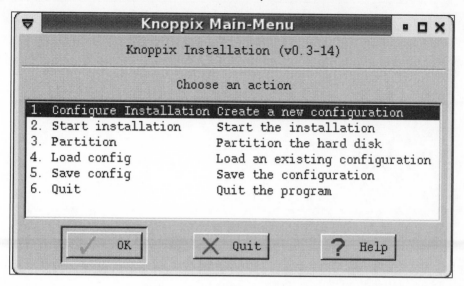

Figure 1.11 Live CD Install to Hard Disk Install Type Selection

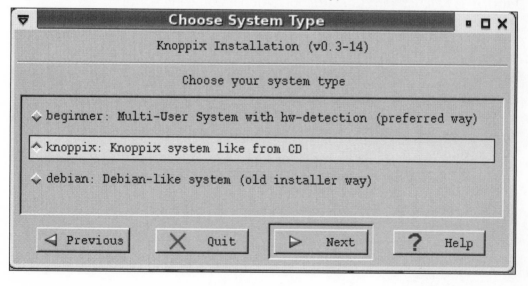

NOTE

If you do not choose any persistent storage option or install this Live CD to a hard drive, the system will revert to its original state and no changes will be saved if the system is rebooted for any reason. You have been warned.

The Portals

Each example company has a complete sample portal for SOX based on the eGroupWare open source groupware suite. Although there are many groupware applications available, we chose eGroupWare for our examples because there were a variety of applications built in and others we wrote and modified to make it a very useful toolkit for SOX compliance activities. Figure 1.12 shows an example of the BuiltRight Construction sample company portal.

Figure 1.12 BuiltRight Construction Sample Company Portal

The eGroupWare suite is written in PHP and provides a framework in which applications can be written, providing common user management and ACLs, a theme engine, and transparent database access. As an example, each of the portal sites was built from the SiteManager application to demonstrate the power of eGroupWare. The SiteManager application allows for Web sites to be built using modules and components, including some of the applications included in eGroupWare itself. Each front page to the portals can be accessed anonymously; however, to work through most of the examples in the book, you will need to log in as one of the sample users listed in the next section. A toolbar icon represents each eGroupWare application, and we have provided a picture of this icon in each applicable section of the book for easy reference. The following is a quick overview of the portals and the eGroupWare applications, and we will be using specific examples throughout the book as they apply to the SOX compliance requirements. The SiteManager module is the only one that does not require logging in to explore, so we will begin there.

SiteManager

http://xfld/builtright
http://xfld/nustuff

The portals for each sample company are essentially the same; only the content is significantly different, so we will cover them together and only point out the differences where they matter. We used SiteManager to divide each portal into several main sections: the main site that loads initially, and the reference section that contains materials and links. Each section has the following functionality:

Main

- **Site Index** A built-in feature of SiteManager for navigation.

- **Home Page** The news application for eGroupWare. These items are defined inside the application and appear on the front page.

- **Login** The gateway to the eGroupWare application suite; you must log in to access this portion of the portal site.

- **Google block** An example of a SiteManager module that provides search capabilities. Since this Live CD is not a public Web site, the "this site" functionality will not work because Google cannot index it.

- **Amazon block** This is another example of a SiteManager module.

Launch Pad

- **The Other Side** Links you to the other portal site.

- **Webmin** Transports you to the locally running instance of Webmin, which is covered in detail in Chapters 6, "Domain 2: Acquisition and Implementation," and 7, "Domain 3: Delivery and Support."

- **Nagios** Transports you to the locally running instance of Webmin, which is covered in detail in Chapter 8, "Domain 4: Monitoring."

Reference

- **Bookmarks and Links** Contains links to all references and sites in the book.

- **Sample Configurations** Contains sample configurations and code listings in the book for convenient reference and download.

- **Knowledge Base** Another eGroupWare application that we will be further demonstrating later in the book.

- **Software and Downloads** Contains open source packages of several applications used in this book.

TIP

You will need to log in to continue exploring the CD. For now, use the following credentials:
Username: *bjohnson*
Password *letmein*
We provide a complete discussion of the user roles in Chapter 5; however, Biff Johnson has administrative access to the eGroupWare portal sites, so use this role to continue to explore the CD. Now that you are logged in, you can access the administrative side of SiteManager from the toolbar.

Home

http://xfld/builtright/egw/home.php
http://xfld/nustuff/egw/home.php

The home application is the simplest of all eGroupWare applications and provides a configurable "front page" view of the system that you can adjust to your preferences. This application is not specifically used in the book and is provided with every default eGroupWare instance.

Admin

http://xfld/builtright/egw/admin/index.php
http://xfld/nustuff/egw/admin/index.php

The admin application is where all users and groups are managed, and application defaults and access control lists (ACLs). Rather than spend several pages discussing the setup of each application, we refer you to the eGroupWare Web site where you will find much documentation on the setup of eGroupWare (http://egroupware.org). However, we do want to illustrate the concept of ACLs. Users with administration rights to eGroupWare such as Biff Johnson have the ability to allow groups of people access to various application data entered by the users. The rights are generally granted for the following types of access:

- **Read** Grant read rights to nonprivate data.
- **Edit** Grant change rights to nonprivate data.
- **Add** Grant rights to add new data.
- **Delete** Grant delete rights to nonprivate data.

Individual users can also grant rights to their own data in some applications; however, this is beyond the scope of this discussion. Not every eGroupWare application supports ACLs and not every type is implemented. However, for those applications in which ACLs are important to our SOX examples, we point this out in the appropriate sections of the book. You can view and maintain Users, Groups, and ACLs by selecting the entity in the Admin module and "drilling" down to the ACL page.

Email

http://xfld/builtright/egw/index.php?menuaction=email.uiindex.index
http://xfld/nustuff/egw/index.php?menuaction=email.uiindex.index

The e-mail application is a full-featured Web e-mail client that supports both IMAP and POP servers. We included this application so you can view the IMAP mailboxes of system users provided by the Courier IMAP suite running on the Live CD. E-mail has become an integral part of business communications, and the importance of this is further illustrated when we discuss workflow notifications in Chapters 5, 6, and 7.

Calendar

http://xfld/builtright/egw/index.php?menuaction=calendar.uicalendar.day
http://xfld/nustuff/egw/index.php?menuaction=calendar.uicalendar.day

The calendar application is one of those "meat and potatoes" types of functionality found in all groupware applications and provides individual and group shared calendaring. Although this application is not specifically used in the book, it would be a useful tool to provide meeting schedules to all persons and groups that will be working on your SOX compliance.

Address Book

http://xfld/builtright/egw/addressbook/index.php
http://xfld/nustuff/egw/addressbook/index.php

The address book application contains address information for all employees and external players in our SOX examples. It is integrated into many of the other applications such as projects and infolog; therefore, it becomes the central place to store information about the people involved in the compliance process.

InfoLog

http://xfld/builtright/egw/index.php?menuaction=infolog.uiinfolog.index
http://xfld/nustuff/egw/index.php?menuaction=infolog.uiinfolog.index

The infolog application is an important application that covers items where tracking and record keeping is important, such as to-do items, telephone calls, and notes. Links to the address book can be established for items and external references and file attachments. This versatile application is well integrated with other modules in which people are involved, and while we do not directly use this application in our examples, this could and should be used heavily in an actual audit process.

Fud Forum

http://xfld/builtright/egw/fudforum/3814588639/index.php
http://xfld/nustuff/egw/fudforum/3814588639/index.php

Fud forum is a full-featured forum application that supports threaded discussions. It is an excellent example of the power of open source, since it was actually developed external to eGroupWare with the FUDForum project (http://fudforum.org/forum). The GPL license allows the code to be distributed and modified, so this application was integrated with eGroupWare.

Projects

http://xfld/builtright/egw/index.php?menuaction=projects.uiprojects.list_projects
http://xfld/nustuff/egw/index.php?menuaction=projects.uiprojects.list_projects

The projects application is a project tracking application. We use this in Chapter 6 to illustrate the tracking of projects that result from our "one-page strategies." This application could be used to track virtually any project, including the SOX consultants' and auditors' billable time and deliverables so you can be sure you are getting what you are paying for.

Wiki

http://xfld/builtright/egw/wiki/index.php
http://xfld/nustuff/egw/wiki/index.php

Wiki is a system of free-form collaboration in which anyone within the eGroupWare portal (subject to optional access controls) can add and modify pages using a WYSIWYG editor. This is another excellent example of an open source application born elsewhere as WikiTikiTavi (http://tavi.sourceforge.net) and integrated into eGroupWare.

Wiki is based on an easy-to-learn markup language similar to HTML, and in addition to the actual pages, content, and links that are created, each page has a header and footer that provides information and allows actions to be taken. We are covering the general concepts of Wiki here since it is used heavily in Chapters 5, 6, 7, and 8 to support various aspects of SOX compliance activities.

Wiki Page Header

At the top of every Wiki page is a header section that provides the following for each page:

- **Navigation links** Provide a way to return to the "top" of the Wiki.

- **Recent changes** Shows a list of recently modified pages in the Wiki system.

- **Search** Allows you to search for text that appears in the pages and categories.

- **Summary** An optional brief summary of the Wiki page you are viewing; common to all versions of the same Wiki page.

- **Category** An optional field where you can categorize your Wiki pages, and search on them later. This is also common to all versions of the same Wiki page.

- **Last changed by the user** ID of the person who last changed the document, which is the version you are currently viewing.

- **Workflow status** If the Wiki page requires a workflow approval chain, this field will show the status of that activity. We discuss workflow in more detail later in the chapter.

Wiki Page Footer

At the bottom of every Wiki page is a footer section that provides the following for each page:

- **Edit this document** Provides a way make changes to the Wiki page. Any change to the page creates a fully new page and saves the previous version as a historical record.

- **View Document History** Allows you to view, compare, and modify any version of the current Wiki page. You will be presented with information of who, when, and how the page was modified, and if you choose to modify a historical version, this becomes the current version of the document.

- **Preferences** Defines your individual display preferences for the Wiki application.

- **Workflow** Allows a page to be submitted for workflow approval, or cancel an existing request. More information on the workflow application is provided in the next section of this chapter.

Bookmarks

http://xfld/builtright/egw/bookmarks/index.php
http://xfld/nustuff/egw/bookmarks/index.php

The bookmarks application tracks links to external Web sites similar to your browser favorites. This is an example of an application integrated with SiteManager, in which the links added to this application are displayed in each portal site as a SiteManager module. We have used the bookmarks application to provide convenient links grouped by chapter to all sites referred to in this book.

News Admin

http://xfld/builtright/egw/news_admin/index.php
http://xfld/nustuff/egw/news_admin/index.php

The news admin application is another example of an eGroupWare application integrated with SiteManager. In our example, we use this application to make announcements on the portal site, such as important meeting announcements, milestones, and so forth. This is a good tool to disseminate any type of publicly accessible information.

Knowledge Base

http://xfld/builtright/egw/phpbrain/index.php
http://xfld/nustuff/egw/phpbrain/index.php

The knowledge base is the last example SiteManager integrated application. We use this in Chapters 8 and 9 to define implementation for applications, IT documentation, and test procedures for SOX controls. The testing of your controls is the criteria on which your audit will be based and is a crucial deliverable.

Workflow

http://xfld/builtright/egw/workflow_users/index.php
http://xfld/nustuff/egw/workflow_users/index.php

The workflow application is one of the most important applications in the entire suite of tools, and we have done significant work in making this a useful tool for SOX compliance. This workflow application was originally based on Galaxia (http://tikiwiki.org/tiki-index.php?page=GalaxiaWorkflow), which was based on OpenFlow (www.openflow.it). The Workflow Management Coalition definition of a workflow is "The automation of a business process, in whole or parts, where documents, information or tasks are passed from one participant to another to be processed, according to a set of procedural rules." Figure 1.13 illustrates the concept of this workflow application.

Figure 1.13 Workflow Application Concepts

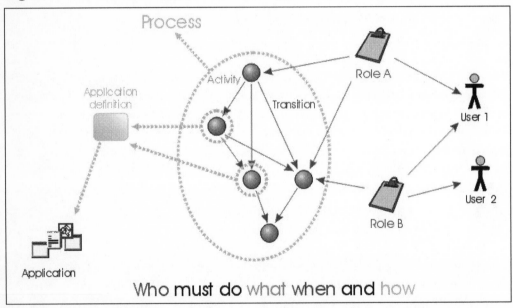

This application is an "activity-based" workflow where processes are implemented as a set of activities that must be completed to achieve some result. One of the obvious uses of this is document approval routing, and we use this application in this capacity and others extensively in Chapters 5, 6, 7, and 8. We even show you how to define your own workflows, since the possibilities of this application are nearly boundless.

Summary

In this chapter, we discussed that although your IT infrastructure may have been part of your normal year-end audit, the Sarbanes-Oxley experience promises to be quite different in terms of depth, cost, and resources. Since Sarbanes-Oxley requires all publicly held companies to prove compliance, it will affect virtually every person in your organization.

While we reserve the discussion of what Sarbanes-Oxley is specifically, we wanted to give you an idea of why this book was written and its intended audience. There are two main focuses on open source as it relates to the Sarbanes-Oxley discussion: first are those of you who have or are considering deploying open source in your IT organization; and second is to illustrate the some of many opportunities to make your life easier and reduce the amount your audit may cost in terms of resources and money by employing open source technologies to help in the monitoring, process, and documentation aspects regardless of your current IT landscape.

We hope this book is useful to many different people. Non-IT management will gain an over-arching understanding of how open source can help reduce their Sarbanes-Oxley costs and how open source fits into the picture. IT management will see how open source can assist with and automate the task of documenting and tracking compliance and internal controls, independent of whether they are derived from proprietary or open source systems, and understand the benefits gained from such an environment. IT/financial consultants will be able to use the tools and technologies on the Live CD as a valuable toolset to improve their clients' IT processes, and hopefully make their SOX compliance a less painful and costly experience. Finally, principals of nonpublic companies who might be considering an IPO can better understand some of the implications SOX will bring to the table, and get an idea of how open source can offset some of the requirements.

We finished the chapter with a look at the Live CD. The CD is based on the XFLD distribution, which was originally derived from the original Knoppix Live CD. We chose this particular distribution because of its low computer requirements. When the Live CD is running, nothing on your original setup is disturbed, because the program runs completely in memory. Since the running image is a virtual file system in memory, changes are not saved between reboots. However, if you want to save any changes, there is an option to save to USB pen drive, ZIP disk, or an available hard disk partition. Additionally, if you want to install the Live CD so it runs from a hard disk as a normal distribution, we provide the means to do that. The portal sites are an integral part of this book because they demonstrate the actual compliance process in real time with many examples of open source tools and applications you can use for your own compliance needs.

Solutions Fast Track

The Audit Experience: An Introduction

- ☑ The Sarbanes-Oxley audit is much more in-depth, costly, and resource intensive than any other audit you might have experienced previously.

- ☑ Sarbanes-Oxley will affect virtually every person in your organization.

- ☑ Companies are compelled to comply if they are publicly held, regardless of size or revenue.

What This Book Is

- ☑ This book is a technical book at heart; however, much material on the business side is presented to place the technology into a frame of reference for SOX compliance.

- ☑ The examples and technologies presented here are based on open source technologies to help you save time, resources, and money.

What This Book Is Not

- ☑ This book is not a road map on how to comply; that would be impossible since every business is unique.

- ☑ This book is not about financial compliance; it is strictly focused on the IT considerations for Sarbanes-Oxley. There are many other references for that particular aspect.

Who Should Read This Book

- ☑ **Non-IT management** Even though you may not be in the IT department directly, you will have an over-arching understanding of how open source can help.

- ☑ **IT management** This book demonstrates open source to assist and automate the task of documenting and tracking compliance and internal controls, independent of whether they are derived from proprietary or open source systems, and outlines the business reasons and benefits derived from such an environment.

☑ **IT/financial consultants** The Live CD provides a valuable toolset that can be used to improve clients' IT processes, and hopefully make their SOX compliance a less painful and costly experience.

☑ **Principals of nonpublic companies** If you are considering an IPO, you should read this book to understand some of the implications SOX will bring to the table, together with an idea of how open source can offset some of the requirements.

The "Live" CD Concept

☑ The Live CD contains a toolset and example configurations used throughout the book to demonstrate open source for SOX compliance needs. The CD is bootable, completely self-contained, and will not disturb any existing operating system that might be installed.

☑ The CD runs completely in memory; therefore, any changes are not saved upon reboot. You can, however, save your changes to a USB pen drive, ZIP disk, or available hard drive partition.

☑ The CD can be installed to an available hard drive by selecting the **install to hard disk** option. A 3GB ext3 partition and a Linux swap partition must be available to perform this function.

The Portals

☑ The CD contains two main portals, one for each of the example companies used throughout the book, BuiltRight Construction and NuStuff Electronics.

☑ We chose eGroupWare as the example open source groupware application because it provides a rich application framework in terms of common user management and access control, a theme engine, and transparent database access. A look at each application in the framework is provided.

Frequently Asked Questions

The following Frequently Asked Questions, answered by the authors of this book, are designed to both measure your understanding of the concepts presented in this chapter and to assist you with real-life implementation of these concepts. To have your questions about this chapter answered by the author, browse to **www.syngress.com/solutions** and click on the **"Ask the Author"** form. You will also gain access to thousands of other FAQs at ITFAQnet.com.

Q: You mentioned other resources that cover the financial aspects of Sarbanes-Oxley compliance. Can you name a few?

A: Here is a short list:

Web Sites

- SEC Spotlight on Sarbanes-Oxley Rulemaking and Reports— www.sec.gov/spotlight/sarbanes-oxley.htm

- The Sarbanes-Oxley Act Forum—www.sarbanes-oxley-forum.com/

- American Institute of Certified Public Accountants (AICPA)— www.aicpa.org/index.htm

- Sarbanes-Oxley Disclosure Information—www.sarbanes-oxley.com/

Books

- *What Is Sarbanes-Oxley?* (ISBN: 0071437967)

- *Manager's Guide to the Sarbanes-Oxley Act : Improving Internal Controls to Prevent Fraud* (ISBN: 0471569755)

- *Sarbanes-Oxley and the New Internal Auditing Rules* (ISBN: 0471483060)

Q: Under what license are the applications and examples on the Live CD being released?

A: All of the software available on the CD, including any customizations, are released under the General Public License (GPL). The example policies and procedures are copyright 2005 Syngress Publishing Inc. This being said, all of your policies and controls should be original and applicable to your own organization, but you may use those provided on the CD as examples to get you started. A copy of the GPL can be found in Appendix C.

Q: What other customized Live CDs are available? Is there one that does "foo"?

A: There are many specialized Live CDs available to do anything from security forensics to massively parallel compute clusters. You can find an exhaustive list at Distro-Watch (http://distrowatch.com). Just select **Search** and specify Live CD (or DVD) as the distribution category.

Q: The Live CD is really cool! Are there tutorials online to show me how to roll my own?

A: There are many online documents outlining how to customize your own Live CD on the Knoppix community Web site (www.knoppix.net). You will find many examples there on how to create your own distribution.

Chapter 2

SOX and COBIT Defined

Solutions in this chapter:

- SOX Overview
- Why IT COBIT?
- Are the Developers of COBIT Controls Crazy? Is This Practical?
- Sustainability Is the Key

☑ Summary

☑ Solutions Fast Track

☑ Frequently Asked Questions

SOX Overview

As a result of the financial scandals at major Fortune 100 companies in 2001, Congress enacted the Sarbanes-Oxley Act of 2002. This act affects how public companies report financials, and significantly impacts IT. Sarbanes-Oxley compliance requires more than documentation and/or establishment of financial controls; it also requires the assessment of a company's IT infrastructure, operations, and personnel. Unfortunately, the requirements of the Sarbanes-Oxley Act of 2002 do not scale based on the size or revenue of a company. Small to medium-sized companies (IT department) will face unique challenges, both budgetary and with personnel, in their effort to comply with the Sarbanes-Oxley Act of 2002.

The Transparency Test...

The CFO Perspective

"It is not clear that the intent of SOX could not have been met with the requirements under Section 302. However, with the requirements included under Section 404, companies need a framework for implementation. COBIT provides a methodical approach to the IT function for Sarbanes-Oxley implementation and support. While using the framework provided, each company will need to customize the approach to its own size and complexity. A multinational, multidivisional organization is different from a single factory domestic company. The authors provide an example for this customization and rightfully point out that SOX will evolve over time, at least for the first few years." — Steve Lanza

What Will SOX Accomplish?

There continues to be much controversy and debate about the effectiveness of SOX. Although most people who are aware of the requirements to comply with SOX (Section 404) believe the intention was good, there exists controversy over whether the existing 302 reporting requirements are sufficient.

If you read Sections 302 and 404, you may see similarities, and subsequently, why a controversy may exist as to whether (Section 404) SOX requirements and compliance were necessary. The next two sections in this chapter include an example of Sections 302 and 404 as they pertain to a company's executive management assertions.

Section 302

In accordance with Section 302, executive management of a public company:

a) are responsible for establishing and maintaining internal controls

b) have designed such internal controls to ensure that material information relating to the issuer and its consolidated subsidiaries is made known to such officers by others within those entities, particularly during the period in which the periodic reports are being prepared

Section 404

In accordance with Section 404, executive management of a public company:

a) are responsible for establishing and maintaining an adequate internal control structure and procedures for financial reporting

b) must report the effectiveness of the internal control structure and procedures

We will discuss Section 302 and Section 404 in later chapters of this book.

SOX: Not Just a Dark Cloud

The initial response to Sarbanes-Oxley may be as yet another drain on your already understaffed, overtaxed IT department; however, this does not necessarily have to be the case. Whether SOX compliance is viewed as just another project, or a strategic opportunity for the IT department to reduce the project backlog, will be determined by how the CFO, CIO, or IT Director positions SOX compliance with executive management. However, because a majority of companies will view SOX compliance as a Finance initiative and may not involve IT, or limit IT's involvement to the project's periphery, this may be easier said than done. Because of this "limited" perception of SOX compliance, the process of positioning with executive management to include IT within this initiative may require significant effort, but will be well worth it.

If properly executed, the SOX compliance process gives CFOs, CIOs, and IT Directors an opportunity to address antiquated systems, personnel resource issues, and documentation/process issues. It will also provide them the opportunity to forge stronger alliances with the business units. IT will be critical to the success of SOX compliance, and the support of the business units will be critical to the success of IT.

TIP

When implementing new processes, procedures, or applications for SOX compliance, the activities should add value to the business unit(s) or the overall business.

Be prepared for change; as auditors gain more knowledge about SOX, their interpretation will change, and subsequently, so will their requirements of your IT organization.

Why IT COBIT?

Sarbanes-Oxley compliance will significantly impact the IT organization of most public companies. However, there is one enormous problem: there is no specific mention of IT in Section 404, and more importantly, there are no specifics as to what controls have to be established within an IT organization to comply with Sarbanes-Oxley legislation.

If there is no specific mention in Section 404 as to what IT needs to do to comply with Sarbanes-Oxley, the logical question would be, "How can I comply with something without knowing what I need to do to comply?" Although there are various standards a company can use for defining and documenting its internal controls—ITIL (IT Infrastructure Library), Six Sigma, and COBIT—the majority of auditors have adopted COBIT.

ITIL is an international series of documents used to aid the implementation of a framework for IT Service Management. The intent of the framework is to define how Service Management is applied within specific organizations. Given that the framework consists of guidelines, it is agnostic of any application or platform and can therefore be applied in any organization.

In many organizations, Six Sigma simply means a measure of quality that strives for near perfection. Six Sigma is a disciplined, data-driven approach and methodology for eliminating defects (driving toward six standard deviations between the mean and the nearest specification limit) in any process—from manufacturing to transactional and from product to service.

COBIT stands for Control Objectives for Information and Related Technology. While the COBIT guidelines have been around since 1996, the guidelines and best practices have almost become the de facto standard for auditors and SOX compliance, mostly because the COBIT standards are platform independent. There are approximately 300 generic COBIT objectives, grouped under six COBIT

Components. When reviewing and applying the COBIT guidelines and best practices, keep in mind that they will need to be tailored to your particular environment.

The Six COBIT Components

COBIT consists of six components:

- **Executive Summary** Explains the key concepts and principles.

- **Framework** Foundation for approach and COBIT elements. Organizes the process model into four domains:

    - Plan and organize

    - Acquire and implement

    - Deliver and support

    - Monitor and evaluate

- **Control Objective** Foundation for approach and COBIT elements. Organizes the process model into the four domains (discussed in a moment).

- **Control Practices** Identifies best practices and describes requirements for specific controls.

- **Management Guidelines** Links business and IT objectives and provides tools to improve IT performance.

- **Audit Guidelines** Provides guidance on how to evaluate controls, assess compliance, and document risk with these characteristics:

    - Define "internal controls" over financial reporting

    - Internally test and assess these controls

    - Support external audits of controls

    - Document compliance efforts

    - Report any significant deficiencies or material weaknesses

In conclusion, although an IT organization is free to select any predefined standards, or even one they develop to assist them in obtaining Sarbanes-Oxley compliance, the mostly widely accepted standard is COBIT. Subsequently, you may find that selecting COBIT will be the path of least resistance to Sarbanes-Oxley compliance.

TIP

COBIT guidelines and best practices will need to be tailored to your environment. Although the enormity of the COBIT guidelines and best practices may appear daunting, it can and should be distilled down to what is pertinent to your environment.

Entity Level Controls versus Control Objectives

Entity level controls consist of the policies, procedures, practices, and organizational structures intended to assure the use of IT will enable the accomplishments of business objectives, and that planned events will be prevented, or detected and corrected.

Control objective is a statement of the desired result or purpose to be achieved by implementing control procedures for a particular IT activity. When developing and documenting your controls, you will want to keep in mind several characteristics so your controls will be as effective as possible:

Key control characteristics include:

- Employees are aware of their responsibilities for the control activities.

- The control is clearly understood.

- The control is effective in preventing, detecting, or correcting risk.

- The operating effectiveness of the control activity is adequately evaluated on a regular basis.

- The standards and assertions required to execute the control are clearly understood.

- Deficiencies are identified and remedied in a timely manner.

- The performance of the control can be documented.

- The controls, policies, and procedures are documented.

TIP

Although the goal is to implement a control that will be 100-percent effective, it is not realistic. Therefore, the objective should be to implement the most effective control within your environment. Be prepared to explain to your auditors how your environment works and why a particular control is effective in your environment.

What Are the Four COBIT Domains?

We'll now briefly describe each COBIT domain.

Planning and Organization

Planning is about developing strategic IT plans that support the business objectives. These plans should be forward looking and in alignment with the company's planning intervals; that is, a two-, three-, or five-year projection.

Acquisition and Implementation

Once the plans are developed and approved, you may need to acquire new applications, or even acquire or develop a new staff skill set to execute the plans. Upon completion of the Acquisition phase, the plans now need to be enacted in the Implementation phase, which should include maintenance, testing, certifying, and identification of any changes needed to ensure continued availability of both existing and new systems.

Delivery and Support

This phase ensures that systems perform as expected upon implementation, and continue to perform in accordance with expectations over time, usually managed via service level agreements (SLAs). In this regard, systems can be related to infrastructure components or third-party services.

Monitoring

The monitoring phase uses the SLAs or baseline established in subsequent phases to allow an IT organization to gauge how they are performing against expectation, and provides them with an opportunity to be proactive.

Are the Developers of COBIT Controls Crazy? Is This Practical?

A cursory review of the COBIT controls described in this section would convince any CEO, CFO, or IT director that implementation of COBIT controls is a daunting task, and the developers of the controls must be crazy. Neither of the aforementioned assumptions necessarily has to be the case. Whether the task of implementing COBIT controls is daunting will depend on how much effort is put into filtering the COBIT controls. Keep in mind that although all the controls center on good, sound practices, even the largest and most well run organization will not be able to implement all of them as defined by COBIT—a good idea, yes, but not necessarily practical. The keys to culling down COBIT controls center on a couple of questions:

- Which controls are appropriate to your environment?
- Of the appropriate controls, which will maximize your efforts?

After you have successfully answered the preceding questions, you will be in a position to reduce the COBIT controls to a manageable and actionable list for your implementation. Prior to executing your list of controls, you should verify your assumptions with your auditor. In addition, as part of your assessment process, you should identify all areas that are not appropriate for your environment, and be prepared to justify and defend these exclusions to your auditors as part of the Gap and Remediation process.

Tables 2.1 through 2.4 outline a partial list of the COBIT controls, and show some of the control objectives for each process cycle and the risk factor to which they relate. For a complete listing, see Appendix A.

Table 2.1 Planning and Organization

	Risk	Control Objective
1	IT plans may not be present in the organization's long- and short-range plans. The organization's plans may not support IT.	Management prepares strategic plans for IT that align business objectives with IT strategies. The planning approach includes mechanisms to solicit input from relevant internal and external stakeholders impacted by the IT strategic direction.

Continued

Table 2.1 continued Planning and Organization

	Risk	Control Objective
2	IT plans may not be updated regularly.	Management obtains feedback from business process owners and users regarding the quality and usefulness of its IT plans for use in the ongoing risk assessment process.
3	IT plans may not be consistent with the organization's goals and may impair the achievement of business objectives.	An IT planning or steering committee exists to oversee the IT function and its activities. Committee membership includes representatives from senior manage-ment, user management, and the IT function.
4	New business processes may conflict with current IT plans, or new IT plans may conflict with current business processes.	The IT organization ensures that IT plans are communicated to business process owners and other relevant parties across the organization.
5	IT activities may not be understood by management or business processes, so conflicts may not be known.	IT management communicates its activities, challenges, and risks on a regular basis with the CEO and CFO. This information is also shared with the board of directors.
6	Changes in the business or IT environment may unknowingly impact IT plans.	The IT organization monitors its progress against the strategic plan and reacts accordingly to meet established objectives.
7	IT architecture may not support the growth of the business or current business goals.	IT management has defined information capture, processing, and reporting controls—including completeness, accuracy, validity, and authorization—to support the quality and integrity of information used for financial and disclosure purposes.
8	IT security levels may not comply with regulatory or corporate policies regarding information protection.	IT management has defined information classification standards in accordance with corporate security and privacy policies.

Continued

Table 2.1 continued Planning and Organization

	Risk	Control Objective
9	IT security levels may not comply with regulatory or corporate policies regarding information protection. IT security plans may not be updated regularly.	IT management has defined, implemented, and maintained security levels for each data classification. These security levels represent the appropriate (minimum) set of security and control measures of each of the classifications and are reevaluated periodically and modified accordingly.
10	Information systems data may not be reliable if systems are not functioning as intended, or errors are not dealt with appropriately.	IT managers have adequate knowledge and experience to fulfill their responsibilities.

Table 2.2 Acquire and Implement

	Risk	Control Objective
1	Program development may not adhere to regulatory or corporate processes and procedures risking data integrity.	The organization has a system development life cycle methodology that considers security, availability, and processing integrity requirements of the organization.
2	Program implementations may not function as intended, risking the integrity of the calculations, data capture, data integrity, or the implementation of unauthorized processes.	The system development life cycle methodology ensures that information systems are designed to include application controls that support complete, accurate, authorized, and valid transaction processing.
3	New application selection may not support business and regulatory objectives.	The organization has an acquisition and planning process that aligns with its overall strategic direction.
4	Business objectives may not be achieved, or undetected processes may be installed in production systems.	The organization acquires software in accordance with its acquisition and planning process.

Continued

Table 2.2 continued Acquire and Implement

	Risk	Control Objective
5	Integrity of the implementation may not be achieved, and the program may not function as intended.	Procedures exist to ensure that system software is installed and maintained in accordance with the organization's requirements.
6	Integrity of the implementation may not be achieved, the program may not function as intended, and unauthorized processes may be installed undetected.	Procedures exist to ensure that system software changes are controlled in line with the organization's change management procedures.
7	System program upgrades may change security settings and allow unauthorized access to protected information.	IT management ensures that the setup and implementation of system software do not jeopardize the security of the data and programs being stored on the system.
8	System program upgrades may interrupt production and network services, corrupting data or other activities.	Procedures exist and are followed to ensure that infrastructure systems, including network devices and software, are installed and maintained in accordance with the acquisition and maintenance framework.
9	System program upgrades may interrupt production and network services, corrupting data or other activities.	Procedures exist and are followed to ensure that infrastructure system changes are controlled in line with the organization's change management procedures.
10	Consistent application of application reporting and transaction processing may not occur, jeopardizing the integrity of the data and financial statement reporting.	The organization's system development life cycle methodology requires that user reference and support manuals (including documentation of controls) be prepared as part of every information system development or modification project.

Table 2.3 Delivery and Support

	Risk	Control Objective
1	Financial data integrity may be compromised if the system is not functioning as intended.	Selection of vendors for outsourced services is performed in accordance with the organization's vendor management policy.
2	Financial data integrity may be compromised if the system is not functioning as intended.	A framework is defined to establish key performance indicators to manage SLAs, both internally and externally.
3	Vendor viability may risk the delivery of programs and subsequent support of the application.	IT management ensures that, before selection, potential third parties are properly qualified through an assessment of their capability to deliver the required service and their financial viability.
4	Vendors have access to protected and sensitive data; confidentiality may be compromised.	Third-party service contracts address the risks, security controls, and procedures for information systems and networks in the contract between the parties.
5	If systems fail, data integrity may be compromised, or business objectives may not be met.	Business continuity controls consider business risk related to third-party service providers in terms of continuity of service, and escrow contracts exist where appropriate.
6	Confidentiality and achievement of business objectives may be breached.	Procedures exist and are followed to ensure that a formal contract is defined and agreed to for all third-party services before work is initiated, including definition of internal control requirements and acceptance of the organization's policies and procedures.
7	Vendor failures may go undetected.	A designated individual is responsible for regular monitoring and reporting on the achievement of the third-party service level performance criteria.

Continued

Table 2.3 continued Delivery and Support

	Risk	Control Objective
8	Financial data integrity may be compromised if the system is not functioning as intended.	A regular review of security, availability, and processing integrity is performed for SLAs and related contracts with third-party service providers.
9	Capacity to retain the source transaction information may be limited.	IT management monitors the performance and capacity levels of the systems.
10	SLAs may not be met.	IT management has a process in place to respond to suboptimal performance and capacity measures in a timely manner.

Table 2.4 Monitor and Evaluate

	Risk	Control Objective
1	Breakdowns in performance may not be detected and corrected in a timely fashion.	Performance indicators (e.g., benchmarks) from both internal and external sources are defined, and data are collected and reported regarding achievement of these benchmarks.
2	Breakdowns in performance may not be detected and corrected in a timely fashion.	IT management monitors its delivery of services to identify shortfalls and responds with actionable plans to improve.
3	Breakdowns in performance may not be detected and corrected in a timely fashion.	IT management monitors the effectiveness of internal controls in the normal course of operations through management and supervisory activities, comparisons, and benchmarks.
4	Breakdowns in performance may not be detected and corrected in a timely fashion.	Serious deviations in the operation of internal control, including major security, availability, and processing integrity events, are reported to senior management.

Continued

Table 2.4 continued Monitor and Evaluate

	Risk	Control Objective
5	Lack of independent assessment could cause structural control deficiencies to go undetected.	Internal control assessments are performed periodically, using self-assessment or independent audits, to examine whether internal controls are operating satisfactorily.
6	System flaws could lead to errors that impact the financial reporting environment.	IT management obtains independent reviews prior to implementing significant IT systems that are directly linked to the organization's financial reporting environment.
7	Controls for outsourced IT assets and facilities may not be sufficient.	IT management obtains independent internal control reviews of third-party service providers (e.g., by obtaining and reviewing copies of SAS70, SysTrust, or other independent audit reports).

What Controls Should I Use?

Let's explore how this intimidating list can be reduced based on the size and complexity of a particular company. For this process, we will create a fictitious company named XYZ Sprockets, a small public company with 90 employees. XYZ Sprockets has only one office, which houses its operations and manufacturing. The company's entire IT staff consists of two full-time employees, one server admin and one desktop technician. Although small, the company is the number-one manufacturer of bicycle gears, currently having 80 percent of the market. It generates $40 million a year in revenue, approximately $10 million per quarter.

When determining what controls you will need to put in place, you'll discover that what XYZ Sprockets does not have and does not support is as important as what the company does have and support. The importance of this will become clear in subsequent chapters. Here is a quick rundown on XYZ Sprockets' IT infrastructure.

Server Room

XYZ Sprockets' server infrastructure is as follows:

- Windows 2000 departmental file servers, one each for Finance, Marketing, and HR
- Active Directory for authentication

Desktops

Here's a look at XYZ Sprockets' desktop inventory:

- Eighty employees in the main office running Windows 98, Windows 2000, and Windows XP
- Ten Windows XP laptops, Microsoft Office, Visio, and Project for desktop applications
- Outlook for e-mail client
- Internet Explorer
- Norton AntiVirus

Outsourced Services

XYZ Sprockets has elected to outsource the following services to BigHosting Inc. to facilitate a small, in-house IT organization:

- VPN services
- Financials in-house developed
- E-mail
- Internet access
- Telecommunications

Outsourced Services

Figure 2.1 diagrams XYZ Sprockets' networking infrastructure.

Figure 2.1 XYZ Sprockets' Network Topology

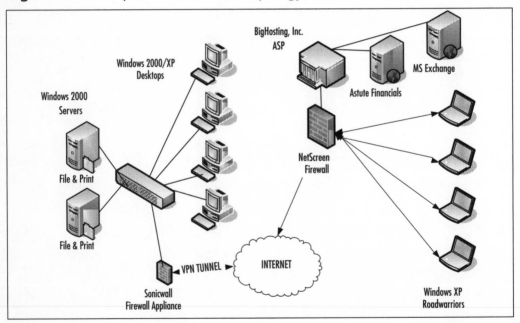

Based on XYZ Sprockets' environment, the list of Control Objectives shown in Table 2.5 could be applicable for the company's SOX compliance. As the majority of the Planning and Organization Control Objectives are related to management function, there is generally little opportunity to reduce the required number of actions.

However, if you review the subsequent domains, note that various Control Objectives have been left off. The missing Control Objectives were not omitted, but rather intentionally left off, as they did not apply to XYZ Sprockets' specific environment. The logic behind customizing the Control Objectives to a specific environment is discussed in subsequent chapters.

Table 2.5 Control Objectives Applicable for SOX Compliance at XYZ Sprockets

Domain	Removed Control Objective
Planning and Organization	N/A
Acquire and Implement	1, 2, and 10
Delivery and Support	5 and 10
Monitor and Evaluate	6

Planning and Organization

1. Management prepares strategic plans for IT that align business objectives with IT strategies.

2. Management obtains feedback from business process owners and users regarding the quality and usefulness of its IT plans in the ongoing risk assessment process.

3. An IT planning or steering committee exists to oversee the IT function and its activities.

4. The IT organization ensures that IT plans are communicated to business process owners and other relevant parties across the organization.

5. IT management communicates its activities, challenges, and risks on a regular basis with the CEO and CFO.

6. The IT organization monitors its progress against the strategic plan and reacts accordingly to meet established objectives.

7. IT management has defined information capture, processing and reporting controls—including completeness, accuracy, validity, and authorization—to support the quality and integrity of information used for financial and disclosure purposes.

8. IT management has defined information classification standards in accordance with corporate security and privacy policies.

9. IT management has defined, implemented, and maintained security levels for each data classification. These security levels represent the appropriate (minimum) set of security and control measures of each classification and are reevaluated.

10. IT managers have adequate knowledge and experience to fulfill their responsibilities.

Acquire and Implement

1. The organization has an acquisition and planning process that aligns with its overall strategic direction.

2. The organization acquires software in accordance with its acquisition and planning process.

3. Procedures exist to ensure that system software is installed and maintained in accordance with the organization's requirements.

4. Procedures exist to ensure that system software changes are controlled in line with the organization's change management procedures.

5. IT management ensures that the setup and implementation of system software do not jeopardize the security of the data and programs stored on the system.

6. Procedures exist and are followed to ensure that infrastructure systems, including network devices and software, are installed and maintained in accordance with the acquisition and maintenance framework.

7. Procedures exist and are followed to ensure that infrastructure system changes are controlled in line with the organization's change management procedures.

Delivery and Support

1. Selection of vendors for outsourced services is performed in accordance with the organization's vendor management policy.

2. A framework is defined to establish key performance indicators to manage SLAs, both internally and externally.

3. IT management ensures that, before selection, potential third parties are properly qualified through an assessment of their ability to deliver the required service and their financial viability.

4. Third-party service contracts address the risks, security controls, and procedures for information systems and networks in the contract between the parties.

5. Procedures exist and are followed to ensure that a formal contract is defined and agreed to for all third-party services before work is initiated, including definition of internal control requirements and acceptance of the organization's policies and procedures.

6. A designated individual is responsible for regular monitoring and reporting on the achievement of the third-party service level performance criteria.

7. A regular review of security, availability, and processing integrity is performed for SLAs and related contracts with third-party service providers.

8. IT management monitors the performance and capacity levels of the systems.

Monitor and Evaluate

1. Performance indicators (e.g., benchmarks) from both internal and external sources are defined, and data are collected and reported regarding achievement of these benchmarks.

2. IT management monitors its delivery of services to identify shortfalls and responds with actionable plans to improve.

3. IT management monitors the effectiveness of internal controls in the normal course of operations through management and supervisory activities, comparisons, and benchmarks.

4. Serious deviations in the operation of internal control, including major security, availability, and processing integrity events, are reported to senior management.

5. Internal control assessments are performed periodically, using self-assessment or independent audit, to examine whether internal controls are operating satisfactorily.

6. IT management obtains independent internal control reviews of third-party service providers (e.g., by obtaining and reviewing copies of SAS70, SysTrust or other independent audit reports).

Sustainability Is the Key

It is critical that SOX compliance be viewed as an ongoing process rather than a one-time event. In cases where you will need to revise, develop, and implement new procedures and controls, it will be vital to your continuing success that these procedures and controls are sustainable. Rest assured that the auditors will return periodically and will want to review evidence of the effectiveness of your ongoing controls—you must walk the walk.

In instances when you will need to revise, develop, and implement new procedures, keep the following in mind:

- Can the frequency of review be maintained (weekly, monthly, bimonthly quarterly, yearly, etc.)?

- How much evidence of review will be maintained, and how will it be stored?

- How disruptive will the review process be to daily functions?

- Can review evidence be systemically produced?

- How much of the review process can be automated?

In conclusion, it is possible for an IT organization, even a small one, to use COBIT to attain SOX compliance. However, you will need to customize and scale the COBIT controls to best fit your environment.

> **TIP**
>
> Keep Control Objectives as simple as possible and automate wherever possible. Get buy-in for new controls or documented processes from business units as soon as possible. IT staff will initially have to re-enforce new controls or processes with business units to facilitate the necessary behavioral change.

Finance and IT organizations of publicly traded companies should be familiar with audits or the need to have, even undocumented, procedures required to manage key IT processes. However, to comply with SOX, the Finance and IT organizations of publicly traded companies will be required not only to formalize and document these processes but also to increase the number and granularity of their audit concerns.

Again, while Finance and IT organizations of publicly traded companies should be familiar with audits, those audits have traditionally been of a cursory nature and typically only covered the following areas:

- Program change control

- Segregation of duties in Finance and IT

- Lack of user access controls and their periodic review

- Weak password controls

- Shared administration access rights

However, to comply with SOX, Finance and IT organizations of publicly traded companies will find that the areas of the audit process have increased (see the next section), and the nature and the complexity of the audit process have changed. No longer will an informal or even a loosely documented procedure suffice; rather, proof will now be the cornerstone to an organization's passing its SOX compliance. To pass SOX compliance, an IT organization will have to show proof of formal documentation, management buy-off and sign-off, and effectiveness of the implemented controls. These controls include:

- Periodic review of effectiveness of controls

- External security controls

- External security change management controls

- File and folder security

- Control of access to sensitive financial data in nonproduction systems

- Testing the backup and restore process

- Physical access controls

- Rapid response to employee and contractor terminations

- Process for reporting, investigating, and resolving security problems

- Data retention policy

TIP

The primary focus of the SOX IT audit will be information security, program change, and data backup and recovery. Where possible, build on what you have, even if the process is not documented or formalized. Processes currently outside the scope of SOX are business continuity planning and operations that do not impact integrity/ access /reporting of financial data.

Summary

In this chapter, we discussed how Congress enacted the Sarbanes-Oxley Act of 2002 in an effort to prevent financial scandals such as those that occurred at Enron and MCI. We also discussed how although Congress had the best of intentions when they enacted the Sarbanes-Oxley Act of 2002; there are some fundamental issues with how the Act was drafted:

- No IT-specific wording for IT compliance
- Section 404 and 302 appear to overlap
- De facto standard for SOX (COBIT) does not scale based on a company's size

Based on the aforementioned issues, we established that small to medium-sized companies will face unique challenges in their effort to pursue compliance of Sarbanes-Oxley Act of 2002. Given the unique challenges with which small to medium-sized companies will have to contend, their ability to leverage SOX and position it with executive management will be critical to their success.

We continued by delving into how the Sarbanes-Oxley Act of 2002 and COBIT came to be synonymous, and how different standards exist, but COBIT has been most widely adopted by audit firms. From there, we learned the six components of COBIT and the four COBIT domains. We continued by drilling further down by defining an Entity Level, a Control Objective, and the difference between the two. Building on the section on COBIT, we established that while the COBIT guidelines are good, standard operating procedures (SOPs) for an IT organization, it is impractical for any company to implement all of the COBIT guidelines as written. From there, we developed a fictitious company to demonstrate how, with planning and knowledge of an environment, the COBIT guidelines could be culled into something more doable and manageable.

Solutions Fast Track

SOX Overview

☑ The Sarbanes-Oxley Act of 2002 affects how public companies report financials and significantly impacts IT.

☑ Sarbanes-Oxley compliance requires more than documentation and/or establishment of financial controls; it also requires the assessment of a company's IT infrastructure, operations, and personnel.

☑ Requirements of the Sarbanes-Oxley Act of 2002 do not scale based on the size or revenue of a company.

☑ Small to medium-sized companies (IT department) will face unique challenges, both budgetary and with personnel, in their effort to comply with the Sarbanes-Oxley Act of 2002.

☑ A vast majority of companies will view SOX compliance as a Finance initiative and may not involve IT, or limit IT's involvement to the project's periphery.

☑ Limited perception of SOX compliance may make it difficult for CFOs, CIOs, and IT Directors to position SOC compliance with executive management.

☑ The SOX compliance process will provide CFOs, CIOs, and IT Directors the opportunity to forge stronger alliances with the business units.

Why IT COBIT?

☑ There is no specific mention in Section 404 as to what IT needs to do to comply with Sarbanes-Oxley.

☑ A company can use various predefined standards for defining and documenting their internal controls—ITIL (IT Infrastructure Library), Six Sigma, COBIT—or develop their own.

☑ The adoption of the COBIT guidelines and practices as a de facto standard is likely because they are platform independent.

☑ There are approximately 300 generic COBIT objectives, grouped under six COBIT Components.

☑ Entity Level Control consists of the policies, procedures, practices, and organizational structures.

☑ Control Objective is a statement of the desired result or purpose to be achieved.

☑ The control is effective in preventing, detecting, or correcting risk.

☑ The operating effectiveness of the control activity is adequately evaluated on a regular basis.

☑ The standards and assertions required to execute the control are clearly understood.

☑ Deficiencies are identified and remedied in a timely manner.

☑ The performance of the control can be documented.

☑ The controls, policies, and procedures are documented.

☑ COBIT is comprised of four Domains:

☑ Planning and organization

☑ Acquisition and implementation

☑ Delivery and support

☑ Monitoring

Are the Developers of COBIT Controls Crazy? Is This Practical?

☑ COBIT controls may appear to any CEO, CFO, or IT Director a daunting task, and that the developers of the controls must be crazy.

☑ Whether the task of implementing COBIT controls is daunting will depend on how much effort is put into filtering the COBIT controls.

☑ The largest and best run organization would not be able to implement all the controls as defined by COBIT.

☑ The keys to culling down COBIT controls center on a couple of questions:

■ Which controls are appropriate to your environment?

■ Of the appropriate controls, which will maximize your efforts?

Sustainability Is the Key

☑ It is critical that SOX compliance be viewed as an on-going process, rather than a one-time event.

☑ Auditors will return periodically and will want to review evidence of the effectiveness of your on-going controls—you must walk the walk.

☑ Where you will need to revise, develop, and implement new procedures, keep the following in mind:

☑ Can the frequency of review be maintained (weekly, monthly, bimonthly quarterly, yearly, and so on)?

☑ How much evidence of review will be maintained, and how will it be stored?

☑ How disruptive will the review process be to daily functions?

☑ Can review evidence be systemically produced?

☑ How much of the review process can be automated?

Frequently Asked Questions

The following Frequently Asked Questions, answered by the authors of this book, are designed to both measure your understanding of the concepts presented in this chapter and to assist you with real-life implementation of these concepts. To have your questions about this chapter answered by the author, browse to **www.syngress.com/solutions** and click on the **"Ask the Author"** form. You will also gain access to thousands of other FAQs at ITFAQnet.com.

Q: Where can I find additional information on COBIT?

A: There is a vast amount of information on the Internet about COBIT. We recommend the following sites as a good place to start:

- **Information Systems Audit and Control Association** www.isaca.org

- **IT Governance Institute** www.itgi.org/

Q: Is it necessary that I use the COBIT guidelines?

A: No. You can follow any predefined standard, or even use your own. However, bear in mind that choosing to use a standard with which your audit company is unfamiliar will extend your compliance process and jeopardize failing compliance.

Q: Can I implement all the COBIT guidelines?

A: Yes, if you have an unlimited budget and unlimited resources.

Q: Can SOX compliance be achieved without any automation?

A: Yes, but since auditors generally prefer evidence of a control to be system generated, you might find it extremely difficult.

Chapter 3

The Cost of Compliance

Solutions in this chapter:

- Overview
- Why Comply?
- Tools and Applications
- The Human Factor
- Walk the Walk

- ☑ Summary
- ☑ Solutions Fast Track
- ☑ Frequently Asked Questions

Overview

Although Section 404 isn't very specific as to what needs to be done to comply with the Sarbanes-Oxley Act, it is very clear about what needs to be reported and attested.

Section 404

In accordance with Section 404 Executive Management of a public company:

- State the responsibility of management for establishing and maintaining an adequate internal control structure and procedures for financial reporting.

- Contain an assessment, as of the end of the most recent fiscal year of the issuer, of the effectiveness of the internal control structure and procedures of the issuer for financial reporting.

It is the responsibility of the CEO and CFO to provide the attestation and sign off on the company's SEC filing. An understanding by the CFO, CIO, or IT Director of what compliance means and how best to comply will be crucial to the success or failure of the compliance efforts. In this chapter, we discuss the consequences of noncompliance and the benefits of compliance, and look at areas that have the potential to impede or facilitate your efforts to comply.

The following is an excerpt from an article published in the February 07, 2005 edition of *Computerworld*, titled "IT role in Sarb-Ox problems is unclear":

> Many clients of Meta Group Inc. "were keeping their fingers crossed that the auditors weren't going to dig as deep in Year 1 around all of the IT areas," said John Van Decker, an analyst at the research firm in Stamford, Conn.
>
> Van Decker expects that up to 25% of accelerated filers—companies with a market capitalization greater than $75 million whose fiscal year ended after Nov. 15—will report material weaknesses to their internal controls. The cause for 30% to 40% of those companies will be IT or application-control deficiencies.
>
> Van Decker and other experts predicted that problems will be more common among small-to-midsize businesses—those with $75 million to $900 million in revenues—whose IT staffs are stretched too thin to effectively deal with compliance requirements.

Given the statistic quoted by Van Decker and the underlying rationale for the small to midsize businesses to have to report material weaknesses, it is even more critical that they use automation as much as possible and are very discriminating in the tools they select.

The Transparency Test...

The CFO Perspective

Small and mid-cap companies are struggling under the weight of 404 compliance. In many cases, the consolidated cost of 404 compliance is turning profitable companies into unprofitable companies. Automation, specifically open source automation, provides a cost containment tool in a world seemingly without help. Automation can help control spending, and assists in standardizing processes. As with any system implementation, you must start with good planning and analysis. A number of tools are available, and it is imperative that you choose the one that is best for your organization. Of course, this analysis should be done in concert with your external SOX support team to ensure it meets the audit requirements as well. Once implemented, as with any process, you need to review it and revise as needed on a regular basis.

Open source as an IT tool for SOX implementation can provide quality advantages over closed source software depending on the number of volunteers willing to evaluate and test it. The key is to map any automation tool into your existing infrastructure and organization. Your company's size and, perhaps more pertinent, experience with open source software should impact your plan. Of course, your IT organization will need to be comfortable with any open source solution, just as with a proprietary solution, that the quality and capability of the software is acceptable. This, however, may be harder for them to evaluate given the nature of the support." — *Steve Lanza*

Why Comply?

If a company does not comply with the Sarbanes–Oxley Act, it will expose itself to the possibility of lawsuits and negative publicity. If a corporate officer, even if unintentionally, files an inaccurate certification, he or she is subject to a fine up to $1 million and 10 years in prison. If a corporate officer *intentionally* files an inaccurate certification, the fine can be as much as $5 million and possible 20 years in prison. When thinking about the severity of the consequences of noncompliance for corporation and corporate officers, we must remember that the intent, although arguably misguided, was to prevent occurrences such as those that happened at WorldCom and Enron—hence the stiff penalties for those at the top.

Therefore, the downside of not complying with the Sarbanes-Oxley Act can be pretty severe for a company's executive management. However, there is, perhaps not as tangible, an upside to complying. If your IT organization is typical, it is understaffed, has not done a technology assessment/refresh (applications/hardware) in quite some time, and activities like documenting and developing policies and procedures have been relegated to the backburner in deference to putting out current fires. By no means are we suggesting that the requirement to comply with Sarbanes-Oxley Act be used as a catch-all or some sort of panacea to fix all the ills that exist in your IT organization. What we are suggesting is that because of the need to comply with the Sarbanes-Oxley Act, opportunities will present themselves to address both SOX deficiencies and other IT organization deficiencies. Moreover, with adequate research and planning, a CFO, CIO, or IT Director can capitalize on his or her compliance effort to address some of the aforementioned problems in the IT organization.

NOTE

With adequate research and planning, Sarbanes-Oxley compliance can be used to correct additional IT organization deficiencies beyond SOX. Failure to comply may negatively affect both a company's executive management and the company.

Tools and Applications

Later in the book we cover the configuration and implementation of various tools and applications that you can use in your effort to comply with the Sarbanes-Oxley Act. Here, we look at a logical grouping of SOX controls and some of the tools that can be used.

As Table 3.1 indicates, in distilling down the COBIT control objectives, you will find that they fit into four main categories: security, change management, monitoring, and logical access. When looking at the possible implementation of a tool or application, it will be necessary to determine what "control objective" it will support and to which grouping it applies. In determining the grouping, you may prevent the acquisition of tools and applications that are redundant. However, bear in mind that some tools may have multiple functions and therefore overlap other tools. In instances where this occurs, it will be necessary, based on your environment, to determine the best tools or applications for the task.

Table 3.1 COBIT Control Objectives Fit into Four Main Categories

Security	Change Management
Virus Prevention Procedure	Application change management
Badge Access control procedure	Database change management
Procedure for monitoring user physical access	Operating system and hardware change management
Environment controls	Network design and change management procedure
Procedure for granting access to data center	Firewall change management procedure
Remote network connectivity procedure	

Monitoring	Logical Access
Monitoring server performance and capacity	Procedure for maintaining applications user access
Network availability monitoring procedure	System authentication password control procedure
Backup/restore procedures	Database and applications security control
Network node backups procedure	Application password administration controls
Network security monitoring and controls	Procedure for granting access to servers/file system OS security controls

Before we delve into some of the tools and applications that you can use to assist with compliance of the Sarbanes–Oxley Act, let's answer a few questions:

Q: Why would I need or want tools or applications to comply with Sarbanes–Oxley?

A: Remember that your processes and procedures will need to be repeatable, so one of the best ways to have a process repeatable is to automate it.

Q: Will a tool or application improve my existing processes?

A: No, a bad process will still be a bad process. However, a tool or application will allow you to put correction in place faster.

Q: Can't I achieve compliance without tools and applications?

A: Yes, but your process will need to be sustainable over time, and again, the best way to do that is to use a tool to automate.

Now that we have defined a framework for organizing the tools and applications, let's look at some of the available tools and applications. Although the majority of the tools are open source, not all of those listed here are. However, the tools and applications listed that are not open source will be a fraction of the cost of mainstream tools or applications.

What's Out There?

The list of tools and applications in the following sections is a representation of the tools and applications that are readily available to assist you with your Sarbanes-Oxley compliance efforts. Later in this book, we cover these tools in more detail and introduce others as well.

Security

Some security tools that can help you with your SOX compliance efforts include Shorewall, Astaro Security Linux, Smoothwall, and Snort. In this section we describe these tools.

Shorewall

An iptables-based firewall for Linux systems. By describing your firewall/gateway requirements via entries in configuration files, Shorewall will read those configuration files, and with the help of the iptables utility, Shorewall configures Netfilter to match your requirements.

Key features of Shorewall include:

- Customizable using configuration files

- Supports status monitoring with an audible alarm when an "interesting" packet is detected

- Includes a fallback script that backs out the installation of the most recent version of Shorewall, and an uninstall script for completely uninstalling the firewall

- Can be used on a dedicated firewall system, a multifunction gateway/router/server, or on a stand-alone GNU/Linux system
- Static NAT is supported
- Proxy ARP is supported
- Provides DMZ functionality
- Support for IPsec, GRE, and IPIP tunnels
- Support for traffic control/shaping

Astaro Security Linux

An all-encompassing network security gateway composed of a firewall, intrusion protection, virus protection, SPAM protection, URL filtering, and a VPN gateway.

Key features of Astaro Security Linux include:

- Stateful packet inspection
- Deep packet filtering
- Application-level intrusion detection
- Content filtering
- Virus detection for e-mail traffic (SMTP and POP3)
- Web traffic (HTTP), whitelists and blacklists
- IPsec and PPTP VPN tunneling
- SPAM blocking, logging and reporting

Smoothwall

Although not as robust or feature rich as Astaro or Shorewall, Smoothwall is another open source firewall. Smoothwall is probably more suited to smaller organizations with simple ruleset requirements.

Key features of Smoothwall include:

- Automated modem/advanced ISDN autoprobing,
- Ethernet ADSL/cable, USB ADSL
- Supports multiple Ethernet cards
- Web manageable
- Has SSH and DHCP capabilities
- Full firewall logging and auditing functionality

Snort

An intrusion detection system capable of performing real-time traffic analysis and packet logging on IP networks. It can perform protocol analysis, content searching/matching. Snort can be used to detect a variety of attacks and probes, such as buffer overflows, stealth port scans, CGI attacks, SMB probes, OS fingerprinting attempts, and more. Snort uses a flexible rules language to describe traffic it should collect or pass, and includes a detection engine using a modular plug-in architecture. Snort has real-time alerting capability as well, incorporating alerting mechanisms for Syslog, user-specified files, a UNIX socket, or WinPopup messages to Windows clients using Samba's smbclient. Snort has three primary uses: as a straight packet sniffer like tcpdump, as a packet logger that is useful for network traffic debugging, and as a full-blown network intrusion detection system.

Monitoring

In this section, we'll discuss monitoring tools that help you comply with SOX guidelines. These tools include Nagios, Big Brother, Tripwire, Sentinel, and Linux-HA Heartbeat. Three backup tools are also described: AMANDA, Bacula, and the Hydra Backup System.

Nagios

A host and service monitor designed to detect network and services performance issues, based on user-defined thresholds. When problems are detected, Nagios can send notifications to administrative contacts via e-mail, instant message, SMS, etc. Current status information, historical logs, and reports can all be accessed via a Web browser.

Big Brother

Similar to Nagios, Big Brother is designed to monitor system and network-delivered services for availability. The network status is displayed on a color-coded Web page in near-real time. When problems are detected, Big Brother can send an alert via e-mail, pager, or text messaging.

Tripwire

A system integrity checker that compares properties of designated files and directories against information stored in a previously generated database.

Sentinel

A fast file scanner similar to Tripwire or Viper with built-in authentication using the RIPEMD 160-bit MAC hashing function. It uses a single database similar to

Tripwire, maintains file integrity using the RIPEMD algorithm, and produces secure, signed logfiles. Its main design goal is to detect intruders modifying files.

Linux-HA Heartbeat

Provides a heartbeat and IP address takeover functions for a high-availability Linux cluster. It supports multiple IP addresses and a simple two-node primary/secondary model. The heartbeat component sends heartbeat packets across the network (or serial ports) to the other instances of Heartbeat. When heartbeat packets are no longer received, the node is assumed dead, and any services (resources) it was providing are failed over to the other node. Heartbeat also has the capability to monitor routers and switches as though they were cluster members using the ping or ping group directives.

Heartbeat can monitor the following typical applications:

- Web servers
- LVS director servers
- Mail servers
- Database servers
- Firewalls
- File servers
- DNS servers
- DHCP servers
- Proxy Caching servers

AMANDA

The Advanced Maryland Automatic Network Disk Archiver (AMANDA) is a backup system that allows a LAN administrator to set up a single master backup server to back up multiple hosts to a single large-capacity tape drive. AMANDA uses native dump and/or GNU tar facilities and can back up a large number of workstations running multiple versions of UNIX. Along with supporting various Linux-based OSs, AMANDA is able to support many different tape backup hardware systems.

Types of hardware AMANDA can support include the following:

- Dell
- HP
- Sony
- Quantum

NOTE

To determine if a particular H/W platform is supported, visit the AMANDA site at www.amanda.org/.

Bacula

A network-based backup program. It is a set of computer programs that allow a system administrator to manage backup, recovery, and verification of computer data across a network of computers of different kinds. Because of its modular design, Bacula is capable of scaling from small to large networks. Bacula is relatively easy to use, and contains many advanced storage management features that make it easy to find and recover lost or damaged files.

Bacula supports:

- Catalog services
- Can write to multiple volumes (i.e., is not limited by your tape drive capacity)
- Many of the same features as Legato Networker. ARCserveIT, Arkeia, etc.

Hydra Backup System

A backup system that contains a backup server, a command-line client, and a graphical client. The clients can be used to administer backup commands to any Hydra server over a network. The backup server allows you to specify which paths to back up, and will store backups on any number of user-defined FTP repositories. You can back up directories daily, weekly, or monthly.

Change Management

Change management involves using E-Groupware tools. In the next section, we define E-Groupware and the modules that are available.

E-Groupware

E-Groupware is a Web-based, multiuser groupware suite developed on a custom set of PHP-based APIs. Modules currently available include e-mail, address-book, calendar, info-log (notes, to-dos, phone calls), content management, forum, bookmarks, and wiki.

Logical Access

In this section we discuss three logical access tools: Samba NTLM, Kerberos, and PAM.

Samba NTLM

Microsoft encrypted security for domains as implemented in Samba.

Kerberos

A single signon authentication protocol, based on tickets. It is a network authentication protocol, and is designed to provide strong authentication for client/server applications by using secret-key cryptography.

PAM

A mechanism for authenticating users. It provides a way to develop programs independent of authentication scheme. These programs need "authentication modules" attached to them at runtime in order to work. Which authentication module to attach depends on the local system setup, and is at the discretion of the local system administrator.

Now that we have identified some of the tools that are available to assist with Sarbanes-Oxley compliance, and assuming the necessary due diligence has been done, we can group them based on Table 3.1. Under normal circumstances, IT organizations generally like redundancy. However, when it comes to Sarbanes-Oxley compliance, configuring tools and applications that are redundant or significantly overlap will require more time and resources and jeopardize your compliance efforts.

TIP

Open source tools should pass the functionality test and same requirements as a proprietary tool. Try to minimize tool redundancy and overlap as much as possible. Choose the tool that's right for your environment—size, complexity, and so on.

The Human Factor

At this point, we will assume that executive management's understanding of the need to comply with SOX is sufficient motivation to drive the necessary changes in their company. Hence, we will not provide reasons for the change, but rather guidance for change and identify what might be an unthought-of obstacle. In general, many people are averse to change, especially change within the organization or company for which they work. Some primary reasons for resistance to change include:

- Fear of the unknown
- The belief that things are fine as they are
- Do not understand what's driving the change
- Believe the change is just another exercise that can be ignored
- WIFM (What's In It For Me) comes into play

Again, assuming executive management has come onboard, the change process can be focused on lower level of employees at the company. To do so successfully, communication is key. Communication can and should be deployed in various ways and repeated consistently and often, via memos issued by executive management, employee meetings, informal meetings, and, if feasible, one-on-one conversations with individual employees.

> Sun Tzu once said, "If you know the enemy and know yourself, you need not fear the result of a hundred battles. If you know yourself but not the enemy, for every victory gained you will also suffer a defeat. If you know neither the enemy nor yourself, you will succumb in every battle."

Lessons Learned...

Tell Me You Didn't

During the course of this book we will touch inevitably touch on various aspects of this chapter, as well as "Prevent Controls and "Detect Controls". However, if there is not a common understanding and goal within the IT Organization responsible for executing your existing and new processes and procedures, your audit will almost assuredly be destined to fail.

Although BuiltRight Construction IT Organization already had various procedures as with most IT Organizations they weren't strictly followed and needed to be modified. So as part of the process of preparing for their Sarbanes-Oxley audit BuiltRight Construction IT Organization updated and re-implemented and tested all of their procedures. Thinking they had done all that needed to be done BuiltRight Construction was fairly confident that they would not have any problems related to IT execution. They couldn't have been more wrong. As part of

Continued

their audit one of the auditors required access to BuiltRight's network in order to test a control so, he asked the Admin for the required access. Without a hesitation the Admin granted the auditor access to the network without following any of the procedures that had been communicated to the auditors. Fortunately for BuiltRight this incident happened during its self-assessment phase and was corrected prior to its real audit. The main point to remember is that you can never test too much to see if the processes that have been defined are the ones people are actually following.

This might seem to be a strange quote to find in a book addressing Sarbanes-Oxley compliance, and in particular, in a section addressing change. If you were to ask any CFO, CIO, or IT director responsible for implementing Sarbanes-Oxley who "enemy" was in reference to, he or she would probably say "the end user," of course. These individuals would be in for at best a surprise, or at worst, a gotcha that could hamper their ability to obtain compliance. The biggest threat in this regard will more than likely come from within the IT organization itself. As a rule, within any company or organization exist what we refer to as *personal processes*. These processes are usually formed on an individual basis with an underpinning of *quid pro quo* (Latin for "something for something," used to generally describe the mutual agreement between two parties in which each party provides goods or service in return for goods or service). If you are not aware that these processes exist and that they can be extremely detrimental to your compliance process, regardless of how good your controls in place are, your controls will almost certainly fail.

TIP

IT staff may not want to or openly embrace change. Communicate, ad nauseam, the need for SOX compliance and the consequences of non-compliance. Understand and manage the personal processes, And don't make assumptions when it comes to change.

To combat personal processes, here are some simple guidelines to keep in mind:

- Overcommunicate to the IT staff what you are doing, what their roles are, and the consequences of failure.

- Get buy-in on the plan and what needs to be done.

- Wherever possible, delegate decisions to the IT staff.

- Bear in mind that change is a process, and usually a slow one.

- Retain responsibility for reaching the ultimate goal.

- Lead by example.
- If necessary, demonstrate any consequences with staff and use community.

Walk the Walk

Table 3.2 is an example of the type of policy BuiltRight Construction might use in its activities to comply with the Sarbanes-Oxley Act, and although BuiltRight Construction is fictional, the procedure and the areas it defines are not. At first glance, the policy appears to be a standard procedure that would have been used by any IT organization prior to Sarbanes-Oxley, so what the big deal? If the Sarbanes-Oxley Act was never drafted, your IT organization would be audited based on traditional audit practices and guidelines. The auditors would give this policy a cursory review, at best, more to ensure that you have a documented procedure than anything else. Now, here is the big deal, aside from being an actual policy used to obtain Sarbanes-Oxley compliance, it contains two very important areas that were added to make the procedure acceptable for Sarbanes-Oxley compliance—5.0 Review and 6.0 Enforcement. Although it is important that you adhere to what you state in your policy, be particularly cautious about what you stipulate in Review; if you can't or won't adhere to it, don't state it. Whether during initial testing after the remediation phase or during a subsequent compliance audit, the auditor will want to see evidence of the effectiveness of the control.

As stated previously in this book, COBIT is merely a detailed set of "Best Known Methods" for IT. Therefore, there is no need to discuss this particular policy's password parameters (password length, password age, etc.); those would need to be tailored to fit your environment. However, we would like to make note of some of the particular areas in the policy to which you must pay special attention:

- **Scope** If your company has other locations, whether domestic or international, it is critical that you define what location your policy affects and which it does not.

- **Review** There are two concerns that you must define well regarding the "Review":

    - **The frequency of review** If the interval between reviews is too long, the auditor will perceive the control as ineffective.

    - **Connect the review of evidence to the CFO** Although the IT manager may perform a review monthly, the CFO will perform a review of the effectiveness of the control and evidence on a quarterly basis.

■ **Enforcement** You may not have to define consequences in all policies, but if you do, you want to ensure that Human Resources reviews them before formalizing and publishing your modified or new policy. Generally speaking, it is a good idea to have information readily available to all employees, using whatever mechanism works best in your environment. Moreover, the employment packet for a new hire should contain a document (which the new employee will sign) stating that he or she has read and understands the corporate policies.

NOTE

It is also a good idea to periodically re-distribute corporate policies and have existing employees review and sign a document stating they have read and understand the policies.

The following outline is an example of a SOX compliance policy:

BuiltRight Construction Company

Information Technology

Section	
Policy Title	Password Control Policy
Approved By:	Joe Manager
Policy Number	123
Issue Date	04/15/2005
Supersedes	

1.0 Overview

Passwords are an important aspect of computer security, and are the front line of protection for employees' accounts. A poorly chosen password may result in the compromise of BuiltRight's entire corporate network. As such, all BuiltRight employees (including contractors and vendors with access to BuiltRight systems) are responsible for taking the appropriate steps, as outlined here, to select and secure their passwords.

2.0 Purpose

The purpose of this policy is to establish a standard for the creation of strong passwords, the protection of those passwords, and the frequency of change.

3.0 Scope

The scope of this policy includes all employees who have or are responsible for an account (or any form of access that supports or requires a password) on any system that resides at any BuiltRight facility, has access to the BuiltRight network, or stores any nonpublic BuiltRight information.

4.0 Policy

4.1 General

All system-level passwords (Win2000/NT) admin, application administration accounts, etc.) must be changed on at least a quarterly basis.

All employee-level and system-level passwords must conform to the guidelines described here.

4.2 Guidelines

4.2.1 General Password Construction Guidelines

Passwords are used for various purposes at BuiltRight, some of which include user level accounts, Web accounts, e-mail accounts, screensaver protection, voicemail password, and local router logins. Since very few systems have support for one-time tokens (dynamic passwords that are only used once), everyone should be aware of how to select strong passwords.

Poor, weak passwords have the following characteristics:

- The password contains fewer than eight characters.
- The password is a word found in a dictionary (English or foreign).
- Names of family, pets, friends, coworkers, fantasy characters, etc.
- Computer terms and names, commands, sites, companies, hardware, software.
- The words *sanjose*, "*sanfran*," or any derivation.
- Birthdays and other personal information such as addresses and phone numbers.
- Word or number patterns like aaabbb, qwerty, zyxwvuts, 123321, etc.

- Any of the above spelled backward.
- Any of the above preceded or followed by a digit (e.g., secret1, 1secret).

Strong passwords have the following characteristics:

- Contain both upper- and lowercase characters (e.g., a–z, A–Z).
- Have digits, punctuation characters, and letters (e.g., 0-9! @#$%^&*()_+|~-=\`{}[]:";'<>?,./).
- Are at least eight alphanumeric characters long.
- Not a word in any language, slang, dialect, jargon, etc.
- Are not based on personal information, names of family, etc.

4.2.2 Password Protection Standards

Do not use the same password for BuiltRight accounts as for other non–BuiltRight access (e.g., personal ISP account, option trading, benefits, etc.). Where possible, do not use the same password for various BuiltRight access needs.

Here is a list of "don'ts":

- Don't reveal a password over the phone to ANYONE.
- Don't reveal a password in an e-mail message.
- Don't reveal a password to the boss.
- Don't talk about a password in front of others.
- Don't hint at the format of a password (e.g., "my family name").
- Don't reveal a password on questionnaires or security forms.
- Don't share a password with family members.
- Don't reveal a password to coworkers while on vacation.
- Do not use the "Remember Password" feature of applications (e.g., Eudora, Outlook, Netscape Messenger).
- Do not write passwords down and store them anywhere in your office. Do not store passwords in a file on ANY computer system (including Palm Pilots or similar devices) without encryption.

4.3 System Policy

- Maximum Password Agn   90 Days
- Minimum Password Lengtn   8 Characters

- Minimum Password Agn   5 Days
- Password Uniquenesn   5 Passwords
- Account Lockoun   n   10 Bad Login Attempts
- Lockout Duration   n   Forever (until admin unlocks)

Change passwords at least once every six months (except system-level passwords, which must be changed quarterly). The recommended change interval is every four months.

If you suspect an account or password has been compromised, report the incident to IT.

5.0 Review

IT Director to annually review current Windows Password policy to ensure current policies are still enforced.

6.0 Enforcement

Any employee found to have violated this policy might be subject to disciplinary action, up to and including termination of employment.

Passwords should never be written down or stored online. Try to create passwords that can be easily remembered. One way to do this is to create a password based on a song title, affirmation, or other phrase. For example, the phrase might be "This May Be One Way To Remember," and the password could be "TmB1w2R!", "Tmb1W>r~", or some other variation.

If we go back to the quality practice of PDCA (Plan, Do, Check and Act) developed in the 1950s, we might start to see similarities between COBIT and the Quality discipline. At it core, COBIT is no more than a quality discipline, much like Deming or Juran, of which the major objective is to have a closed looped process that drives continuous improvement. If we were to apply the quality approach to a control objective, it would look something like Figure 3.1. The concept of Figure 3.1 could be applied to a manual process; however, it tends to work best when automation is used. The define policy/control objective would drive the requirements, functionality, and configuration of the application or tool, which would in turn drive the functionality and configuration of the application or tool for monitoring/reporting, whereas the cycle continues to repeat.

Figure 3.1 Quality Control Process Cycle

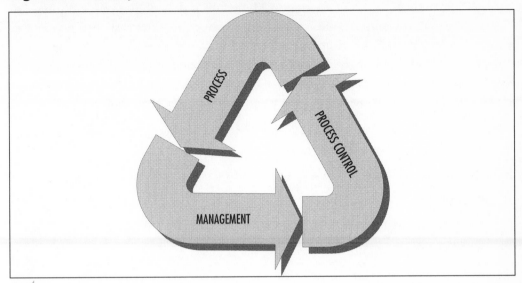

TIP

Think of COBIT as a quality process.

Definition/Implementation, Execution and Managing/Monitoring of Control Objective should follow a closed loop process.

Your policies should not contain any activities your organization can't sustain.

Summary

In this chapter, we discussed the need for SOX compliance and the possible consequences of noncompliance—lawsuits, negative publicity for the company, and fines for executive management. Although it's important to understand the consequences, it is paramount that you realize that with planning, knowledge, and a great deal of work, it is possible to comply with the Sarbanes-Oxley Act, even in a small company. To this extent, we looked at some applications and tools that are readily available to assist in compliance with the Sarbanes-Oxley Act. Regarding application and tools, it is imperative that you minimize the number of applications and tools you select, maximize their capabilities, and minimize overlap.

The remaining two areas we discussed were "The Human Factor" and "Walk the Talk." While perhaps not as interesting to IT people as the applications and tools discussion, it is just as vital that you evaluate and manage these items as they pertain to your environment. In "The Human Factor" section, we discussed reasons why employees, including IT staff, may not embrace the changes that SOX compliance may bring, and steps to try to effectively negate any resistance to change. Given the importance of change management, we re-emphasize these steps here:

- Overcommunicate to the IT staff what you are doing, what their roles are, and the consequences of failure.

- Get buy-in on the plan and what needs to be done.

- Wherever possible, delegate decisions to the IT staff.

- Bear in mind that change is a process, and usually a slow one.

- Retain responsibility for reaching the ultimate goal.

- Lead by example.

- If necessary, demonstrate any consequences with staff and user community.

Finally, we discussed "Walk the Talk," and the importance of the following:

- Keep your policies/procedures and or controls as simple as possible.

- You have to be to sustain whatever you implement.

- If you can't sustain it or won't, do not define it.

Solutions Fast Track

Overview

- ☑ It is the responsibility of the CEO and CFO of a company to provide the attestment and sign off on the company's SEC filing.

- ☑ CFO, CIO, and IT Directors must understand what compliance means.

- ☑ There are significant consequences of noncompliance.

Why Comply?

- ☑ There are significant consequences of noncompliance.

☑ If a company does not comply with the Sarbanes-Oxley Act, it will expose itself to the possibility of lawsuits and negative publicity.

☑ If a corporate officer intentionally files an inaccurate certification, the fine can be as much as $5 million and possible 20 years in prison.

☑ Opportunities will present themselves to address SOX deficiencies and other IT organization deficiencies.

☑ CFO, CIO, or IT Director can capitalize on their compliance effort to address some of the aforementioned problems in their IT organization.

The Human Factor

☑ Executive management should initiate the communication process, setting the tone and explaining the process.

☑ Communication can and should be deployed in various ways and repeated consistently.

☑ Informal and personal processes are as big a threat to compliance as poor procedures and controls are—Quid Pro Quo.

☑ Change is very difficult on an individual level, and extremely difficult on an organizational or company level.

☑ Change is a process.

Walk the Talk

☑ The previous audit process was fundamentally done at a cursory level and there was no need to show evidence.

☑ If you can't sustain it, do not state it in your policy.

☑ Auditors will want to see evidence of control effectiveness and review.

☑ Identify as much as you can in the initial discovery phase.

☑ Don't minimize the importance of review.

☑ With a few modifications, you may be able to use existing policies.

Frequently Asked Questions

The following Frequently Asked Questions, answered by the authors of this book, are designed to both measure your understanding of the concepts presented in this chapter and to assist you with real-life implementation of these concepts. To have your questions about this chapter answered by the author, browse to **www.syngress.com/solutions** and click on the **"Ask the Author"** form. You will also gain access to thousands of other FAQs at ITFAQnet.com.

Q: Are there any other repercussions if a company fails to comply with the Sarbanes–Oxley Act?

A: Yes. In addition to possible litigation and negative publicity, a company could possibly be de-listed if it fails to comply with the Sarbanes–Oxley Act.

Q: Are open source tools really effective for complying with the Sarbanes–Oxley Act?

A: If done properly, yes. Keep in mind that applications and tools are merely one piece of the puzzle in your efforts to comply with the Sarbanes–Oxley Act. Just as important will be your ability to customize the COBIT guidelines to your environment, select the best application or tool for your environment, and configure them correctly.

Q: Are the applications and tools listed in this chapter the only ones available?

A: Absolutely not. Many sites on the Internet offer open source tools for free, and proprietary tools for a very low cost. A few good places to start are:

- **Shareware downloads** www.download.com/
- **Open source downloads** http://freshmeat.net
- **Open source projects** http://sourceforge.net/

Q: How important is it to customize the COBIT guidelines to our environment?

A: Very important, for two reasons. This process has the potential to reduce the number of activities you will need to undertake, and will provide requirements for the type of applications and tools you may want to deploy.

Q: How important is change management?

A: Very important. You can have the best policies, applications, tools, and controls in place; however, you will never be able to completely eliminate the "Human Factor." Therefore, if you fail to address the area of change management, you may fail Sarbanes–Oxley compliance regardless of your other efforts.

Q: Can I really use some of my exiting policies?

A: Yes. You may have to make some slight modifications, but as long as they are documented and support a control, they can be used.

Chapter 4

Why Open Source?

Solutions in this chapter:

- **The Open Source Model**
- **Closed Source Application Development**
- **Open Source Application Development**
- **The Business Case for Open Source**
- **Assessing Your Infrastructure**
- **Case Studies: Introduction to the Sample Companies**

☑ **Summary**

☑ **Solutions Fast Track**

☑ **Frequently Asked Questions**

The Open Source Model

In this chapter, we initially take a brief departure from Sarbanes–Oxley to discuss open source software, its developmental methodology, and some of the benefits that can be realized by its adoption into your organization. Undoubtedly, you have had some exposure to the phenomenon, whether in the actual deployment of various projects, or at the very least, you may have read about open source in trade periodicals, news publications, or other sources. The purpose of this book is not necessarily to educate you on the philosophy of open source per se, but rather to have an understanding of the underlying concepts and some of the possible misconceptions surrounding the subject so you can gain the most benefit from the technologies presented here. Before we discuss the pros and cons of the open source model, we should spend a few minutes discussing how software is developed in general, and highlight the differences between this and closed source methodology.

The Transparency Test...

Open Source Licenses

The General Public License (GPL) is by far the most popular, widely used, and sometimes controversial license in the open source arena; however, it is not the only one by any means. When most people talk about an open source-compatible license, they are usually referring to a license that has been reviewed and certified by the Open Source Initiative (OSI), a nonprofit organization whose sole purpose is to promote the idea of Free/Libre/Open Source Software (FLOSS). Here, we take a brief look at three examples of OSI certified licenses and how they differ.

GNU General Public License (GPL)

The GPL is termed a "strong" license, because it is completely incompatible with proprietary software. The GPL compels a user to make the source code available when distributing any copies of the software, and all modifications to the original source must be licensed under the GPL. In addition, if any GPL licensed source code is incorporated into another project (known as a "derivative work"), the entire project must be released under the GPL. For this reason, GPL licensed software cannot be mixed with proprietary offerings because it inherently would render the proprietary source GPL licensed as well. Users are free to make copies and changes, redistribute, and charge money for derivative works as long as the source code is available and a copyright notice is attached.

Continued

Lesser GNU Public License (LPGL)

The LPGL is essentially the same as the GPL, with a notable exception. Unlike the GPL, which requires the source code for the "derivative work" to be licensed under the GPL and the source be made available, the LPGL allows binary-only linking of applications, typically libraries, with any other application, including proprietary software. Thus, under the terms of the LPGL, the original source and any changes made to it must be made available along with a copyright notice; however, if a binary version of it is used by a nonfree application, the source of that application is not required to be released under the LPGL.

BSD/Modified BSD License

By contrast, the original Berkeley Software Distribution (BSD) license and the more recently modified version of it are the most permissive in nature. These basically say that users are free do to with the software whatever they like, including modify the original source or incorporate it into another project. Users are free to redistribute their derivative works without any requirement to make the source code or any of their modifications available. The only requirement is that the original authors be acknowledged in the license that does accompany the released application, whatever it may be. The only difference between the Modified BSD License and the Original BSD License is that an advertising clause was removed.

Closed Source Application Development

Figure 4.1 is a simplified diagram of the typical development cycle of your average software project.

Figure 4.1 Proprietary Software Development Model

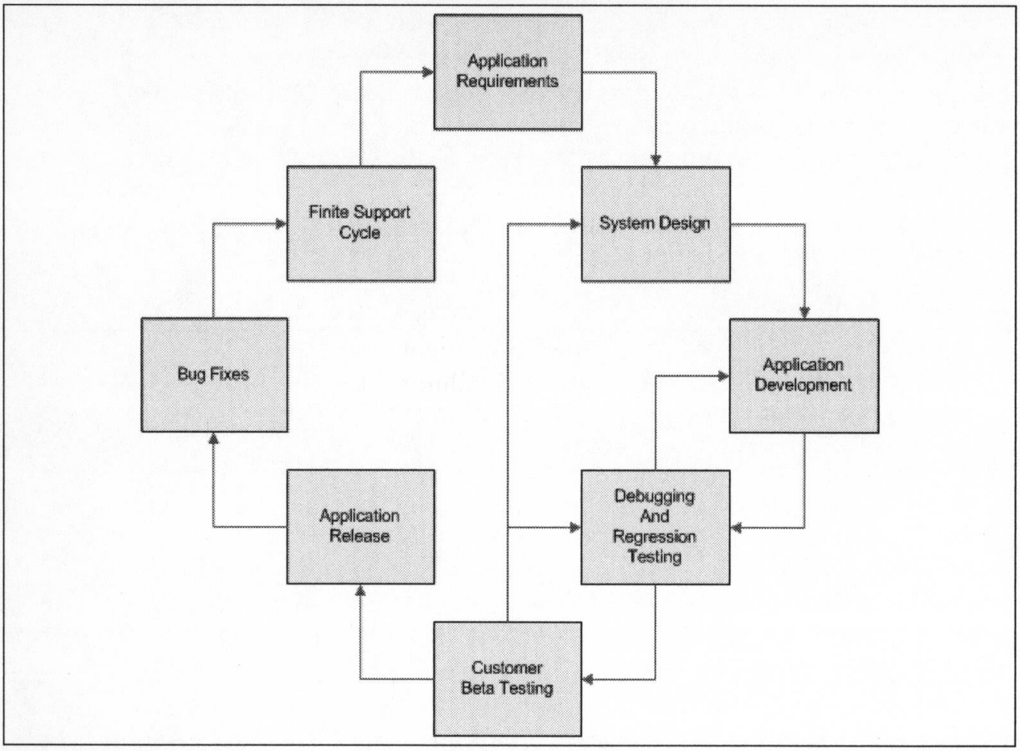

NOTE

Although the diagram in Figure 4.1 is useful for our discussion, many aspects of the software development model may not be represented in detail. The goal of this section is to give you a flavor of the typical development considerations and major phases in both open and closed source projects, and some of the fundamental differences that drive each.

Application Requirements

When a company sets out to develop a product, the first step is to decide what need its product will satisfy or what functionality the company wishes its product to provide. This set of requirements can come from many sources such as customer feedback, expertise of those involved in the venture, or your basic "light bulb" type of idea. The point is that the company defines the set of parameters and functionality that its product will encompass, and the feature set is influenced by factors such as time to market and competition. Because this is often a formal process, significant time, energy, and financial resources can be devoted to the project during this stage to determine the marketability and feasibility of the project, and importantly, the potential profitability to offset the development costs.

Because a significant portion of a closed source company's revenue stream comes from the prospective sales of the application, most software companies attempt to select projects that will maximize their ability to generate profits, either by identifying a "vertical market" in which they can write a specialized application and charge a comparatively large sum for each software license, or developing an application that has mass appeal where the company might not necessarily charge as much per license, but make up the difference with volume sales. As with any for-profit model, it is important to note and is completely understandable that a software company's motivation *must* be for the maximum salability of its product for the least amount of research and development costs accrued.

System Design and Application Development

The system design phase involves describing the problem in terms of a solution or set of solutions. During this phase, the requirements are hashed out, the blueprint of the result is devised, and the blueprint is usually broken out into the conceptual user interface and the technical details necessary to meet the requirements. On the user interface side, the design can be driven by various inputs such as designer preference, look and feel requirements dictated by the customer, cultural considerations, or simply as demanded by the system structure. The technical design, however, has other goals such as performance and efficiency, and code abstraction and modularization.

One of the important design goals of any modern software company is to extract as much general functionality into modules or libraries so it can reuse this functionality in other applications. The identification of common or repeating functionality, also known as *design patterns*, and abstraction of these enables a company to leverage its research and development costs by spreading the fruits of its coding labor across multiple projects. Interestingly, if a company does not have the time or expertise to develop certain aspects of its application, it can choose to purchase code libraries from other sources. As we will see later, this is an important concept with open source; however, the approach is subtly different.

Once the logic of the system design has been described and the user interface specification is complete, the company will then employ a team of developers to actually write the code based on the functional design. The size and expertise of this team are characteristically based on factors such as the development budget, how quickly the company wishes to deliver its product, and the complexity of the design. This team of developers may go back to prior steps in the process in an iterative fashion, but the result is to put physical code to the logical design.

Debugging and Regression Testing

Depending on the size and scope of the project, the company may employ a team of testers to debug the software and perform regression tests with prior versions for compatibility, and possibly identify the points where data from older versions may need to be converted to be compatible with the new version. Often, problems found at this stage merit a revisit to the system design phase in the event a major flaw in the original specification is discovered. The design is then modified, and sometimes it is necessary to go all the way back to the application requirements to clarify and/or reestablish expectations so the design can move forward. It is also at this point that a company may decide to pare down an application's features, especially problematic ones so they can reasonably meet any previously established deadlines. A company has to weigh the pros and cons between how much to test and what features to keep while still maximizing potential sales.

Customer Beta Testing and Application Release

Once a company decides the application is ready for prime time, almost every project of note goes through some type of customer trials. These customers may be existing users of a previous version of the product or users of other offerings the software company might have. Another tactic software companies may deploy, especially if their product fits into a specialty or niche market, will be to recruit beta sites that in the course of their businesses would appropriately test the major features of the application in exchange for deeply discounted pricing once the software "goes gold" and is finally released.

Just when you would think the company could breathe a sigh of relief now that its development efforts have molded an idea into a tangible product, the sales and marketing machine (which may have been in motion far before the actual release) and customer support now need to spend their time and effort to get their customer base to adopt and, most importantly, pay for the software the company just spent large sums of money to develop.

Bug Fixes and Support Cycle

Once the application has been released, customers respond fairly quickly with issues they are experiencing; whether they are bugs that manifest themselves or "random features" that always seem to crop up, the company usually has a laundry list of bugs and feature changes to make, especially if the application is a 1.0 release. The company now has the option of devoting enough developer resources to fix each pending issue, but the more realistic scenario is that the list is prioritized and a budgeted number of resources are devoted to fixing bugs, while the remainder is allocated to developing the next version or another product. Thus, some bug fixes may be pushed into subsequent releases or never fixed at all. The successful software company finds the right balance between public relations and minimizing support expenditures.

Open Source Application Development

Generally speaking, the term *open source* refers to a method of software development where volunteer developers contribute to a particular project and donate all of their source code and documentation efforts to the public for the benefit of all. Altruistic as this may sound, most people who get involved with open source at the coding level do so for several reasons. Some developers may join to avail themselves of the expertise of other developers on the project and benefit from their work, some desire peer recognition, and some simply may be paid by a company to develop software for a need the company has and the resulting application is released to open source. We will explore this in greater detail in a moment; however, the salient point is that very often, interested individuals both drive the requirements of the software project and directly develop the result to their own satisfaction. In contrast to the closed development model, Figure 4.2 diagrams a typical open source development cycle.

Figure 4.2 Open Source Software Development Model

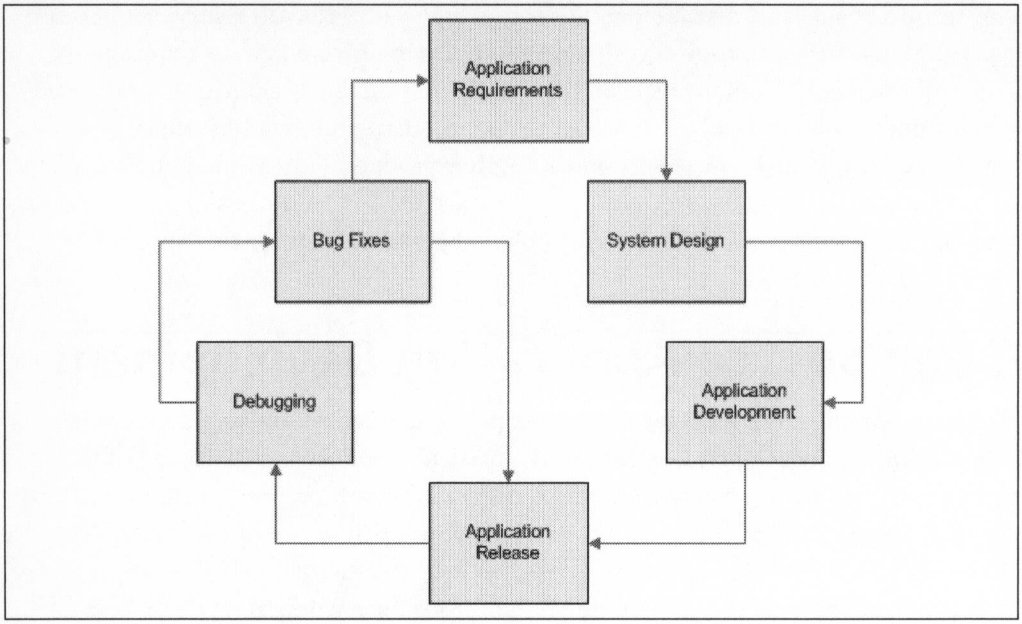

Application Requirements

An open source project's application requirements are typically derived from the following scenarios:

- **Developer driven** The most frequent reason for a project to be started in the first place is that a developer or group of developers decide to embark on a new software project, possibly for fame and fortune, but more likely to solve a personal need they are having either at work or in their personal lives.

- **End-user driven** In this setting, a user or group of users who have a common problem or desire a widget to fulfill a particular software need look at the software landscape in over-the-counter (OTC) and/or existing open source projects. Regardless of whether the OTC applications did not fit their needs or were too expensive, the reason to turn to open source is not important here; what is important is that in this scenario, the end user typically locates an already existing project. End users then download the current version and begin contributing to the application requirements by articulating their needs and desirable features to the project developers via mailing lists, Internet relay chat (IRC), or project forums.

- **Company driven** There are many reasons why a company might be motivated to develop and release an application under the GPL. For one, they might need a specialized application but have limited developer resources. In this example, they would pay their staff to get the project off the ground and spend some effort to rally a community of developers to enhance the application. Another example would be a company that releases a version of its software as open source while offering for sale an enhanced version of the application with more features. Other companies may contribute to the development of a project and offer per-incident support or support contracts as a revenue stream. Open source offers many opportunities for companies with or without developer resources to realize a revenue opportunity.

TIP

Any open source licensing restriction actually applies to only the *licensees* of a project's source. Original developers of an application can do what they like with their source, including selling a proprietary version if they so desire. Only derivative works or improvements to a version the developer may choose to release under an open source license are affected.

System Design and Application Development

Whatever the source of the application requirements, most open source efforts are hacked about in a decidedly closed fashion in the beginning until the core developer decides it is usable enough to release for early feedback and begins to attract other hackers to add to the design features and development. The difference between a programmer who is paid to develop a piece of software he neither uses nor particularly cares about and the community that springs up around an open source project that consists of people interested in using the software and adding features *they* find useful may explain the reason why the quality of code for the latter is so characteristically high. The Internet makes volunteer involvement via distributed and parallel hacking eminently possible, and as we will see in the release and debugging stages, this is crucially important to the success of the FLOSS phenomenon.

Another aspect we discussed in the design and development of proprietary software is the goal of code reuse. This also holds true with open source software. Where a company might desire to leverage its own development efforts across many projects, it perceives to be in its best interest to keep its intellectual property proprietary in nature so that nobody can steal its ideas and form a competitive product. Companies are free to develop interoperability as they see fit within their own products. Open source software, however, tends to employ the UNIX design philosophy (upon which Linux and many open source projects are founded) of writing many small applications that do one thing very well and stringing them together to perform a more complex task. Interoperability is achieved by fiercely supporting and employing standards so that many different projects work together, and the net result is that code reusability is taken to a much greater extreme.

NOTE

Sometimes, companies will decide to release a software application that they previously developed as closed source for many reasons. Examples may be that the software is in danger of becoming obsolete, but the company does not have the developer resources to continue to innovate and maintain the software; or a company may be transitioning from software sales to being service providers, and opening its software would generate or expand its customer base. Netscape Communications was one of the notable firsts with its release of its well-known Communicator Web browser suite, which later became the Mozilla Foundation. Others include Borland's Interbase (now know as the Firebird project), and more recently, Sun Microsystems has released the Solaris 10 operating system under Common Development and Distribution License (CDDL). The CDDL is one of many licenses approved by the OSI; a full listing can be seen at www.opensource.org/.

Application Release, Debugging, and Bug Fixes

As Eric Raymond so famously stated and is often quoted: "Release early. Release often. And listen to your customers." In contrast to a closed source project, where release happens when the company is convinced it is of sufficient quality to be able to charge money for and not completely upset their customer base, most open source projects release their code as often as possible. Although it may seem that users would choose not to muck about with something that might be buggy and wait for a "stable" release (although there are plenty that fall into this category), they will often embrace early releases for several reasons. First, they are regularly stimulated and rewarded with new features, and this fosters a constant flow of communication in the form of bugs and feature requests/refinements, particularly when they see one of their own requests quickly incorporated into the application. Second, it contributes to the rapid stability of an application, because debugging happens in consort between the developers and *the actual users of the project* rather than by the developers of a closed source project who attempt to envision how their user base might use the product.

Many small incremental releases are also rewarding to the developers, who see their work being used and problems being fixed continuously, which gives them a sense of accomplishment very early in the process. This is sufficient to keep most developers interested in continuing to develop while recognizing the contribution of others to the project. It is a truly win-win situation.

Another famous quote often cited comes from Linus Torvalds, the creator of the Linux operating system: "Given enough eyeballs, all bugs are shallow." In other words, the chance that someone will find a bug in a piece of software is the greatest when many people are using the software, and having access to the source code means that someone, somewhere, is very likely to see the solution where the original developer of the code may not be able to find it so quickly, much less have a fix for it. In fact, many users are also hackers and will often report a bug and submit a patch to fix the bug they found all in one go—clearly not an option for any user of a closed source application. Thus, the quality of open source tends to be very high because of the constant peer review of developers, users, and hackers who make up the project community.

The Business Case for Open Source

As we have seen, there are many compelling reasons to consider the use of open source in your organization. When examining the pros and cons, it is important to understand some additional factors that ultimately make the decision a good or bad one. Now that you have a better understanding of how open source is developed, the next logical question one might ask is, "What's the catch?" Here we discuss some of the more practical considerations in introducing open source into your environment.

Free ! = No Cost

While open source software is freely available, and you could theoretically run any one of thousands of projects available without spending any money, therein lies a problem. Because there is so much choice (a good thing), users could and would spend significant time finding software suitable for their needs that also plays well with their OSS brethren (maybe a bad thing). This being the case, we will examine three ways in which open source can, and maybe should, cost you money.

Distribution Vendors

Linux is a shining example of the power and success that open source software can achieve. One often-overlooked fact is that Linux is actually only the kernel of the operating system, not the thousands of applications that run on top of it. Because this is the case, there are many collections of software known as *distributions* put together by various people and companies. One example is the Debian project, which is a Linux distribution maintained by thousands of volunteers all over the globe. At last count, there were more than 16,000 distinct packages in the Debian distribution. Many businesses that deploy Linux, however, choose to use a distribution that is tested and supported by a company. Red Hat's Enterprise Server and Novell's SuSE are two example Linux distributions provided by companies that charge for the regression and integration testing they perform on the packages offered in the distribution and the after-sale support of these products.

Project Developers

In addition to distribution vendors, some project developers also provide per-incident and/or support contracts for the software they help develop as a means to make a living while donating their development efforts back to the project. Charging for deployment assistance or one-off custom integration tasks is also very common.

In-House

Some companies that may not have any in-house development expertise may choose to sponsor development, either in general to ensure that a project continues in a healthy manner, or for a specific set of features the company needs. This allows a company to lower costs by embracing open source, while ensuring that they get the features they need to meet their business goals and mitigating the risk that their implementations might otherwise pose. Sometimes, it is as simple as a project donation without any particular goal in mind other than to reward the developers or give them equipment or Internet bandwidth to ensure the project has the capability to continue uninterrupted.

Lastly, a company may employ in-house developers to steer an open source project in the direction they wish it to go, while leveraging the benefits of outside resources for a myriad of details such as development, testing, and documentation.

Does It Really Save Money?

We have discussed how the implementation of open source software in your IT environment is not necessarily free of cost. While there are many opportunities to donate time, human resources, and money to your distribution vendors and favorite projects, the simple fact is that there are no software licensing fees associated with an open source project. This means that once you decide to deploy an open source undertaking for the life of that project, you will not be burdened with initial or subsequent fees for the use of the software unless you elect to pay for some form of support. Because this makes sound business sense and is an ongoing cost even with proprietary software, you actually pay for only support when you use open source software.

Another consideration is that many large OTC software applications are of sufficient size and complexity that significant money is spent in customizing that software in your business to work the way you want it to. Because you are paying for deployment in this regard, a one-time sponsored development can be in some cases significantly less expensive than paying a company to customize the OTC package. Because you also have access to the source code, you mitigate any risk of the company that performed the customizations being hit by the proverbial truck and going out of business. You have the option of continuing support of your customizations with in-house developers or finding another source that can continue the maintenance of the code. Another tangible cost-saving feature lends itself to the quality of open source, which tends to be high for reasons previously discussed, contributing to its efficiency, performance, and capability to run on older hardware that can save companies significant money by extending the usable life of the hardware and older PCs.

Other intangible benefits can reduce a company's overall IT expenditures such as better security. For example, it is now a widely accepted fact that open source software tends to be more secure than closed source offerings. Wikipedia (http://en.wikipedia.org/wiki/Security_by_obscurity) defines "Security through obscurity" as the attempt to use secrecy (of design, implementation, etc.) to ensure security. The premise of this is that if the methodology of an implementation is not revealed, an attacker is not likely to discover any vulnerabilities because he does not have access to the implementation details. In practice, this is far from the truth. One look at the pace at which Microsoft releases security updates for its products supports this position, because once a security flaw is revealed, it is the sole responsibility of the company to provide a patch to deal with the breach. In the open source world, however, if a vulnerability is discovered, it reverts to the "many eyeballs" approach, and typically, severe security weaknesses are patched far faster than their nonfree counterparts are.

Get Off the Merry-Go-Round

Microsoft can and should take credit for being one of the main contributors to the wide acceptance of personal computing over the last couple of decades. However, it is no secret that Microsoft has grown into a company with more than $35 billion in annual revenue by stifling the competition with unfair, monopolistic business practices. Limiting choice and dictating predatory pricing models ultimately resulted in an indictment and conviction of this behavior by the Department of Justice in 2000. In the end, open source software offers freedom, not necessarily in cost, although this is a demonstrable benefit, but in choice.

Platform-Agnostic Architecture

Open source software is more than Linux. Linux has gained much fame and fortune over the past 10 years, but there are many other wildly successful examples such as the Apache Web server and Samba. One of the advantages that open source enjoys is having a passionate yet diverse support organization made up of people with all types of needs, desires, and agendas. This is a good thing because anyone who wants to can port the project to run on his or her own favorite hardware or operating system. Thus, open source projects tend to have broad support across multiple architectures, particularly prominent projects. From a Sarbanes-Oxley point of view, this is important because many companies run their IT systems on a multitude of different platforms and technologies, and it is instructive to understand where free software fits into the equation.

Open Source and Windows

Most of the major open source projects (other than operating systems such as Linux to state the obvious) run on a Windows platform. As we will see a bit later in the chapter, this can be helpful when assessing your infrastructure, as most companies have some type of Windows software deployed in their organizations; in fact, open source software is useful even if your IT infrastructure is completely Windows based using nonfree software. For the purposes of Sarbanes-Oxley, the main goal is to avoid any deficiencies that could lead toward a material weakness, if a risk is identified and no in-house closed source solution lends itself to immediate remediation, there is most likely an open source solution that can be used or modified to mitigate the risk and satisfy the auditors. We will examine these projects in detail in the remaining chapters of the book, but for now, suffice it to say that a primarily Windows-based platform does not prevent the use of open source software to assist in your compliance requirements.

TIP

If you are interested in investigating the many open source projects that are available on the Windows platform, you should visit The OSSwin project (http://osswin.sourceforge.net). This site contains information about most OSS applications that can be run natively in a Windows environment, including many applications outside the scope of this book that we will not cover.

Mixed Platforms

In today's business IT environments, there is a good chance that you are using a mix of technologies, particularly if your business is related to technology, health care, research, or manufacturing, to name a few. Not too long ago if you needed to run a UNIX and Windows environment side by side, your IT infrastructure may have looked something like this:

- Windows and UNIX network segments physically separate
- Windows using domains or Active Directory, UNIX using Network Information Systems for authentication
- Engineers with UNIX workstations also have Windows box for e-mail, Web browsing, and Microsoft Office applications for documentation

This is not necessarily a bad setup, and some environments may still be similarly laid out; however, when considering IT controls for Sarbanes-Oxley it is best to keep your environment as simple as possible. The more complex the environment, the more work will be needed in all phases of the compliance process to get through your audit. Even if you survive the audit process with a few strands of hair intact, bear in mind that you will have an ongoing compliance requirement, and complexity breeds overtime. The good news is that open source software fits well in a mixed environment; you will be able to use this to help you wrap your arms around the job to be done, and we intend to help you from both a business and technical perspective.

Migration: a Work in Progress

If you are already a part of the Linux revolution and are migrating some of or your entire IT infrastructure away from proprietary systems, you'll need to consider a few things about Sarbanes-Oxley compliance. You must keep in mind that section 404, *Management Assessment of Internal Controls*, means that every IT system that touches, contributes to, or in any way supports the financial apparatus of the company, and thus the reporting thereof, is affected by the act. Any changes as a work in progress that may make up the support infrastructure for the financial controls identified for your business processes must be stringently documented. Any deviations must be subjected to the appropriate approval chain and documented as well.

Assessing Your Infrastructure

Now that we have covered open source software in some detail as an adoptable platform and some of the reasons why you should consider this in your own organization, we will continue with a 20,000-foot overview of the two aspects of SOX compliance that will be covered in detail in the rest of the book.

Regardless of whether you already have open source software deployed or wish to augment your environment, you need to have the ability to certify your methods and configurations in a demonstrable way. The way to accomplish this is with internal controls, which we will cover in depth in Chapter 5, "Domain 1: Planning and Organization." These controls universally will fall into two categories of prevention controls and detection controls; however, all controls share the following characteristics and constraints:

- **Testable** A well-defined test is in place to validate the control.

- **Repeatable** The same test yields the same result every time.

- **Sustainable** The ability to maintain your controls and certification processes over time.

Lessons Learned...

A Word on Linux Distributions

Something to always keep in mind when evaluating any software for your enterprise in the context of SOX is whether the software meets your needs primarily on two key points, whether they be open source or not. You should ask yourself some important questions:

Continued

■ **Functionality** Can the software do what I need it to do, and can it be modified to suit our business processes? If so, how do these changes affect other dependent systems? Who else is using the software who can contribute mind share back to the developers to make it a better and, important to our discussion, compliant offering?

■ **Support** Who will answer my auditor's questions regarding the technical bits of the application that I do not already know the answer to? From a change management perspective, how do I know whether application ABC plays nice with XYZ?

Using Linux as an example, your selection criteria will depend in part on your goals for open source, whether it is to serve as a one-off application or two, or you will be basing your entire core infrastructure on open source. The more you are considering the latter, the more valuable a distribution becomes. In the writing of this book, we have been conscious not to advocate any particular Linux vendor, as the concepts and principles are truly neutral. That being said, however, you must consider that the auditors' experience with open source may be limited, in some cases very limited in fact. Therefore, using a recognized distribution such as Red Hat's Advanced Server or Novell's SuSE Enterprise will in all likelihood save you a fair amount of time and energy in documenting and validating the origin of your open source infrastructure.

Now, for the exception that proves the rule: We have seen the successful use of community driven distributions such as WhiteBox Linux and CentOS in roles throughout the enterprise as the basis for its core infrastructure. The salient points are that these distributions are based on vendor-supplied source RPMs in accordance with the GPL and recompiled unmodified, and in most cases are the binary equivalents of their commercially distributed brethren. Any differences due to compile time environmental variances are usually minor and documented.

You might choose to use Debian, Gentoo, or one of the many other fine Linux distributions out there in the wild, and many of these distributions offer compelling features in the areas of performance, security, and stability. In fact, the Live CD used as a companion to this book is based on the XFLD distribution, which is based on the original Knoppix distribution, which in turn uses Debian as its core. That is a wonderful example of the power of open source. However, it is very important to communicate with your auditors to make sure they have an understanding of your environment, and sometimes that involves using a toolset that both of you can come together on as a basis to move forward with your compliance audit. Ultimately, the choice is yours, but this one should be considered.

Open Source for IT Systems

One of the positive aspects is that you may very likely have the hardware in–house and experience minimal acquisition needs to leverage open source for your SOX needs. Another is you may very likely have some in-house expertise to more easily incorporate the ideas of the remaining chapters in this book. One of the disadvantages is that your need for documentation of the various systems may be greater than a purely OTC environment, because early in the process the auditors we encountered had much more knowledge of proprietary systems. Therefore, it seemed like a long road to consensus that an environment with open source could pass the certification process. As more information about the auditing process becomes standardized and auditing firms gain more core competency in this arena, it is expected that this will become less of a factor in the future. Some of the major infrastructure-related areas that may appear on the radar screen of SOX compliance include:

- System security access controls
- System availability reliability
- Data backup and retention

Open Source to Support Proprietary Systems

Although you may not have the in-house expertise, don't despair; there is plenty of opportunity to use OSS in non-OSS environments, and we will show specific technologies and methods that you can employ to accomplish this goal. We will be looking specifically at:

- Workflow and approval mechanisms
- Document and revision control
- Policy and procedure management
- Reporting, monitoring, and escalation

Case Studies: Introduction to the Sample Companies

Because 404 and 302 compliance touch virtually every IT infrastructure mechanism in your environment, the best way to present the many technologies we must cover in an intuitively understandable way is to provide the solution in the context of a typical business operation. Because one of the core goals of this book is to illustrate the use of open source software in virtually any environment, the best way to do so is to present two companies with very different architectures. The following examples may or may not track closely with your own business; however, we have endeavored to cover as many scenarios as practical, so you may need to do a bit of creative thinking when considering how these may map to your organization. Although this book is primarily IT related and technical, some brief business and financial background is provided so that the readers can get a feel for the size of their operations and understand the differences between the two. In each chapter, a section is devoted to the fast track CD, which contains fully configured and documented examples of open source solutions that are appropriate for each company as it relates to Sarbanes-Oxley compliance. Since this is a bootable CD, we will show you exact running configurations that can be demonstrated in real time to illustrate open source in action starting with Chapter 5. Of course, these companies are fictitious, and any resemblance to an actual company is strictly coincidental.

BuiltRight Construction Company

BuiltRight Construction Company is a small regional developer of tract homes and small commercial buildings. It has one central office that houses its operations, which span architectural design, project management, building, and property management. The company currently has 150 regular employees and uses a roster of 300 trade subcontractors for building its various construction projects. They have some real estate holdings and rental properties and recently ventured into offering property management; both the construction and property management divisions are housed at its corporate headquarters. BuiltRight currently has approximately $30 million in cash and investments, and quarterly revenues of approximately $5 million. Because of the potential costs imposed by regulatory compliance, the BuiltRight board of directors is currently contemplating a plan to change the organization back to a privately held company.

IT Infrastructure

BuiltRight Construction is currently a completely Windows-based IT environment on both the client and server sides. The main aspects of its infrastructure are as follows.

Server Room

- Windows 2000 departmental file servers, one each for Finance, Marketing, and HR

- Active Directory for authentication

- Oracle Financials completely outsourced to Trusty DBA Services, Inc., which is an online application service provider with per-seat licensing for each member of the finance department

- Microsoft Exchange for groupware/messaging services
- Cisco PIX firewall/VPN

Desktops

- One-hundred employees in the main office running Windows 2000 and Windows XP
- Fifty superintendents and field engineers with Windows XP laptops connected to the central office via VPN
- Microsoft Office, Visio, and Project for desktop applications
- Outlook for e-mail client
- Explorer Web browser for Internet ASP financials access

Network Topology

Figure 4.3 illustrates BuiltRight Construction's network topology.

Figure 4.3 BuiltRight Construction's Network Topology

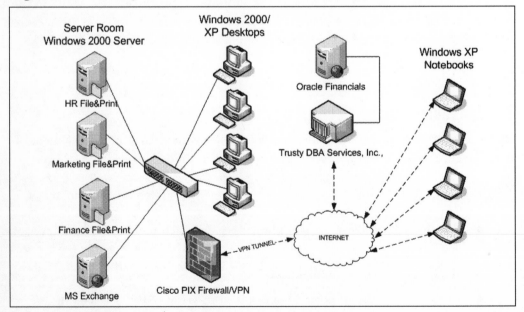

NuStuff Electronics, Inc.

NuStuff Electronics is a successful semiconductor designer of baseband communication chips for original equipment manufacturers (OEMs) of digital telephones. Operations span the globe with offices in India, Japan, Singapore, the United Kingdom, and two offices in the United States. The majority of the design work is done in India, and research and development on new products are primarily done in the UK branch, with corporate headquarters in the United States and the remaining offices performing sales and customer support. NuStuff outsources its manufacturing needs to contract electronics fabrication firms and has approximately 800 employees worldwide. NuStuff has $60 million in assets and quarterly revenues averaging $20 million.

IT Infrastructure

Because electronic design automation (EDA) tools have strong historical roots in UNIX, NuStuff has already embraced open source and Linux technologies to a great extent. NuStuff recognized early on the cost-saving benefits of migrating away from proprietary UNIX and Windows systems on both the client and server sides for engineering, while concurrently maintaining mostly Windows-centric clients for nonengineering and support personnel. To consolidate its IT infrastructure as much as possible, the company has standardized on Linux in the server room and eliminated as many Windows servers as possible, although it does have a few proprietary and legacy applications that run in only a Windows environment.

Server Room (General, Sales, Support, and Executive)

- SAN storage for network services and departmental file services
- Red Hat Advanced Server Linux servers in a high-availability cluster for network services such as DNS, FTP, and HTTP
- Oracle Financials managed with in-house DBA and a financial analyst on staff
- OpenLDAP directory and Samba for cross-platform, single-sign-on authentication services
- Scalix for groupware/messaging services
- Astaro Firewall/VPN with dedicated interoffice IPsec tunnels

Server Room (Engineering and Design)

- Solaris and Linux engineering computer farm
- SAN storage for engineering data
- Separate VLAN for engineering traffic

Desktops (Sales, Support, and Executive)

For the most part, all nonengineering staff fall into this category from an IT desktop standpoint.

- Windows 2000/XP desktops for general support staff, XP laptops for field sales
- Microsoft Office and Open Office for desktop applications
- Mozilla Firefox Web browser for Internet/intranet access
- Microsoft Outlook, Mozilla Thunderbird for e-mail clients

Desktops (Engineering and Design)

Because the engineering team already has Linux workstations for EDA design work, the NuStuff IT department has strived to consolidate the engineering footprint to one desktop per user. To achieve this goal, it has deployed:

- CentOS Linux workstations
- Open Office for desktop applications
- Mozilla Firefox Web browser for Internet/intranet access
- Mozilla Thunderbird for e-mail client

Network Topology

Figure 4.4 illustrates the interoffice topology for NuStuff's global operations, followed by Figure 4.5, which diagrams NuStuff's corporate headquarters IT landscape. We then illustrate with a bit more detail how NuStuff's network services are provided with a high-availability cluster solution (see Figure 4.6). Each of these topics will be explored in more detail in subsequent chapters.

Figure 4.4 NuStuff Electronics' Interoffice Network (Global Operations)

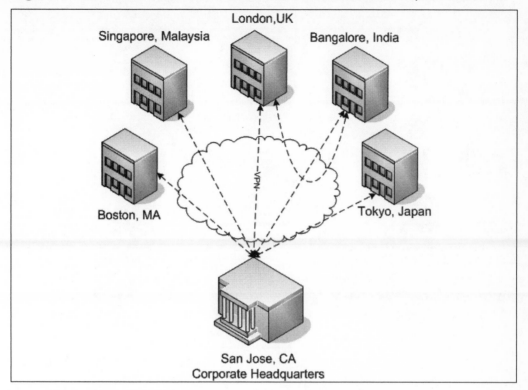

Figure 4.5 NuStuff Electronics' Network (Corporate Office)

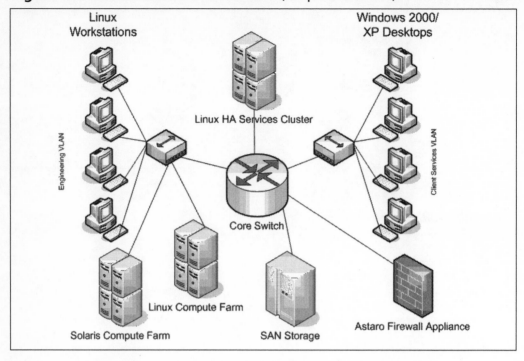

Figure 4.6 NuStuff Electronics' Network Services Cluster Detail

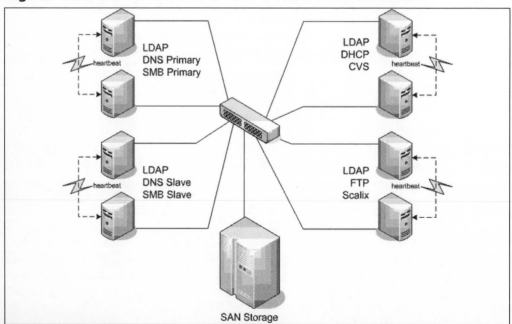

Summary

In this chapter, we set aside the Sarbanes-Oxley discussion for a moment to investigate the entire open source phenomenon and the fundamental differences between it and nonfree software. After an examination of closed source development, we examined the open source methodology in some detail and articulated the tangible and intangible reasons why open source software can save you money and give you freedom of choice. Because of the rapid development cycle and the "release early, release often" mentality, the bar of quality and security is raised owing to massively parallel peer review of the source code. When a bug is identified by an end user, often he or she is a hacker who also supplies the fix, or at least a directed report on how to reliably reproduce the bug for the developer to test. Linux Torvalds' "Given enough eyeballs, all bugs are shallow" theorem essentially states that someone, somewhere, will know the fix to a bug no matter how difficult it may seem to the original developer.

We continued by examining the use of open source in your environment. We learned that there are many opportunities for the use of OSS software, even if you are currently on a primarily Windows-based infrastructure, as most prominent open source software runs on diverse architectures, including Windows. This investigation was further refined by discussing the two main ways in which open source software fits into the SOX compliance equation, both as elements of your IT infrastructure and as support systems such as document control, system monitoring, workflow, and approval management. We also discussed some of the items you should consider if your environment is in a state of transition. One must be diligent to document and subject any changes to the same approval and testing mechanisms as those identified for internal controls procedures.

When evaluating your IT infrastructure, your internal controls universally fall into the categories of prevention and detection; however, all controls share some common characteristics and constraints. All controls must be testable; a well-defined test must be in place to validate the control. All control tests must be repeatable; the same test should yield the same result every time. All control tests should be sustainable; that is, they should enable you to maintain your controls and certification processes over time.

In conclusion, we introduced the sample companies that will be used as case studies for the remainder of the book to illustrate concrete examples of open source software deployment as the subject of certification, and the use of open source software in the compliance process. The sample companies demonstrate two completely different architectures; BuiltRight Construction is a small public company with an infrastructure based entirely on Microsoft Windows and other closed source technologies, and NuStuff Electronics is a medium-sized global organization with a mixed platform environment.

Solutions Fast Track

The Open Source Model

☑ The quality of open source tends to be very high because of the constant peer review of developers, users, and hackers who make up the project community.

☑ The General Public License (GPL) is the most common open source license in use today, but there are many others.

☑ The GPL main features are that it compels one to make the source code and a copy of the license available when distributing copies of the software, and that all modifications to the original source and any source it is tied to also be licensed under the GPL.

☑ The Lesser GNU Public License (LPGL) requires the source code available for the LGPL licensed project, but allows for binary-only linking to other applications and does not require that application to be licensed in any particular way.

☑ The Berkeley Software Distribution (BSD) license allows users to do whatever they like to the software with no restrictions.

Closed Source Application Development

☑ Application requirements are driven by external factors such as existing customer requirements or ideas, and internal requirements such as resource limitations, development costs, and time-to-market considerations

☑ System design and development is usually a formal process involving transforming the requirements into a saleable product. The company may choose to develop the application entirely or integrate and/or purchase libraries from other sources to augment their development efforts and reduce time to market.

☑ Debugging and regression testing may cause the design or requirements to change in an iterative process.

☑ Beta testing and application release almost always involves customer trials of some sort. Once the application is released, the marketing engine starts and sales become the primary focus.

☑ Bug fixes and support are usually provided, usually at additional cost if this was not built in to the purchase price. The company must balance the division of resources between fixing what has already been written and developing the next release; therefore, some bugs might not be fixed as the company drives the priorities.

Open Source Application Development

☑ Open source development is typically a group of interested individuals and/or volunteer developers who have a personal need to fulfill.

☑ Application requirements are driven by three factors: developers who have a personal need, users who join existing projects and articulate their desires directly to developers, and companies that wish to leverage external developer and community support for their own software projects.

☑ System design and development involves coding in parallel. Interoperability and the leveraging of other open source libraries and projects are achieved by fierce adherence to published standards.

☑ Release and debugging happen on a very rapid cycle. The users are stimulated by new features and seeing the project grow with their direct input, and developers get immediate quality feedback about their code. Very often, bugs are fixed as they are discovered, since the source is available to anyone who cares to look.

The Business Case for Open Source

☑ Deploying open source can have costs associated, such as purchasing a support contract from distribution vendors, paying project developers for specific functionality that your organization requires, and hiring in-house developers to work on a project and leverage the community support. In addition, you might consider a donation to help defray project costs.

☑ Open source can save money in many ways. There are no initial license fees to pay, deployment costs are usually not more expensive, and often less, since closed source deployments may require customizations. High reliability and security reduce costly downtime.

☑ Intangible benefits include freedom of choice and less risk, since having access to the source ensures the continuation of a project regardless of whether a company goes out of business or decides to end-of-life a product.

Assessing Your Infrastructure

☑ Open source is platform agnostic; most prominent projects run on most platforms, including Windows.

☑ Having a proprietary infrastructure does not prevent the use of open source for Sarbanes-Oxley compliance; many projects can be used to augment your environment and assist in making the compliance process less painful.

☑ Having open source already deployed can survive an audit; all IT environments have the same compliance requirements regardless of platform.

Case Studies: Introduction to the Sample Companies

☑ BuiltRight Construction is a small public company with an infrastructure based entirely on Microsoft Windows and other closed source technologies. We will illustrate how open source can be leveraged in later chapters despite the fact that their architecture has not currently deployed OSS in their environment.

☑ NuStuff Electronics is a medium-sized global organization with a mixed platform environment consisting of Microsoft Windows, Sun Solaris, and Linux technologies. In the remainder of the book, we will show you what aspects of NuStuff's existing deployments of open source technologies will fall under the scrutiny of the auditors, and the considerations that arise from having a cross-platform architecture.

Frequently Asked Questions

The following Frequently Asked Questions, answered by the authors of this book, are designed to both measure your understanding of the concepts presented in this chapter and to assist you with real-life implementation of these concepts. To have your questions about this chapter answered by the author, browse to **www.syngress.com/solutions** and click on the **"Ask the Author"** form. You will also gain access to thousands of other FAQs at ITFAQnet.com.

Q: I would like to know more about open source. Are there any other books or Web sites where I can get more information?

A: The short answer is, plenty! A Google search of the term *Open Source* reveals 199,000,000 results, so although there are far too many to catalog in one list, here is a short list to get you started:

Web Sites

- Open Source Initiative www.opensource.org/
- Free Software Foundation www.fsf.org/
- Open Source News http://osdir.com/
- Linux Online http://linux.org

Books

- *The Cathedral & the Bazaar: Musings on Linux and Open Source by an Accidental Revolutionary* (ISBN: 0-596-00108-8)
- *Open Sources, Voices from the Open Source Revolution* (ISBN: 1-56592-582-3)
- *The Success of Open Source* (ISBN: 0674012925)
- *Understanding Open Source and Free Software Licensing* (ISBN: 0596005814)
- *Succeeding with Open Source* (ISBN: 0321268539)

Q: Why does some open source software run on Windows? Isn't that contrary to the mind-set of the open source movement?

A: Although *Linux* and *open source* may be synonymous in many people's minds, the fact is that the open source development model existed for many years before Linus Torvalds released his university project into the wild. The motivations that drive open source projects—such as freedom of choice, lower cost, increased security and better quality—are not a function of platform, rather a philosophy of the individual contributors of each project. If their infrastructure happens to be Apple, Solaris, or Windows, this does not preclude or prevent anyone from taking advantage of the open source paradigm.

Q: If open source software is frequently updated after bugs are found and the code is always changing, does that mean that an attacker would have more difficulty trying to exploit systems based on open source software than on Windows-based systems?

A: The fact that the code may be on a rapid development cycle might deter a lazy attacker, but certainly not a determined one. In addition, as many open source projects mature, they tend to have maintenance releases for those users who wish to deploy a "stable" version, so the rapid-development cycle tends to not be applicable in these cases, however the security needs remain the same. The real security advantantage is the rapidity in which exploits that are discovered are fixed in the code. Anyone can develop an exploit to either open or closed source; however, the flipside cannot be said. Whereas anyone can develop a fix for the open source exploit, in closed source you are betting the farm on the closed source provider having the expertise and priorities to close the hole. Transparency in this regard, not the changing codebase, is what differentiates open and closed source for security.

Q: How complicated is using Linux or open source?

A: If you haven't seen a modern distribution of Linux, we highly encourage you to do so—you may be pleasantly surprised. Linux has come a long way in the past 10+ years, and we think it rivals any available operating system out there, for both corporate and personal use. In the past, one of the main problems with Linux was the distinct lack of software that was not specialized for some obscure IT or scientific need. That has now changed with the advent of contemporary software such as KDE and Gnome, OpenOffice, Evolution, and Firefox—the list goes on. The main point is that there is sufficient high-quality and mature open source software that combined with Linux to make a compelling choice. If you want to try Linux without installing it, we recommend downloading Knoppix (www.knoppix.org), which is a full desktop Linux distribution that runs entirely on CD and memory without disturbing your computer's existing OS, or you could simply run the Live CD included with this book that is actually a derivative of Knoppix! You be the judge.

Chapter 5

Domain I: Planning and Organization

Solutions in this chapter:

- Overview
- The Work Starts Here
- What Work?
- What Do Planning and Organization Mean?
- Working the List
- FastTrack CD
- Policy Management

☑ Summary

☑ Solutions Fast Track

☑ Frequently Asked Questions

Overview

When we first thought about Chapter 5 and how to start it in a manner that would drive home the significance of the information we planned to cover, we immediately thought of a quote that until now we had been incorrectly attributing to General George Patton, "People who fail to plan, plan to fail." We offer our apologies to Stewart Turcotte, the "owner" of those words.

The author Gustav Metzman once said, "Most business men generally are so busy coping with immediate and piecemeal matters that there is a lamentable tendency to let the 'long run' or future take care of itself. We often are so busy 'putting out fires,' so to speak, that we find it difficult to do the planning that would prevent those fires from occurring in the first place. As a prominent educator has expressed it, Americans generally 'spend so much time on things that are urgent that we have none left to spend on those that are important.'" When we ran across this quote, we immediately knew it was the right one to use here. The words *business men* can easily be replaced with *IT professionals*, and in doing so sum up the existence of most IT professionals and articulates why COBIT identified planning and organization as one of their domains. As part of daily life within IT organizations, fires tend to get the highest priority, and unfortunately, the areas in which IT can really add value to a company, such as planning and documentation, are usually relegated to the back burner.

In this chapter, we look at the numerous control objectives in the Planning and Organization domain, and based on our experience offer suggestions on how a small to medium-sized company might reduce them to a manageable process.

The Work Starts Here

Before delving into the various control objectives of the Planning and Organization domain, we reiterate that although COBIT is the de facto standard that the majority of audit firms have adopted, and the practices defined within COBIT are generally good practices to have, most large companies find the implementation and sustaining activities daunting, if not impossible. Therefore, as part of this chapter, we focus more on illustrating how, with the appropriate processes and documentation, a small to medium-sized company can effectively comply with relevant COBIT guidelines, while not overburdening their IT organization with COBIT controls to the point at which documentation and paperwork become their main focus.

In Chapter 3, "The Cost of Compliance," we discussed the opportunity for a CFO, CIO, and IT Director to capitalize on their Sarbanes-Oxley Act compliance effort to position their IT organization as a strategic advantage in their company. Well, it all starts here. If you were to ask the majority of CFOs, CIOs, and IT

Directors how IT was perceived at their company, most of them would say, "Executive management views IT as a necessary evil, nonvalue overhead," or even worse, "They just fix computers; don't they?" However, if you were to ask them, "In an ideal world, how would you like your IT organization to be perceived?" the answer would be vastly different. The majority of CFOs, CIOs, and IT Directors would say that they believe their IT organization can be a used as a strategic advantage to the company, one capable of improving employee productivity and contributing to the bottom line of the company. Now, we are not suggesting that the Sarbanes-Oxley Act is some sort of magic wand that will transform a company's opinion of its IT organization regardless of its competence or effectiveness. However, what we *are* suggesting is that if the aforementioned issues are not barriers, COBIT and SOX compliance could provide the bridge from a reactive day-to-day IT organization to strategic IT organization. Although policies are a part of every COBIT domain, the majority of the work resides in Domain I, because this is where you will need to examine the policies, processes, and practices your company currently has (documented or not), and which ones will be needed. Later in this chapter, we provide you with some examples of processes and policies to assist you in your process.

What Work?

If there is one thing that needs to be overemphasized, it is the concept that COBIT and SOX are two distinct entities. Again, COBIT is a set of platform-agnostic guidelines developed to allow an IT organization to implement BKMs (best-known practices). Sarbanes-Oxley Section 404's focus is on internal controls over financial reporting, period. Therefore, in conjunction with developing an overall IT strategy, you will have to look at your various IT functions to determine (1) which IT activities are relevant to your financial reporting process and (2) of these functions, which are significant to the financial report process. This activity is not only critical for work within the Planning and Organization domain but also paramount to your successful execution of subsequent domains. In addition to enabling you to define your work activities, it will also enable you to define the scope of your SOX audit. Defining the scope of your audit will enable you to keep your activities on track, and more importantly, keep your SOX audit and auditors on track. The latter will probably be the more difficult task.

The major tasks you will need to accomplish include:

- Development of IT plans process
- Development of IT plans

- Determination of your IT activities on financial reporting systems
- Determination of significances of your IT activities on financial reporting systems

As every IT environment is different, the goal of this and subsequent chapters concerning COBIT domains is to illustrate that the COBIT guidelines can and should be customized, and the value of said guidelines. Keep in mind, for the sake of illustration purposes, that the application of these guidelines for this chapter and subsequent chapters were applied to NuStuff and BuiltRight. Consequently, the stated guidelines should be used as examples to guide you through the process of your planning and scoping activities as you determine the specifics of your environment.

What Do Planning and Organization Mean?

In Chapter 2, "SOX and COBIT Defined," we established a high-level definition for the COBIT Planning and Organization domain: "Planning is about developing strategic IT plans that support the business objectives. These plans should be forward looking and in alignment with the company's planning intervals; that is, a two-, three-, or five-year projection." Now, we will look at the specifics of each of the control objectives of the Planning and Organization domain and attempt to summarize and distill the various control objectives to lend them more to the structure of a small to medium-sized company.

Given the diversity of functions an IT organization might support based on its particular company's requirements, it would be presumptuous of us to assume we could create a one-size-fits-all template for you to use. That being said, our intent is to give an example, based on our experience, of how the COBIT guidelines can be pared down to better accommodate the resources and structure of a small to medium-sized company. To do so, we will use BuiltRight Construction as the company that needs to come into compliance with the Sarbanes-Oxley Act. If a particular control objective of the COBIT Planning and Organization domain or an individual item is not applicable to BuiltRight, NuStuff, and/or generally would not apply to a small to medium-sized company it has not been listed as part of the guidelines presented here. For a complete list of the COBIT guidelines, see Appendix A, "COBIT Control Objectives."

Although some of the items identified in this and subsequent chapters concerning the COBIT domains will not strictly adhere to the guidelines previously given, as stated as a main objective of this book, they can assist you in repositioning your IT organization.

1. Define a Strategic IT Plan

Although none of the items in Section 1 can be eliminated as part of the effort to simplify the "Define a Strategic IT Plan" control objective, it might not be as complicated and time consuming to satisfy as you might expect.

1.1. IT as Part of the Organization's Long- and Short-Range Plan (Repositioning)

IT issues and opportunities are assessed and captured in the overall business objectives. If your IT organization currently has no input in the planning process, this may be an opportunity to correct that issue.

1.2. IT Long-Range Plan (SOX & Repositioning)

IT Long-Range plans should be developed with input from business process owners. Regardless of the process, you will need to ensure that your IT plans are linked to the business process owners.

1.5. Short-Range Planning for the IT Function (SOX & Repositioning)

IT Short-Range plans should be a subset of the IT Long-Range plans. Again, the business process owners should be in agreement with the objectives, timing, and results.

1.6. Communication of IT Plans (Repositioning)

Although COBIT states that management is responsible for communicating IT long-range and short-range plans to business process owners, by assuming this role you can capitalize on another opportunity to change the image of your IT organization.

1.7. Monitoring and Evaluating of IT Plans (Repositioning)

This is control work in conjunction with 1.7, expect now you are measuring your organization against what you communicated you'd do, and reporting the results back to the business process owners.

1.8. Assessment of Existing Systems (SOX & Repositioning)

Whether for SOX, COBIT, or budget planning, the first step in moving in any given direction is to determine where you are.

2. Define the Information Architecture

This section deals with the storage of financial data such as databases, spreadsheets, and so forth. For NuStuff Electronics, you might need to retain each of these items, whereas for BuiltRight Construction, this section will be substantially less because of the nature of their outsourced Oracle data.

2.3. Data Classification Scheme (SOX)

Establish a structure for the classification of data (i.e., categories, security levels, etc.). Although this should be done, depending on your company it might be a monumental task. Therefore, keep in mind the scope of what you need to accomplish for SOX—systems that are materials in the financial reporting process.

2.4. Security Levels (SOX)

Security levels should be defined and maintained for any security access above general access, such as systems that are material in the financial reporting process.

3. Determine Technological Direction

Whereas items 3.2 and 3.3 would be nice to have for an IT strategic plan, they should not be critical for SOX compliance.

3.1. Technological Infrastructure Planning (Repositioning)

This can be incorporated into planning.

3.5. Technology Standards (Repositioning)

IT management should define technology guidelines to facilitate standardization. Most IT organizations have long been pushing standardization and have met with various levels of success; if yours has met with resistance, this is an opportunity.

4. Define the IT Organization and Relationships

This section deals with organizational issues, and we have eliminated the obvious choices for our example companies, since neither uses contracted staff related to financial operations. Please make particular note of item 4.1, as it is very important to note that it stipulates IT Planning *or* Steering Committee, not IT Steering Committee.

4.1. IT Planning or Steering Committee (SOX & Repositioning)

There is no need to have a planning or steering committee, but you should have a defined planning process.

4.2. Organizational Placement of the IT Function (Repositioning)

There is no requirement of SOX concerning IT and organizational placement. However, COBIT does recommend that the IT organization be the place to ensure authority, critical mass, and independence from user departments.

4.3. Review of Organizational Achievements (SOX & Repositioning)

The process to ensure the IT organization continues to meet the needs of the company. This process should be tied into executive management.

4.6. Responsibility for Logical and Physical Security (SOX)

There is no requirement to have a dedicated person in this role, but there will be a need to define where the function resides—could be defined in job descriptions.

4.10. Segregation of Duties (SOX & Repositioning)

From a SOX perspective, you should not have the approver of an action be the same person as the implementer. Depending on the size of your IT organization, you may need to add personnel to address this issue.

4.12. Job or Position Descriptions for IT Staff (SOX & Repositioning)

Job descriptions should already be a normal part of your structure. If not, you should develop them to be able to better articulate the function with IT, and they will be needed as part of SOX.

4.14. Contracted Staff Policies and Procedures (SOX)

Hopefully, there are standard processes in place at your company to protect its IP (Intellectual Property). If so, you should be able to extend those processes to meet this control, as it relates to the financial reporting process.

5. Manage the IT Investment

By eliminating "Cost and Benefit Monitoring" and Cost Benefit Justification," we do not intend to suggest that these are not important items or that an effective IT organization would not need to be cost effective. Rather, in the context of what we are attempting to demonstrate, that these items can be deferred and/or be addressed as part of another project.

5.1. Annual IT Operating Budget (SOX)

This control can be met by a standard company yearly budget planning process.

6. Communicate Management Aims and Direction

As stated in Chapter 2, SOX compliance requires two types of control: "Entity Controls" and "Control Objectives." The significance of this as it relates to Communicate Management Aims and Direction is that with the exception of Control Objective 6.3, the remaining items should be addressed at the Entity level.

6.3. Communication of Organization Policies (SOX)
Simply put, you will need a mechanism for conveying organizational policies to the employees. This process can be accomplished via an intranet site or a printed document. Whatever the method, it would be advantageous to capture the employees' acknowledgment.

6.8. Communication of IT Security Awareness (SOX)
Same as Control Objective 6.3, but as it relates to IT security.

7. Manage Human Resources

Personnel issues have been covered in previous chapters; however, we will formalize some of these items for SOX compliance.

7.3. Roles and Responsibilities (Repositioning)
Covered as part of job descriptions.

7.5. Cross-Training or Staff Back-up (Repositioning)
If yours is a typical IT organization in a small company, cross-training is like documentation—something you will get to eventually. Although not required by SOX, cross-training is a control for COBIT.

8. Ensure Compliance with External Requirements

Although this section contains important business objectives, if your organization must meet compliance requirements such as HIPAA or OSHA standards, no items require our examination for SOX compliance. Therefore, in this case, we can safely eliminate this section for most businesses—but there will be exceptions.

9. Assess Risks

Risk assessment from an IT perspective is also an important subject to undertake as a normal course of capacity planning and disaster recovery. However, from a strictly SOX perspective, these activities are covered elsewhere and do not serve a purpose in the current discussion, so again we can safely skip this section for now.

10. Manage Projects

As stated previously, good, sound project management will be crucial to the success of your Sarbanes-Oxley compliance process. This statement might appear to be an oxymoron when you review this section; however, you must keep in mind that from a SOX perspective, the removed items will not be germane.

10.1. Project Management Framework (Repositioning)

    Throughout this book, we have touted good project management skills and methodologies. This is where you would develop the methodologies surround this discipline within your IT organization.

10.2. User Department Participation in Project Initiation (SOX & Repositioning)

    As with the planning process, user involvement is critical. This should be defined as part of your methodology.

10.4. Project Definition (SOX & Repositioning)

    This should be defined as part of your methodology.

10.5. Project Approval (SOX & Repositioning)

    This should be defined as part of your methodology.

10.11. Test Plan (SOX)

    Although the specific of your test plan should be incorporated into a project plan, the overall methodology should follow your change management process.

10.13. Post-Implementation Review Plan (SOX & Repositioning)

    Should be defined as part of your project methodology, and should be closed loop by inclusion of the requester as part of the review—formal sign-off is recommended.

11. Manage Quality

Quality management is an important part of IT planning, since it is the bar by which you validate your delivery goals of products and services in an organization. In the interest of keeping SOX control objects to a manageable list, however, no specific items in terms of compliance are applicable in this section, with the possible exception of testing your environment and controls. As we will see in Chapter 8, "Domain 4: Monitoring," testing will be an important part of your compliance activities; however, this is a bit different from the COBIT intent for this section, so we will leave this discussion for later.

The Transparency Test...

The CFO Perspective

As with anything you do, planning is the key to success, and becomes more critical the more complex and interdependent an activity becomes. Given the stakes, time pressures, and interdependency of SOX compliance, it is clear that the first step is to properly analyze and plan your activities. As a small company, you will be tempted to shortcut this step—don't! Given the limited resources and high time pressure of implementing SOX in a small company, planning is even more critical than at a larger organization that can afford to catch up with added resources. As the author points out, good practices are good practices, no matter what name they are given and regardless of the size of your organization.

Working the List

If you are a little confused as to why some items were eliminated and other weren't, keep in mind that COBIT and SOX compliance are not synonymous. COBIT Guidelines were developed prior to SOX and were intended to provide IT organizations with guidelines for "Best Known Practices. The focus of SOX compliance is to ensure the accuracy of financial reporting data and/or the systems that support this data.

If you recall, a note at the bottom of Control Objective 4 pointed out a subtlety of item 4.1, which stipulates IT Planning *or* Steering Committee, not IT Steering Committee. Although various sources may tell you that you must have an IT Steering Committee in place to comply with the Sarbanes-Oxley Act, this is not true. If your organization already has one in place, or if you want to put one in place as part of Sarbanes-Oxley compliance, fine. If not, then it merely means that you will have to do a little more work to effectively address this area.

For example, since NuStuff Electronics does not have the type of organizational structure that lends itself to having an IT Steering Committee, this is where we will start. The first thing you will want to do is document your current process for capturing projects. If your IT organization is like most, project activity usually comes in via two mechanisms: Management and Departmental groups. If this information has been captured and is readily available, this is fantastic news. If not, you will need to gather as much information from management and the department heads as possible so you can develop your overall IT plan. Once you have this information, you will need to synthesize it and present it to the originator for concurrence. As with any quality process, this task should be documented as well and be a closed loop process. After completing this process, you will have to get buy-in on your IT strategy from executive management via a formal presentation, a one-on-one meeting with the CEO, CFO, and so forth… whatever the mechanism, make sure you capture it in writing as part of your process.

Assuming we have completed the aforementioned steps, let's see how this information may translate into forms and processes for SOX. The following example represents a single-page strategy that partially fulfills SOX requirements for the items in Control Objectives 1, 3, 4, 5, and 10. Figure 5.1 represents the NuStuff Electronics IT Road Map, which, in conjunction with the single-page strategy, should fulfill the remaining SOX requirements for the items in Control Objectives 1, 3, 5, and 10.

NuStuff Electronics Inc.

Information Technology

Single-Page Strategy

Program	Server capacity
User Champion	Big boss
Owner	Sam customer
Program Manager	Joe IT
Project Priority	1

Purpose and Scope

The existing Engineering server environment may not adequately support the needs of the Engineering Group during the next cycle of product engineering, particularly if multiple product lines and are under development during the same time. Subsequently, it would be advantageous for NuStuff Electronics to allocate the necessary funds to increase the existing server computer farm environment.

Benefits

Increased servers should improve product development cycle time, as contention for resources will be reduced. Additional benefits include new hardware that may allow NuStuff to leverage 64-bit processing where appropriate in the computer farm environment.

Impact

If NuStuff elects not to allocate the appropriate budget to perform the server capacity increase product, development cycle times may be artificially elongated. The elongated cycle times may result in a negative impact to Engineering's schedule and delivery dates.

Financial Summary

Table 5.1 summarizes NuStuff's headcount, expense, and capital costs for sustaining and increasing server capacity.

Table 5.1 NuStuff's Costs for Sustaining and Increasing Server Capacity

Costs	Sustaining Server Capacity	Increasing Server Capacity
Headcount	NA	0
Expense	0	0
Capital	NA	$50,000

Figure 5.1 NuStuff Electronics Example IT Road Map

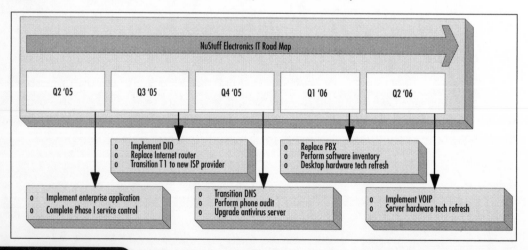

With the identification of two more documents, we will have completed the remaining items in the Planning and Organization domain. Generally, perhaps outdated, most companies will have organizational charts for the various departments. If yours is such a company, you will merely need to update what you have; if not, you will need to create two new documents: Functional and Reporting organizational charts. Figure 5.2 is a standard organizational chart based on reporting line structure. Figure 5.3 may be new to some, but it is a simple functional chart broken down by function versus people as with a standard organizational chart. With the development of the charts in Figures 5.2 and 5.3, we have now addressed the remaining organization item in number 4, which completes the first COBIT domain.

Figure 5.2 NuStuff Electronics Example IT Organizational Chart

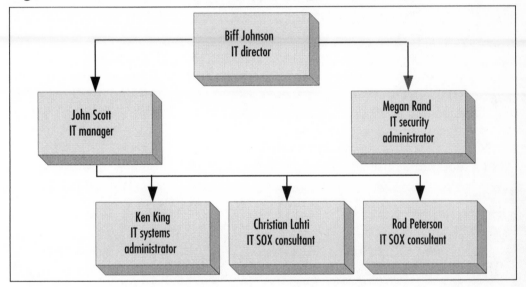

Figure 5.3 NuStuff Electronics Example IT Functional Chart

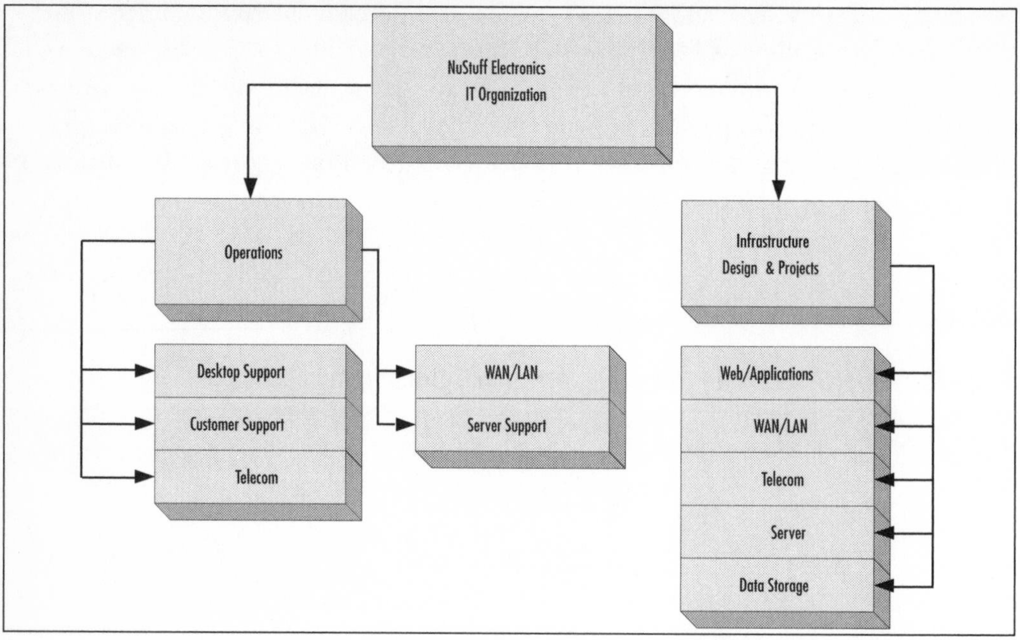

Now that we have discussed the basic process and forms needed for the first COBIT domain, we need to encapsulate them into an open source automated tool.

Lessons Learned...

"I Have to Do WHAT?"

Although some creative liberties were taken in Chapter 1 with the depiction of how the IT manager got involved in his company's SOX compliance efforts, the kernel of the story is true. However, what the story does not tell is that once the IT manager came up to speed on what would be required to implement and maintain SOX, his next reaction was, "I have to do what?" Given the fact that his staff was already limited, budgetary constraints were straining the capacity of his environment and adding to the IT work backlog, he just could not see how he would be able to put another thing on his plate. It wasn't until he had an opportunity to have a couple of in-depth meetings with the auditors that he started to understand the COBIT guidelines and the SOX requirements. With his newfound understanding, he was able to take a step back and look objectively at his envi-

Continued

ronment and what had to be done to achieve SOX compliance. From his objective viewpoint, he began to realize that although there was never a formal name for them, he had already implemented the majority of the process and documentation he needed.

The lesson learned from his experience is that good practices are good practices, no matter what name they are given. Look at what you have in place, and if they are good IT practices, you will be able to tailor them to meet the needs of SOX compliance.

FastTrack CD

We are now ready to begin with concrete examples. If you recall in Chapter 1, the FastTrack CD is a bootable "Live" version customized for this book to demonstrate SOX concepts and practices using open source technologies. If you have not already done so, now would be a good time to insert the CD and boot your computer. Once you have done so and you are viewing the XFLD desktop, you may select either the BuiltRight Construction or NuStuff Electronics portal. Appendix D, "CD Contents at a Glance," has a complete listing of the CD contents; however, we will mainly be using the portal sites built for the book.

NOTE

The CD will not touch your existing hard drive, so you can safely boot it from any suitable system that meets the minimum requirements (listed in Chapter 1). If your system does not boot from the CD, make sure you have set your BIOS to boot from CD before any hard drive in the system.

The Players

http://xfld/builtright/egw/addressbook/index.php
http://xfld/nustuff/egw/addressbook/index.php

To demonstrate the concepts in the remainder of the book, we need to introduce you to the list of players who make up our sample companies. We have used the same names and roles for both BuiltRight Construction and NuStuff electronics so you will be able to interchange between the two with a minimum of confusion. Tables 5.2 through 5.4 include listings from the BuiltRight Construction portal; however, the names and roles are identical in both.

Table 5.2 Employee Listing

Name	Position
Mark Anderson	Finance Controller
Harry Black	Facilities Manager
Jane Brown	CEO
Nancy Green	Business Analyst
Biff Johnson	IT Director
Ken King	IT System Administrator
Marsha Lexington	HR Administrator
Shawn Lundy	Accounts Payable
Megan Rand	IT Security Administrator
John Scott	IT Manager
Joe Smith	CFO
Brent Tooney	Accounts Receivable
Mary Wright	Controller

Table 5.3 SOX Auditor Listing

Name	Position
Molly Fairbanks	IT SOX Auditor
Charles Morrison	Finance SOX Auditor

Table 5.4 IT SOX Consultant Listing

Name	Position
Christian Lahti	IT SOX Implementation Consultant
Rod Peterson	IT SOX Process Consultant

TIP

The password for all of the aforementioned employees and auditors is **letmein.**

The password for the SOX consultants is different because, well, it's our login and we are not going to give you our password, right? It would be a violation of the Password Policy!

Policy Management

http://xfld/builtright/egw/Wiki/index.php

http://xfld/nustuff/egw/Wiki/index.php

The first step in defining the scope of work for your SOX compliance is to define a set of policies as a company in support of the business objectives. While we could spend several chapters creating an exhaustive list of policies, we have narrowed the list to a few examples from which we will derive procedures, strategies, and project plans for implementation throughout the book. We chose to use the Wiki eGroupware application to define the policies; since each change has full document history, "Wiki-fied" HTML is easily learned, and the very nature of a Web application makes for an ideal distributed collaboration environment. You can apply these principles to your environment accordingly.

TIP

Wiki supports access control, and all documents in the Wiki application are readable by all persons in the system. A group called the "Policy Editors" has been created to restrict access to the editing of existing policies, consisting of those individuals who would be responsible for defining and refining the policy documents. The initial page does not have this restriction in place, so currently anyone can define a new Wiki page, but the editing of subsequent versions can and should be restricted. In your environment, you should consider creating groups for every role for which you might use Wiki.

BuiltRight Corporate Policy Documents

From a version history perspective, most of the provided examples are fairly simple, and in all likelihood, your policies will go through much iteration before actually placing them into production. With the CD loaded, you should visit the BuiltRight portal and log in as Charles Morrison, one of the outside auditors, and from here, you can select the Wiki application from the toolbar.

Administrative Access Control Policy

The Administrative Access policy covers the Windows servers and applications. This policy is straightforward, and the version you are viewing is the final version. Selecting version history at the bottom of the page reveals that Biff Johnson originally authored the draft of this policy, and Molly Fairbanks subsequently reviewed the policy and added questions for clarifications. Biff then made the clarifications and the policy was deemed version 1.0.

Change Management Policy

The Change Management policy is one of the most complicated, since the scope of this document covers many practical implementation details. You will notice quite a bit of verbiage related to the procedural execution of the policy statements. While you might think that this should be left to the implementation pieces later, we discovered that the auditors were happier with this level of detail when the procedures defined or clarified the policy statements. Again, this was an interaction between Molly and Biff.

Data Backup and Restore Policy

The backup policy defines standards for what is backed up and when, tape rotation, offsite storage, and restore procedures. The IT manager John Scott drafted the policy, with Molly then providing further feedback.

Firewall and Intrusion Detection Policy

Perimeter defense is an important capability to demonstrate from a SOX perspective, since it represents entry points into the network and is prone to attack from external sources. A solid policy for dealing with protection and attack mitigation is one of the major issues with which you will deal. A multiple layered approach of protection, detection, and escalation works best, although the BuiltRight policy is somewhat simple. See NuStuff for a more robust approach.

Malicious Software Policy

This policy falls under the same category as the Server Environmental policy, ensuring uninterrupted and secure access to the company's financial data and other related systems.

Network Device Configuration Backup Policy

This policy is an example of a subpolicy related to change management. You will be required to demonstrate the ability to control change in your IT environment, and quantify how, when, and why any change occurred. This will become more apparent in later chapters when we implement change management.

Network Security Monitoring and Controls Policy

This policy covers both security and availability of the financial systems and servers. Several subpolicies can be derived from this parent class.

Oracle New User Account Creation and Maintenance Policy

The Oracle policies are identical for both BuiltRight and NuStuff. However, those implementations are handled differently, since one company outsources its applications and the other keeps them inhouse.

Oracle New User Password Policy

This policy is different from the Windows password policy to illustrate special application needs or limitations. You might have to define several subpolicies for various applications and systems in your environment.

Physical Building Access and Badging Policy

This policy is an example of a subject that is indirectly related to IT; IT is not explicitly responsible for controlling access to the building; however, it can be impacted from a security standpoint if the building is breached. For this reason, it falls under the scope of IT SOX compliance

Server Room Access Policy

This policy is another example of the indirect relationship between operational responsibilities versus the operational consequences of a policy violation. You should look to other areas in which IT may not own the process but might be adversely affected by violations to stated business policies.

Server Room Environmental Policy

This policy relates to the reliability and availability of the critical systems, a core component of the IT SOX compliance mission. The BuiltRight process is essentially manual, where we will see a more automated approach in the NuStuff policy.

Windows Password Control Policy

Windows password policy enforcement is straightforward, and the policy reflects the capabilities of the server environment. Strong password controls are essential in preventing successful unauthorized access attempts, and the auditors are bound to ask for a solid policy from which your procedures will stem.

Windows System Security Policy

Locking down systems is important so a baseline of operations can be established. By defining the approved system services, change can be controlled and quantified, and hacking opportunities are diminished as much as possible.

NuStuff Corporate Policy Documents

NuStuff has a much more complex environment; with multiple operating systems and platforms, their policy documents are necessarily going to be more complex in some areas. You will notice, however, that the basic overall SOX compliance requirements are similar for both companies, and as mentioned previously, the scale is not linear. Here are the same policies for NuStuff that cover the same business processes; however, several are expanded or subtly different in other ways.

Administrative Access Control Policy

The administrative access policy covers the access to servers, data, and applications. This policy has been expanded to include the multiplatform considerations that NuStuff has compared to BuiltRight.

Change Management Policy

This policy is fundamentally the same as BuiltRight; however, the implementation details will be significantly different in subsequent phases. It contains similar procedural language

Data Backup and Restore Policy

This policy is also expanded for a much bigger environment. One interesting inclusion in this policy is the snapshot technologies employed by NuStuff's Linux servers in contrast with no similar functionality provided by the Windows servers that BuiltRight employs.

Firewall and Intrusion Detection Policy

Whereas BuiltRight has only employed a policy of log file review, NuStuff has deployed an active intrusion detection system (IDS), and this document reflects the parameters of this functionality.

Malicious Software Policy

This policy is the same; only the names and faces of the software have been changed to protect the innocent.

Network Device Configuration Backup Policy

This policy began the same; however, the auditors who reviewed this policy asked different questions than the BuiltRight auditors did, which resulted in a different final version. This was done to illustrate that some aspects of your policies will be derived from the collaborative process, and you might not end up with exactly the same policy as everyone else—this is simply an artifact of the human element in the equation.

Network Security Monitoring and Controls Policy

NuStuff has chosen to expand this policy to include active monitoring of the network.

Oracle New User Account Creation and Maintenance Policy

This policy is the same; however, the implementation details will be different.

Oracle New User Password Policy

This policy is the same; however, the implementation details will be different.

Password Control Policy

Since NuStuff has unified its authentication using LDAP directory services, it has the flexibility to add more complex controls to its password policy. We will see later how this is achieved, even for the Windows clients.

Physical Building Access and Badging Policy

This policy is fundamentally the same.

Server and Operating System Security Policy

This policy has been expanded to include multiplatform considerations.

Server Room Access Policy

This policy is the same; the requirements and risks exist for both companies.

Server Room Environmental Policy

Whereas BuiltRight chose to implement a policy based on a manual process, NuStuff has deployed some automation for their environmental controls. We will see this process further defined later in the chapter for escalations of anomalies that might occur.

Defining Your Own Policies

We have included a template for your convenience to define your own policies, which you can do by following these steps:

- Load either the BuiltRight or NuStuff portal and select **Sample Configurations**.

- Select the policy template; a standard HTML block listing will appear in your browser. Copy this to the clipboard and press the **Back** button to return to the portal.

- You can now log in as any "role" you desire and edit the first Wiki page to include a link to your new policy page. Even though the page does not yet exist, you should follow the same Wiki styles as the other policy definitions. A question mark will appear next to your entry once you save the page, which means that Wiki understands that a page is supposed to be linked there and is giving you the opportunity to define the page.

- Click the **question mark link** and you will be transported to a new blank page. Select **source view** from the WYSIWYG toolbar and past the template into the code window.

- Press the **Preview** button to revert the view to the WYSIWYG editor. You can now modify the policy to your own liking; be sure to add a summary and optional searchable keywords in the category fields.

- Pay attention to the Wiki page title. The squished together page name is standard Wiki nomenclature; however, you will most likely want to unsquish the title so it appears as a normal title. Wiki will work out the linking details as long as you leave the page name alone.

For complete Wiki documentation and numerous markup examples, visit
the WikiTikiTavi Web site at http://tavi.sourceforge.net.

Policy Approval Workflow

http://xfld/builtright/egw/workflow/index.php
http://xfld/nustuff/egw/workflow/index.php

Once you have gone through the iterations of defining your policies, the next step is
to submit them for approval between the appropriate parties who need to sign off
on these items and make them "official." If there is one thing that brings a smile to
an auditor is seeing a chain of approval attached to every control and business process in the organization, and the workflow application is ideally suited for this task.
Not all Wiki pages in general need approval, so it is up to you to decide whether a
page is submitted. For the purposes of our examples here, we are requiring approval
of policies before they are placed into production. With this in mind, any Wiki page
can have any one of three states displayed in the upper left:

- **Not Submitted** The initial default state of a Wiki page. A page may never
  need to be submitted, so this is what it will remain as. In this state, a workflow link appears in the footer to allow you to initiate a workflow approval
  (see Figure 5.4).

- **Pending** The state in which a policy has been submitted for approval and
  is somewhere in that process. A Cancel workflow link is added to the
  footer to allow a previous workflow request to be cancelled. Page editing
  and access to history are disabled in this state as well, so no changes can be
  made until the workflow is either cancelled or completed.

- **Closed** The state in which a policy has completed a workflow approval
  cycle and was ultimately accepted or rejected. You will not be able to
  submit this page for workflow approval again, but need to make an edit to
  force a new version that will revert to the Not Submitted state.

For each of the aforementioned policies, a single workflow has been defined
called Corporate Policy Approval Workflow, and Figure 5.4 shows how this workflow instance was derived.

Figure 5.4 Policy Approval Workflow Diagram

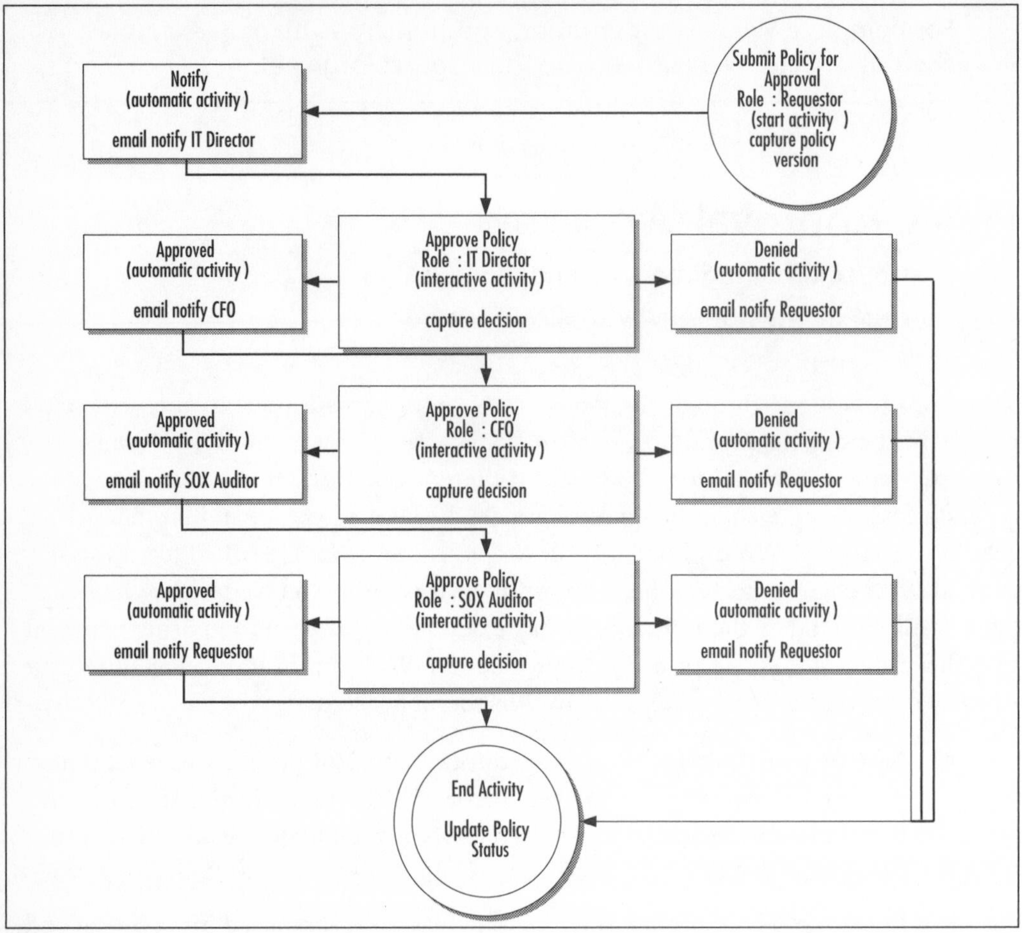

Workflow Roles

Each step in the activity that requires interaction with the system (i.e., the approval steps) has an associated role. There are four roles for this workflow process: the Requestor, CFO, IT Director, and SOX auditor. Role members are defined as:

- **Requestor** The person who actually submits the policy for approval and is dynamically assigned at runtime to the currently logged in ID. Typically, for policies, the IT manager or person who last updated the policy will be the Requestor for submission.

- **CFO** The company CFO, namely Joe Smith. He is the default person assigned to this role; however, Mary Wright is also assigned to the CFO role for this policy as a backup for Joe. In Joe's absence, Mary should fill this role.

- **IT Director** Again, this is Biff Johnson. The IT Manager John Scott serves as the backup for this role.

- **SOX Auditor** The role members for this are both Molly Fairbanks and Charles Morrison. Since a default person has not been assigned to this role, both Molly and Charles will receive notifications, and either can "grab" an existing policy request and approve or deny.

Workflow Activities

In addition to the defined roles are several types of activities at various points in the workflow process:

- **Start/End activity** The point at which a new instance of the workflow is begun or completed.

- **Interactive activity** Any activity that requires human intervention, such as the capture of information or a decision to be made. In this example, all of the approval activities are interactive.

- **Automatic activity** Any activity with no human requirement. All of the notify activities are automatic, and send out e-mail notifications to the appropriate roles associated with the next step in the process

Defining Your Own Policy Approval Workflows

Chapter 8 has a comprehensive "how-to" on defining a workflow from start to finish, but we did want to touch on the subject here to get you thinking about your own approval chain. The workflow application is a fairly involved process to define from scratch, so the place to start is to identify the activities and states your work-flow process would encompass. It is helpful to use a diagramming application, and Dia is an open source diagram creation program released under the GPL license included on the Live CD. We will be seeing many different types of workflow over the next several chapters, and approval routing is probably the simplest of the bunch, the process consisting mainly of:

1. Defining approval levels (called activities), such as IT Approval, Finance Approval, etc.

2. Defining the code that captures the decisions and routing activities based on those actions.

3. Defining the roles for the levels of approval, such as IT Director and Controller.

4. Adding persons to those roles.

5. Assigning the appropriate roles to their corresponding approval levels.

6. Optionally assigning a default person for the role.

7. Defining your workflow as a target for Wiki submissions.

By far. the easiest approach is to modify one of the existing workflows in our example, placing your own roles and role members, and perhaps adding an approval level once you have run through the tutorial in Chapter 8. In any case, this was the first of many uses for the workflow application that we apply toward SOX activities.

Summary

In this chapter, we discussed the difference between SOX and COBIT. We also discussed a basic process for developing IT strategic plans in an effort to comply with the Planning and Organization domain. Finally, we looked at some real-world examples of forms and processes used to comply with the Sarbanes-Oxley Act. In summarizing this chapter, there are three fundamental things you should take away with you:

- Let your unique organizational structure drive the applicable domain items.

- When developing processes, ensure that they follow a good quality methodology, such as PDCA (Plan, Do, Check, and Act).

- Above all, if you have existing processes that are good sound processes and are already ingrained within the organization, customize and modify them to work within COBIT.

We also explored the definition and approval routing of your IT business policies, which form the core of your IT strategy and are the basis from which all procedures grow. Several policies are outlined as a representative set of items you will need to consider for SOX compliance. You can define or modify your own policies; we give you the details on how to accomplish this. You can also define or modify the policy approval workflow process if it does not suit your needs.

We also looked at the first concrete examples on the Live CD in the context of planning and organization. Once you have identified your controls as an organization, it is important to state this in a policy that can later be applied by implementing solutions later in the book that fulfill the requirements of your policies. In addition, we introduced the "approval" type of workflow, the first of many workflow categories we will explore in the remaining chapters. The approval workflow in this example demonstrates the ability to route specific versions of your policies to a chain of approval.

Solutions Fast Track

Overview

- ☑ The nature of IT lends itself to firefighting.
- ☑ Planning tends to be a back-burner activity for most IT organizations.

☑ To comply with Sarbanes-Oxley, IT organizations will have to learn the discipline of planning, and force themselves to adhere to this new discipline.

The Work Start Here

☑ COBIT is the de facto standard, which the majority of the audit firms have adopted.

☑ With the appropriate processes and documentation, a small to medium-sized company can effectively comply with relevant COBIT guidelines.

☑ If implemented correctly, COBIT controls do not have to be so burdensome where paperwork becomes the main focus for an IT organization.

What Do Planning and Organization Mean?

☑ COBIT guidelines can be tailored to better fit a small to medium-sized company's structure.

☑ There is no one-size-fits-all template; COBIT guidelines can and should be customized to a company's particular IT organization.

Working the List

☑ COBIT and SOX compliance are not synonymous.

☑ COBIT guidelines were developed to facilitate IT organizations in deploying "Best Known Practices."

☑ The Sarbanes-Oxley Act was drafted to ensure the accuracy of financial reporting data and/or the systems that support this data.

FastTrack CD

☑ The players for the example portals are presented together with background information.

☑ General information on the eGroupware applications is available in Chapter 1, in which we focus on the specific SOX aspects of the portal applications Wiki and Workflow.

Policy Management

☑ Many example IT policies are presented for both BuiltRight and NuStuff, together with a discussion of the similarities and differences of each. This illustrates the baseline requirements for SOX.

☑ In our examples, the final policy versions are submitted for approval to become officially "live." In SOX compliance, one very important aspect is the signoff from management on IT practices in support of the business goals, and the workflow application is discussed in detail for this purpose.

Frequently Asked Questions

The following Frequently Asked Questions, answered by the authors of this book, are designed to both measure your understanding of the concepts presented in this chapter and to assist you with real-life implementation of these concepts. To have your questions about this chapter answered by the author, browse to **www.syngress.com/solutions** and click on the **"Ask the Author"** form. You will also gain access to thousands of other FAQs at ITFAQnet.com.

Q: Can I really customize COBIT?

A: Yes. However, prior to formalizing any processes or documentation based on your customizations, you will want to run it by your auditor.

Q: Can the customization really be that simple?

A: Yes, as long as you allow your environment to drive the process. However, keep in mind that you will need to justify your decisions.

Q: Can I use the example forms?

A: Yes, you can use any example forms, but you should format them to work best in your environment. These examples were developed to cover many of the items in the Planning and Organization domain.

Q: Is there a particular type of environment in which COBIT works better?

A: No. The COBIT guidelines are platform and environment agnostic.

Q: If COBIT is so cumbersome, why should I use it?

A: Because the guidelines are sound. However, we should apply another quality principle when looking at COBIT guidelines: the 80/20 rule.

Q: Can I use my exiting policies?

A: Yes, but you may have to make some slight modifications. The main thing to remember is that they need to be documented and support a control. By using a tool such as Wiki, the collaborative effort between you and your auditors becomes much easier to manage and track.

Q: I am interested in learning more about Wiki collaboration in general; where can I get more information?

A: Wiki is fast becoming an important collaboration tool, and we have applied it to some very specific functions. There are many Wikis in the open source world (in fact, a freshmeat.net search yielded 118 projects!). Here are a few of the most popular:

- WikkiTikkiTavi, what eGroupware is based on— http://tavi.sourceforge.net/.
- Twiki, a full-blown collaboration server—http://twiki.org/.
- Tiki CMS/Groupware, an interesting content management system Wiki— http://tikiwiki.org/.
- PhpWiki, WikiWikiWeb clone written in PHP—http://phpwiki.source-forge.net/.

Chapter 6

Domain II: Acquisition and Implementation

Solutions in this chapter:

- Overview
- Evaluating In-House Expertise
- Automation Is the Name of the Game
- What Do Acquisition and Implementation Mean?
- Working the List
- FastTrack CD

☑ Summary

☑ Solutions Fast Track

☑ Frequently Asked Questions

Overview

Although we tried diligently, we could not come up with a quote that spoke directly to the second COBIT domain of Acquisition and Implementation. However, we were able to find a quote by James F. Bell, who once said, "To face tomorrow with the thought of using the methods of yesterday is to envision life at a stand-still. To keep ahead, each one of us, no matter what our task, must search for new and better methods—for even that which we now do well must be done better tomorrow." Thinking about this quote, we felt it was not only clear and relevant but also powerful enough to stand on its own. At the risk of diminishing the quote, we will venture to relate it in the context of this chapter. Let's assume that an organization, yours or anyone else's, has followed the COBIT guidelines and has implemented an IT environment that complies with said guidelines. Given the changes and advances in technologies, and the ever-changing requirement of the particular business, it would be fool hearted, if not negligent, to assume that the implemented methods, practices, and infrastructure could persist without evolving as requirements and needs change. The intent of the second COBIT domain is to set up guidelines for processes, practices, and policies to ensure that a company's IT organization continues to meet the needs of the company, by evolving with those needs.

In this chapter, we will look at the numerous control objectives in the Acquisition and Implementation domain, and based on our experience, offer suggestions on how a small to medium-sized company might be able to reduce them to a manageable process.

Evaluating In-House Expertise

In an ideal world, every IT organization would have the expertise to execute the COBIT guidelines and implement the necessary open source or proprietary tools identified in this book to obtain compliance with the Sarbanes-Oxley Act. However, as we all know, this is not the case. As a general rule, an IT organization's skill sets and expertise are usually related to its current environment, and not necessarily to another IT discipline not contained within that environment, or introduced by Sarbanes-Oxley. Since the focus of this book is how to effectively use open source to obtain compliance with the Sarbanes-Oxley Act, and since open source primarily runs on Linux and UNIX-based operating systems, any organization that would like to avail itself of the majority of the open source tools should have minimum level of expertise in these areas.

If your company has already deployed open source in your organization to any significant degree, you probably have the necessary expertise to evaluate and implement the necessary open source tools to assist you with your Sarbanes-Oxley compliance. If your organization does not have the aforementioned discipline and/or you are uncertain about your organization's expertise level, it does not necessarily prevent you from taking advantage of the open source tools listed in this book or open source tools in general. However, what it does mean is, prior to committing to open source as part of your Sarbanes-Oxley compliance efforts, or to assist in fulfilling some of the COBIT guidelines, you will first need to determine what skill sets you have in your organization and whether they are adequate. When evaluating the necessary skill set, you will need to look at two general aspects:

- Linux and UNIX experience
- Open source experience

It may appear somewhat peculiar to some of you that we've separated Linux and UNIX experience from open source experience, as Linux is considered open source. However, in the context of this discussion, when we say "open source" we are referring to applications versus operating systems, where the expertise needed for each category may be slightly different. We do not want to deter you from using open source by any means, but rather leave you with the knowledge that you might have to consider your options for in-house staff and outsourcing.

Deployment and Support Proficiency Considerations

To properly evaluate the expertise needed to support open source, you must examine your existing infrastructure and determine the extent to which open source will play a part in your overall strategy. One of the advantages of Linux, for example, is that if deployed for a specialized purpose, such as Web servers or databases, there tends to be very good setup and support options for these applications. However, if Linux is going to be deployed on your desktops, the skill sets required to maintain adequate levels of support might be quite different. Universally, it is desirable to have a staff knowledgeable in both operating systems and the applications you plan to deploy and support in your organization, but since this may not be realistic or even necessary, there are a few things to keep in mind. Figure 6.1 depicts the external support options typically available to open source.

Figure 6.1 Open Source Support Stack

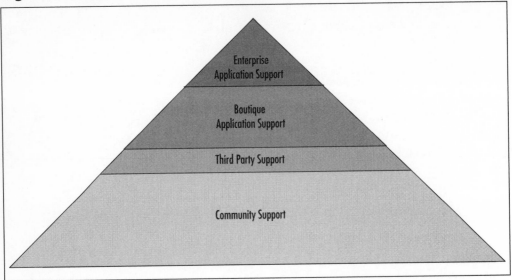

At the top of the support chain are large enterprise vendors such RedHat and Oracle. If your intention is to deploy these distributions and applications, the importance of in-house expertise might not be as critical due to the availability of vendor deployment expertise and support contracts. As we covered in Chapter 4 ("Why Open Source?"), often the primary developers of an open source application offer paid-for installation and support, good examples being Sugar CRM and MySQL. Finally, there are companies that specialize in open source support, providing consulting for a wide variety of applications you might want to deploy in your organization. However, your selection may be limited depending on your geographical location, since these companies tend to be local or regional. By far the most common avenues for support are community driven via documentation (some being better than others), mailing lists, forums, and discussion lists. From a SOX perspective, the majority of applications you might consider—such as eGroupware, Nagios, LDAP, Samba, and Webmin (all examples that we use in this book)—all have very good to excellent documentation and support channels. Depending on your deployment goals, general skills you will be looking for include:

- A solid ability to roll your sleeves up and dig in to solve problems that arise. While the mature projects in open source have good documentation and best-known deployment practices, much of Linux and open source can involve trial and error to adapt to your specific needs, which is why the need for an adequate test environment is important and discussed later in the chapter.

- A good understanding of TCP/IP, networking, and the Linux Standards Base (www.linuxbase.org/), which outlines the general layout of a Linux system so you know how and where configuration files and data are generally stored.

- Solid research skills to navigate forums, mailing lists, and Internet resources, an important addition to any good system administrator, regardless of platform, and open source is no different.

- From a SOX perspective, a very good understanding of security in general, OS hardening, PAM/NSS, and file and application security to ensure that your deployments are rolled out in a secure fashion (more on this in Chapter 7, "Domain 3: Delivery and Support").

TIP

To evaluate someone's Linux and open source skills, give him or her a standardized test such as the A.P. Lawrence's Linux Skills Test, which can be found at http://aplawrence.com/Tests/Linux.

Addressing Deficiencies

If after evaluating your in-house expertise you determine that deficiencies exist, there are several ways to effectively address them, each approach with its pro and cons:

- If time and resources permit you can elect to train existing staff. This could be the best long-term solution, but because of the steep learning curve, mistakes could be numerous in the short term.

- If budget and management allow, you can elect to hire consultants, which would address your short-term requirements and potentially your long-term requirements. The caveats to our previous statement are 1) you will need to ensure that you source qualified consultants, and (2) the consultant you elect to use should have a methodology and planning for transitioning the new environment to your in-house staff.

- If budget and management allow, you can elect to hire additional resources to fill this requirement. However, hiring an unknown entity under these circumstances may add more risk of failure to your process.

- A combination of any of the preceding points.

Automation Is the Name of the Game

In implementing COBIT guidelines, complying with Sarbanes-Oxley, or installing a new application within your infrastructure, the ability to automate existing and potential new functions will be paramount. Not to lament the problems of a small to medium-sized company, but if yours is typical, resources and activities are always at odds—too few resources and too many activities. That said, one of the goals that should be specified as part of the Acquisition and Implementation of potential applications for your environment is the ability to automate new requirements and some of your existing requirements. In doing so, you will be able to better leverage existing resources, and possibly stave off the need to add additional resources.

In addition to managing resources effectively, another objective of the IT managers at our fictitious companies was to (as much as possible) take the "people" out of the "process." Initially, they decided to specify this as a requirement purely from the knowledge that behavioral change is usually difficult and takes a considerable amount of time. Conversely, when you automate tasks via an application, any required changes can be effected, if not in real time, in a fraction of the time. However, as they progressed through their Sarbanes-Oxley compliance and automation efforts, they quickly realized that this process yielded additional benefits they hadn't initially determined. One area that rapidly became apparent was that the automation process was forcing them to better define their processes by removing subjectivity from them. The other benefit they realized was that by eliminating subjectivity in their processes and removing the human element as much as possible, they could better demonstrate that the processes were being executed as defined— and from a Sarbanes-Oxley compliance perspective, this ability is crucial. Since you are reading this book, we assume that you are somewhere in the IT management chain, and therefore need to assert to management or your auditor that the processes as defined is how they are implemented. Therefore, if you remember nothing else, remember this: Without some type of automation, how comfortable would you be making this assertion?

The Transparency Test...

The CFO Perspective

The authors again emphasize the value of planning as it relates to a well-run project. This is especially pertinent with the enormity of Sarbanes-Oxley compliance and the consequences of not meeting your timeline. Given the focus here on small and mid-sized companies, resources will clearly be an issue all through the process. The correct use of automation can have a significant favorable impact on all aspects of the project size, timing, and cost. As with most projects, you need to clearly define the needs and ensure that project creep does not find its way in, thus eliminating the benefits automation offers. Containing any project is not easy, and the natural tendency will be to let the program continue to creep, thus adding some element of timing and cost risk. The project needs to keenly focus on Sarbanes-Oxley certification, and automation done properly can help achieve this end.
— *Steve Lanza*

What Do Acquisition and Implementation Mean?

In Chapter 2, "SOX and COBIT Defined," we established a high-level definition for the COBIT Acquisition and Implementation domain: "Once the plans are developed and approved, there may be a need to acquire new applications or even acquire or develop a new staff skill set to execute the plans." Upon completion of the Acquisition phase, the plans now need to be enacted in the implementation phase, which should include maintenance, testing, certifying, and identification of any changes needed to ensure continued availability of existing systems and new systems. In this chapter, we look at the specifics of each of the control objectives of the Acquisition and Implementation domain and attempt to summarize and distill the various control objectives to lend themselves more to the structure of a small to medium-sized company.

In Chapter 3, "The Cost of Compliance," we cautioned you about minimizing overlap as much as possible in the applications you select for your environment. Well, now we would like to add another caution: Given that there are no acquisition costs associated with open source tools, the tendency might be to over-implement. Our point is this: If you implement open source applications based on a specific requirement versus your total environment, you will likely discover that you have overimplemented, thereby increasing your environment resource and skill set requirements rather than reducing them.

Whether for COBIT or Sarbanes-Oxley compliance, we will again use BuiltRight Construction and NuStuff as companies that need to come into compliance. If a particular Control Objective of the COBIT Acquisition and Implementation or an individual item is not applicable to BuiltRight, NuStuff, and/or would not apply to a small to medium-sized company it has not been listed as part of the guidelines in this chapter. For a complete list of the COBIT guidelines, see Appendix A, "COBIT Control Objectives."

Neither BuiltRight nor NuStuff performed any in-house development activities; thus, only a few Control Objectives apply to either fictitious company. Therefore, what we will do is identify Control Objectives that might not necessarily appear to pertain to these companies, ones that you may want to consider from a different aspect, and/or ones that will feed into other processes that you might need to consider. It is also noteworthy to mention that even if your organization does not perform in-house development, you will want to be able to articulate this and demonstrate it to your auditor.

1. Identify Automated Solutions

This section as it pertains to COBIT deals with identification of Automated Solutions, and more specifically, systems that were developed in-house. Although you might think you are in the clear because you have no development staff, you will need to consider any applications you had developed by consultants and contractors. For clarity in this section, we again state that the scope of Sarbanes-Oxley is any system that is significant in the financial reporting process.

1.1 Definition of Information Requirements (Repositioning)

The COBIT practice states that a methodology should exist to ensure that business requirements are met for existing systems and future development activities. Perhaps not as it relates to development, but this is an area you may want to look to as you prepare your plans and evaluate open source tools.

1.10 Audit Trails Design (SOX)

The COBIT practice states that an organization's system development life cycle methodologies specify that systems have the capability to track activities via audit trails. Even if you do not have any in-house developed systems or systems provided by a consultant or contractors, you might still not be in the clear. If you have systems that have been significantly customized or modified, you will want to examine them.

1.15 Third-Party Software Maintenance (Repositioning)

Although by its very nature, open source cannot be sold, some commercials companies have embraced open source as part of their business model by providing third-party support. In a good IT organization, application support should always be included in the overall plans.

2. Acquire and Maintain Application Software

This section as it pertains to COBIT deals with design elements of systems developed in-house. However, keep in mind that heavily customized or modified systems may fall in this category from a SOX perspective.

2.2 Major Changes to Existing Systems (SOX and Repositioning)

COBIT states that major system changes should follow a process similar to a systems development process, and should contain Change Management.

2.8 Definition of Interfaces (SOX)

COBIT basically states that the system development life cycle methodology should include the requirement that all system interfaces are properly specified, designed, and documented. If you have systems that are significant in your financial reporting process and feed into your financial system, you will also need to include the interface as part of your testing and certification.

2.14 IT Integrity Provisions in Application Program Software (SOX)

COBIT basically states that the application should routinely verify the tasks performed by the software to help ensure data integrity and provide rollback capabilities. As this provides a "Prevent Control," it may be a requirement to use to evaluate future application and/or interfaces you may need to implement.

2.15 Definition of Interfaces (SOX)

COBIT defines that unit, application, integration, system, load, and stress testing should be in accordance with your project test plan. However, from a SOX perspective, if you use production data as part of this process, in essence you have placed your test environment in production, and therefore, all SOX production environment criteria now apply to your test environment.

3. Acquire and Maintain Technology Infrastructure

This section as it pertains to COBIT deals with the acquisition and maintenance of systems related to your IT infrastructure. Depending on the processes you identified to implement from the previous domains, this could impact your open source tools selection.

3.3 System Software Security (SOX)

COBIT states that the setup of system software to be installed does not jeopardize the security of the data and programs. This is true from a SOX perspective as well. If an infrastructure type system interfaces with your financial system (e.g., monitoring, etc.), it too will need to follow the same guidelines as your financial system.

3.5 System Software Maintenance (SOX and Repositioning)

This is in line with 1.15 of Identify Automated Solutions.

3.6 System Software Change Controls (SOX)

As part of your Change Management Process, procedures for system software changes should identified and documented.

3.7 Use and Monitoring of System Utilities (SOX)

This particular control is in line with 3.3, but expands it to include system utilities.

4. Develop and Maintain Procedures

This section as it pertains to COBIT deals with the development and maintenance of procedures for system development activities. However, as previously established, customized or significantly modified systems also fall under this umbrella.

4.1 Operational Requirements and Service Levels

COBIT states that the system development life cycle methodology should ensure the timely definition of operational requirements and service levels. When looking at open source systems and/or application acquisition, you will want to ascertain SLA methodology management and processes.

4.3 Operations Manual

COBIT states that operational manuals should be prepared and kept up-to-date as part of system development methodology. Again, remember that customized or significantly modified applications will also need to be considered.

5. Install and Accredit Systems

This section as it pertains to COBIT deals with the installation and verification of systems before and after migration to production. As with NuStuff or BuiltRight, the Control Objectives in this section are not germane, but we would like to make a few general statements. At the risk of belaboring points already covered, keep in mind that:

- If required, the focus of these activities should only pertain to systems/applications significant in the financial reporting process.

- Customized or significantly modified applications will also need to be considered.

- Control Objectives listed in this section should be incorporated into your Change Management Procedure, whether specific to application/software development or a general Change Management procedure.

For specifics on these Control Objectives, refer to Appendix A.

6. Manage Changes

This section as it pertains to COBIT deals with change and the management of that change. If you haven't noticed, the various COBIT Control Objectives fundamentally exist in each domain, and are merely restated as they pertain to a particular domain. Therefore, to avoid redundancy we will cite the previous Control Objectives as they apply to this section and guidelines for Change Management.

6.1 Change Request Initiation and Control (SOX and Repositioning)

COBIT states that change requests for system maintenance and supplier maintenance should be standardized, and have a formal change management procedure. Specific elements should include categorization and prioritization of end-user communications.

6.2 Impact Assessment (Repositioning)

COBIT states that procedures should be developed and put in place to assess the proposed change to the environment. At any point of impact, testing should be performed, whether it be functional or integration.

6.3 Control of Changes (SOX and Repositioning)

COBIT states that Change Management and software control and distribution are integrated with a configuration management system. The change control system should be automated.

6.4 Emergency Changes (SOX and Repositioning)

COBIT states that parameters should be established for defining emergency changes and the procedures that control these changes when circumstances require circumvention of normal processes. All and any changes should have prior approval of IT management and be recorded. This should and could be part of your overall Change Management Process.

6.5 Documentation and Procedures (SOX and Repositioning)

COBIT states that the change process should ensure the appropriate documentation and procedures are updated accordingly when a change occurs to the system. This should and could be part of your overall Change Management Process.

6.6 Authorized Maintenance (SOX)

COBIT states that procedures should be in place to ensure that personnel with system access are monitored, and do not perform unauthorized activities. This can be addressed as part of the access policies and procedures.

Working the List

At the risk of belaboring a point a point, "SOX compliance and COBIT compliance are two distinctly different entities. This point can't be stressed enough, because as you progress through your Acquisition and Implementation phase, the two can easily and probably will become convoluted. It is at this point that you will need to refocus yourself and your activities to accomplish the primary goal of Sarbanes-Oxley compliance. Even though one of the stated goals of this book was to enable you to reposition or position your IT organization within your company via COBIT, the main objective of this book is Sarbanes-Oxley compliance using open source and COBIT as vehicles with which you may be able to derived additional benefits beyond compliance.

The process for working the list of Control Objectives will be similar to that discussed in Chapter 5. We will be using our fictitious company NuStuff to drive the process of customizing the Control Objectives in the COBIT Acquisition and Implementation domain. As in Chapter 5, the Control Objectives listed will also be a combination of SOX and COBIT, but each will be clearly identified. Again, your particular environment should drive your customization activities, and you should work with your auditor prior to finalizing your efforts.

Lessons Learned...

Project Management Is Key

This should be understood, but project management will be a key factor in the success or failure of your effort to obtain Sarbanes-Oxley compliance. Yes, as IT professionals or executive management, we have managed our share of projects, and we will assume that some of those projects have been successful. We will also assume that few people, if any, have ever been responsible for a project that touched every aspect of their IT organization and the company in general. Well, that is precisely what you will have to contend with to obtain Sarbanes-Oxley compliance; the scope of this project is that wide reaching. Any project under which one of the COBIT domains would fall under normal circumstances could be considered a viable project by itself, but the combined total of all of these projects becomes the overarching task for which, as of today, the consequences are so severe that failure cannot be an option. After recovering from what a former employee deemed "analysis paralysis," we realized that the fundamentals of good project management still applied:

Continued

- Project Definition and Scope
- Shared Vision
- Role and Responsibilities
- Accountability
- Project Plans

Even though the task at hand may seem daunting, if you keep the objective in mind and apply good, sound project management, your chances of success will be greater.

FastTrack CD

In this section we will discuss automation and workflow.

Automation and Workflow

Automation is key to being able to demonstrate compliance and sustain it over time. As you saw in Chapters 1 and 5, we introduced the concept of the workflow automation to assist in achieving this goal and how it can be used to automate what would otherwise be a paper- or resource-intensive process. The practical applications of this application are nearly limitless; any process that can be translated to an electronic equivalent is a good candidate for process automation via the workflow. For BuiltRight Construction and NuStuff Electronics, we defined several example workflows that fall into several categories, and tie directly back to the policy documents and Control Objectives outlined in Chapter 5.

Figure 6.2 shows the categories of workflow automation that fall under the scope of SOX compliance, and how they tie in to the overall goals of your compliance objectives.

In the remainder of this chapter, we walk through sample implementations for BuiltRight Construction and NuStuff Electronics that highlight some of the important considerations for introducing change to your organization, and how you can automate many aspects of this task. Any change can and should be applied to the same automation process, which is important for SOX since your auditors will expect justification, sign-off, and documentation of any change in your environment that might affect your financial systems and/or reporting chain.

Figure 6.2 SOX Workflow Automation Categories

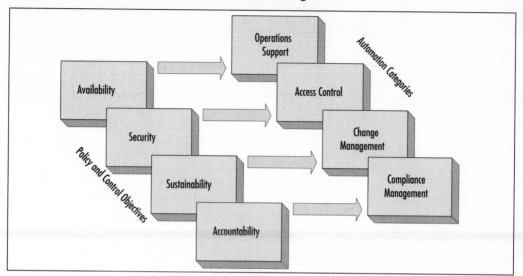

BuiltRight Construction Example Implementation: Web Server Migration

BuiltRight has an important Web site that it maintains for its supervisors that allows them to log in from construction sites to view, modify, and update their subcontractor scheduling. This Web application has a database that tracks hours worked, rates of pay, and other information, and has been identified as a mission-critical application for BuiltRight's business objectives. Since it contains sensitive information, an evaluation of the existing infrastructure revealed that some areas need improvement. The application consists of Microsoft's IIS Web server and an Access database.

Availability and Security

BuiltRight has historically had some instability problems with the current IIS implementation. As a prevention strategy, their administrator reboots the system weekly to prevent system lockups and other failures that seem to randomly occur. Again, Apache has been identified as a suitable platform based on its well-known stability and reliability.

Because of the sensitive information contained in the application, and the fact that it is accessible outside the firewall, security is an important consideration. BuiltRight has experienced a compromise of their current IIS server that resulted in the loss of important contractor information and the deformation of the Web site, so in comparing IIS to Apache, it has been determined that Apache will serve as a better security platform based on vulnerability information available. Since BuiltRight's server environment is Windows based, Apache and MySQL will be installed on the Windows server to leverage in-house platform expertise. Migration of all external Web services to Linux is being considered as a phase-two project. PHP will replace ASP as the scripting language for the converted application.

Sustainability and Accountability

Since this will be introducing change in the environment, approval and signoff of the key stakeholders is a key deliverable, and since this is mission critical, your SOX auditor will want to see these items in place. By implementing the change management workflow, we can be assured that the right people are aware of the intended changes and have approved the project to move forward. Since we are capturing this approval routing in a database, this can be later included in the infrastructure reviews covered in more detail in Chapter 8.

NuStuff Electronics Example Implementation: Intrusion Detection System

NuStuff Electronics has recently become aware of port scanning intrusion attempts on their main corporate firewall. By reviewing the firewall logs, they have determined that there have been almost daily attempts to find open ports to penetrate their network, but what is not known is if any of these penetration attempts have been successful. To improve the security and threat response of the IT organization, management has decided to deploy Snort intrusion detection systems (IDSes), which will tell them when port scans are attempted, and if and when any known exploits have penetrated their firewall. The main objectives this project addresses are discussed next.

Availability and Security

Security is one of the most important aspects of SOX compliance. The consequences of successful penetration from an external hacker are significant depending on the extent of privileges an attacker is able to gain, such as theft, alteration, or destruction of your company's critical intellectual property and proprietary information. NuStuff has opted to implement a detect control to quantify the penetration attempts from the outside, and define a specific process to deal with specific threats that are discovered as part of the detection process.

TIP

There are many types of IDSes, including host, network, and file based. This subject requires far more information than can be covered in this chapter. However, the SANS (SysAdmin, Audit, Network, Security) Institute, which is the largest source of information on security training and certification available, has a comprehensive FAQ regarding IDS at www.sans.org/resources/idfaq/. We cover more open source solutions in Chapter 8.

Sustainability and Accountability

Again, since this is augmenting your security infrastructure, your SOX auditor will want to see the control objectives, policies, procedures, and signoff of the key stakeholders for this project. In addition, we cover the issues of security in more detail in Chapter 7.

Infrastructure Change Request Workflow

http://xfld/builtright/egw/workflow/index.php
http://xfld/nustuff/egw/workflow/index.php

Figure 6.3 demonstrates the general process for the change management approval workflow. While it may seem somewhat complicated at first, it is actually straightforward. From a change management perspective, this captures the information needed for SOX and follows the change through to production deployment. Since this is automated, there is little effort necessary to capture and document the controls necessary for SOX compliance, while still maintaining the good IT practices based on the COBIT framework.

Figure 6.3 Infrastructure Change Request Workflow

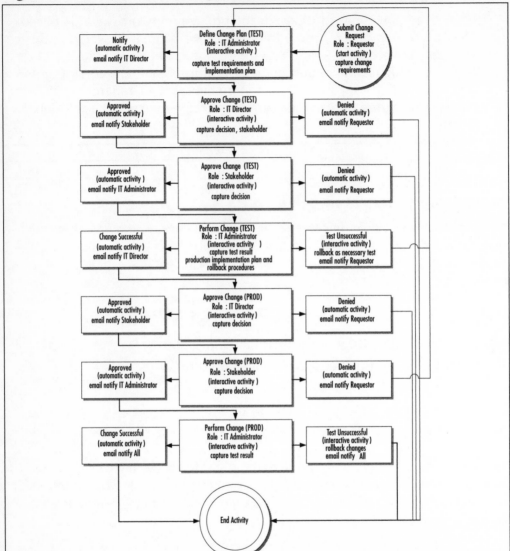

Workflow Roles

The roles for this workflow and their members are:

- **Requestor** The requestor is the person who submits the infrastructure change request. This is limited to the IT Staff group, since this workflow is for IT-specific changes.

- **IT administrator** The administrator is responsible for gathering the change requirements and procedures and performing the actual change. Again, this role is assigned to the IT Staff group, with Ken King being the default assignee for this role, since he is the IT administrator.

- **IT director** Biff Johnson is the IT director, responsible for approving the original request and the transition into production. The IT manager, John Scott, serves as the backup for this role.

- **Stakeholder** The stakeholder can potentially be anyone in the company. This role is defined as the person who would own the process as a result of the change, or the main beneficiary of the change itself. The IT director role defines the stakeholder in his approval process for routing purposes. For our examples, the following people were selected to fulfill this role. Because the Finance group at BuiltRight Construction primarily owns and uses IIS applications, Mark Anderson was chosen as the stakeholder of this change. All roles have at least one backup, so CFO Joe Smith was also selected for the role. Although the IDS is purely an IT-driven function at NuStuff Electronics, the goal is to improve security, and the main beneficiaries are the business owners of the data being protected. Because this is globally deployed, the key stakeholder chosen for this process is the CEO Jane Brown, ensuring she is apprised of the security measures being implemented in the company. There is no backup for this role because it is dynamically chosen by the IT director at runtime.

Workflow Activities

This workflow has two types of activities associated with it: start/end activities and interactive activities. The former workflow is the point where a new instance of the workflow is begun or completed. The latter workflow has several different types of interactive activities associated with it:

- **Definition activities** The IT administrator fills in the requirements and procedures to implement the change in a test environment, and defines the implementation and rollback plans for production.

- **Approval activities** The IT director approves the plan and assigns the key stakeholder initially. Both sign off on both test and production stages.

- **Implementation activities** The IT administrator performs the changes in test and production. Please note that the test implementation and the production definition activities are combined in the same step, since the production plan is only necessary if the test implementation plan is successful.

■ **Automatic activities** These activities automatically send out e-mail notifications to the appropriate roles associated with the next step in the process following an approval, denial, or result of a change implementation, both in test and production.

Implementation Planning

http://xfld/builtright/egw/workflow_users/index.php
http://xfld/nustuff/egw/workflow_users/index.php

The first step in implementing any change is to define what the change will be, how it will be implemented, and what recovery procedures need to be taken if something goes wrong. Here are the implementation plans for our sample projects.

BuiltRight Construction Web Server Migration

Since the purpose of this chapter is to demonstrate the important aspects of SOX compliance as it relates to change in your environment, this will not be an exhaustive tutorial on how to actually perform an IIS to Apache and Access to MySQL migration. Rather, we will focus on the main points to illustrate the things you should consider from a project perspective in general. With that in mind, the following is the overall major bullet-item plan for BuiltRight's migration.

Test Procedure

■ Build Apache server and MySQL on Windows on test network.

■ Convert Access database to MySQL using Access2MySQL (www.fonlow.com/zijianhuang/dbconverter/access2mysql.html).

■ Run ASP2PHP converter script (http://asp2php.naken.cc/).

■ Fix any unresolved conversion issues.

■ Internally test application with Finance and Field supervisors.

Production Procedure

■ Refresh MySQL database with latest data set.

- Bring Apache server onto production network.

- Add firewall SNAT rule to point to Apache server.

- Enter data into both systems for a probation period of one week to field any issues. Finance personnel test this data internally, and field supervisors test the data externally.

- Upon successful probation period, retire IIS server.

Rollback Procedure

- Bring down Apache server.

- Bring up IIS server.

- Restore firewall SNAT ruleset to previous values.

NuStuff Electronics Snort IDS

Again, this is not designed to be a comprehensive Snort tutorial so we will cover the project from a high-level overview to demonstrate the documentation capture and workflow requirements for SOX. In yet another example of the power of open source, we will be using another Live CD distribution for our Snort IDS needs based on a Knoppix derivative called the Network Security Toolkit (NST).

Test Procedure

- Download and burn the latest NST Live CD (www.networksecuritytoolkit.org/nst/index.html).

- Boot Live CD on test network and set root password.

- Use *ifconfig* to determine/set ip-address.

- From test workstation, log in to NST Web interface.

- Select **Bleeding Snort** ruleset.

- Start Snort IDS.

- Use IDS Policy Manager for Windows to tune ruleset (www.activeworx.org/programs/idspm/).

- Use Metasploit on NST Live CD to test IDS.

NOTE

Metasploit is a collection of tools, scripts, and applications gleaned from known security exploits in the wild. The Metasploit framework provides a consistent and easy to use Web interface for executing these tests; however, they are *strictly* provided for legal penetration testing and research purposes only. Please be sure to get management signoff before using these on your own network, and of course, only your own network. See www.metasploit.com for more information.

Production Procedure

- Boot Live CD on test network and set root password.
- Use *ifconfig* to determine/set ip-address.
- From test workstation, log in to NST Web interface.
- Select **Bleeding Snort** ruleset.
- Start Snort IDS.
- Use IDS Policy Manager for Windows to tune ruleset (www.activeworx.org/programs/idspm/).

Rollback Procedure

- Shut down the NST Live CD system.

More Lessons Learned...

Building an Effective Test Environment

Once your policies and control objectives have been identified and defined, the next step in the process is to identify application software that satisfies your objectives. In most cases, you will not have every control objective necessary for compliance met at the beginning of your compliance cycle. Whether you choose to self appraise or have a company assist you in the preparation for your SOX

Continued

audit, the initial assessment of your environment will yield areas that you need to address in any of the four main categories of availability, security, sustainability, or accountability. You may have to deploy new software or make considerable changes to existing configurations to mold them into a SOX friendly mode. In the face of a major augmentation or change, this will obviously require planning and testing before deploying into your production environment.

This being the case, to what point do you need to replicate your current environment; how close is close enough?

The unfortunate answer is, it depends. What you need to deploy into production might be very simple and superficial, or it might be a new and completely independent system from your existing infrastructure. In these cases, your test environment would be tailored to reflect the needs of the application rather than any systems you might already have deployed. On the other hand, if you are implementing something that will integrate with your present architecture to any degree, you will need to simulate this environment accordingly to adequately test your integration efforts. For illustration, if we use the examples given in this chapter for our sample companies, the security example would require the networking pieces to be in place, such as a firewall with a similar ruleset and similar networking topology. To adequately test the Web migration project, you would need server hardware of similar specifications with the same software installed as your intended production target. The advantage of using open source is there will be no licensing issues from a software perspective for your lab systems.

Another important consideration for your test lab that might otherwise be overlooked is the subject of storage. It is good to remember that Production Data in a test environment = Production Data. A common example is the replication of a financials database to a test server to test a change or operation that would otherwise have an effect on your production server that would be difficult to roll back, such as closing a period. Whatever the need to have this type of data in your test environment, you must subject this to the same security and access controls that you would apply to production.

Implementation

http://xfld/builtright/egw/projects/index.php
http://xfld/nustuff/egw/projects/index.php

http://xfld/builtright/egw/infolog/index.php
http://xfld/nustuff/egw/infolog/index.php

We will not spend too much time in this section other than to highlight the capabilities of some open source projects to assist in the project management, tracking, and deployment aspects of your implementation. As highlighted in the sidebar "Project

Management Is Key," keeping track of the various tasks and subtasks is important to ensure everything stays on track and focused on the end result. There are two main applications in the eGroupware suite to assist in the deployment stage: InfoLog and Projects. Depending on the complexity of your project, you may choose to use either the simpler InfoLog application to just assign tasks to users, or the full-blown Projects module, which is a complete project management application with milestones, jobs, time tracking, and Gantt charts. For our example implementations, we have chosen to use the Projects module for BuiltRight Construction, and just InfoLog for NuStuff Electronics to give you an idea on how you might use these applications for your own needs. Visit the portals on the CD to view the projects for our sample implementations.

Documentation

http://xfld/builtright/egw/phpbrain/index.php
http://xfld/nustuff/egw/phpbrain/index.php

Documentation is also an integral part of any ongoing IT function, and the Knowledgebase module is a very good tool for making this available to the right people. Documentation can be separated into categories, and each category can have its own set of permissions. On the sample portal sites, we have set up the following examples to give you an idea how this facility can be useful. As usual, this is not exhaustive by any stretch, and is just meant to give you an idea of what you might use the Knowledgebase application for.

- **IT user documentation** It is important to disseminate information to your users to help them "help themselves." Our simple examples include instructions on how to change their password, and the corporate hardware standards for desktops and laptops.

- **IT administration** We have placed documents for administrators here, mostly based on the operational workflows discussed earlier in the chapter.

- **HR documentation** In an effort to illustrate that not only HR documentation can go here, we included an HR section with a sample Employee Handbook. Other departments to consider would be finance, sales and marketing, engineering, and so forth, and since you can define permissions on a per-category group, you can control access to sensitive documentation, such as monthly finance close procedures and budgets.

Other Change Management Workflow Examples

http://xfld/builtright/egw/workflow/index.php
http://xfld/nustuff/egw/workflow/index.php

Firewall Change Request

This workflow is an example of where it is important to capture the approval of IT management for the test procedure and rollback plan. This differs from the General Infrastructure workflow, since the key stakeholder is IT, and this workflow is strictly designed with SOX documentation in mind. Figure 6.4 illustrates the simplified change request.

Figure 6.4 Firewall Change Request Workflow

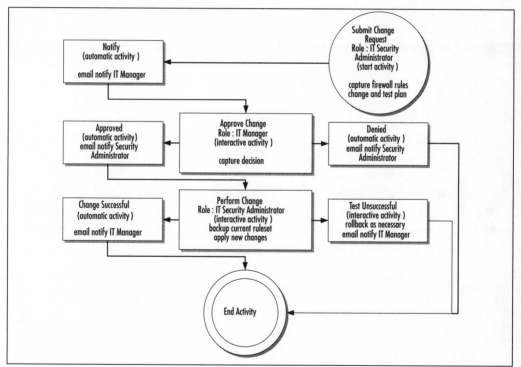

Workflow Roles and Activities

The IT security administrator is responsible for gathering the change requirements and procedures and performing the actual firewall change. The IT security administrator is the only person who can submit such change requests, and this role is assigned to Megan Rand, with Ken King serving as backup. The IT manager role is responsible for approving the original request, and since segregation of duties plays an important part of SOX compliance, John cannot serve in the backup role of IT security administrator by definition. Biff Johnson serves as the backup for this role.

The workflow is straightforward: the IT security administrator submits the workflow with the rules that need to be modified or added, and the IT manager approves or denies the request. On approval, the IT security administrator performs a backup of the current ruleset and applies changes. The test plan is executed, and the new rules are kept or the previous rules are reinstated if there is a problem. Implementing this workflow does not add to the workload of any IT staff, and effectively captures change activity for later review.

Oracle Change Request

The Oracle Change Request is very close to the General IT Change request; however, there are subtle differences. Figure 6.5 shows the workflow activity.

Workflow Roles and Activities

This workflow is designed to capture major changes to the financial system, including patches, upgrades, and interface or database changes. The requestor for this workflow is anyone in Finance, or the business analyst, so a group has been defined for the entire Finance department. The business analyst is responsible for translating the user's requirement into a solution plan that can be submitted for approval. If the business analyst is also the requestor, he or she needs to play both roles. The IT director is part of the approval chain and has first say for approving the intended change. Since the key stakeholder in this case is Finance, the CFO is the next stop in the process. Once approval has been granted, the business analyst will perform the change in test. If the change is unsuccessful, the workflow loops back to the requirements gathering stage so it can be revised and corrected.

> **TIP**
>
> In the event of an outsourced application, the business analyst role can be performed by someone outside the company. In this case, you will need to provide a login to the eGroupware system for this person, and if you decide to make the Web site available outside your firewall to grant access to external partners, you should ensure that the server is encrypted via SSL. For information on how to perform this type of instal-

lation, refer to the Installation and Security Guide available on the eGroupware Sourceforge project page at http://sourceforge.net/project/showfiles.php?group_id=135305.

Figure 6.5 Oracle Change Request Workflow

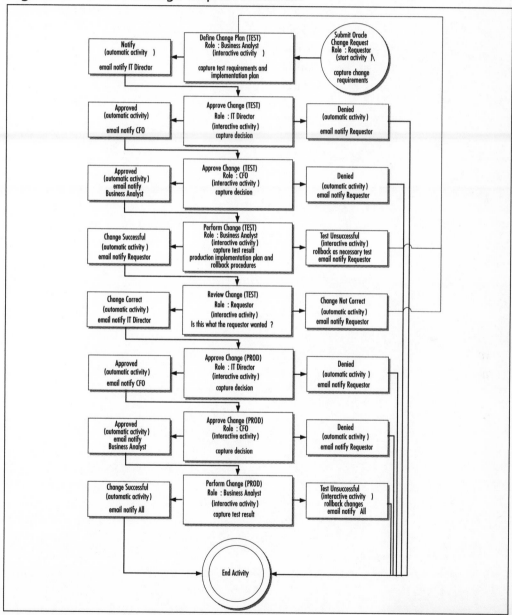

At this point, an additional step has been added to the workflow to ensure that the requestor can review the change in the test environment to make sure it fulfills his or her original requirements. Again, if the requestor does not think the problem has been solved, the workflow loops back to the requirements gathering stage so it can be revised and corrected. The workflow then continues with approvals from the IT director and CFO, and a step to implement the change in production.

Summary

In this chapter, we discussed automation and why it should be a key component of any small to medium-sized company's Sarbanes-Oxley compliance activities. We also developed guidelines by which you can assess your in-house expertise as they relate to the skill sets that will be necessary to use open source tools. We also provided actions and alternatives for acquiring the necessary skill set if it does not currently exist within your organization.

Additionally, we looked at the various control objectives of the Acquisition and Implementation domain, and identified those that relate specifically to Sarbanes-Oxley compliance, using our fictitious company as an example. In summarizing this chapter, there are three fundamental things you should take away with you:

- Let your unique organizational structure drive the applicable domain items.

- Automation will be critical, but resist the urge to over implement.

- Use of good project management methodologies will better position your compliance effort for success.

The remainder of the chapter shows examples of automation, project planning, and tracking for the sample companies. BuiltRight construction has decided to redeploy a Web application to improve availability and security. The project consists of migrating an IIS Web server using ASP scripting and an Access database to an Apache server using PHP and a MySQL database. NuStuff Electronics has opted to augment its security infrastructure with an IDS. Snort has been selected as a network-based detection system, since it is the leading open source solution and there is copious documentation and several books written for its deployment. To leverage the hard work of the open source community, the NST Live Security CD will be deployed since it contains both the Snort IDS and a testing framework. These project examples are then put through the COBIT framework for approval, planning, and implementation, using the example workflow, project management, and documentation modules on the Live CD. The chapter closes with a discussion of additional example change management workflows where there might be special considerations, such as the need for additional activities on one side of the spectrum and the desire to simplify the generic change management workflow on the other, which ultimately demonstrates the flexibility of the system.

Solutions Fast Track

Overview

- BKMs (best known methods) change and evolve over time.

- Domain II of COBIT allows and facilitates evolution of IT environments.

- An IT organization's objective should be to meet the needs of the company.

Evaluating In-House Expertise

- Open source expertise is focused on primarily two areas: operating systems that mainly consist of Linux, and applications that are platform independent. Since most open source is designed to run on Linux, your organization may need a minimum level of expertise with UNIX-like operating systems.

- The open source support stack consists of vendor distributions such as RedHat and Novel, developers such as Sugar CRM and MySQL, third-party support organizations, and community support.

- If any deficiencies are identified, you can choose to train existing staff, add additional staff, hire external expertise, or any combination thereof to effectively deploy open source into your environment.

Automation Is the Name of the Game

- Automation of existing and potential new functions will be paramount.

- There are four main areas of automation opportunity: operations support, access controls, change management, and compliance management. Each of these addresses the control categories of availability, sustainability, security, and accountability.

- Automation will allow you to better manage resources, both existing and future resources.

- Resist the temptation to over implement open source tools.

- The acquisition cost for open source can be low or nonexistent, but you will need to invest in resources.

What Do Acquisition and Implementation Mean?

- Having the right skill sets will be crucial to success.
- Minimize application overlap as much as possible.

Working the List

- The line between COBIT and SOX can become convoluted.
- The main objective is SOX compliance, of which IT repositioning is an added benefit.

FastTrack CD

Four main categories of automation talk directly to your control objectives: (a) operations support sustains availability objectives; (b) access controls reinforce security objectives; (c) change management supports sustainability objectives; and (d) compliance management sustains accountability objectives.

- Changes introduced into your IT environment must have the proper approval and acknowledgment from the key stakeholders. Change management is a key SOX compliance objective, and this chapter demonstrates that automation workflows can be leveraged to accomplish this.
- An effective test environment will ensure your project's successful rollout and integration.
- Production Data in a test environment = Production Data, and should be subjected to the same security and access controls.
- Implementation can be streamlined and managed effectively through the use of project management and tracking tools.

Frequently Asked Questions

The following Frequently Asked Questions, answered by the authors of this book, are designed to both measure your understanding of the concepts presented in this chapter and to assist you with real-life implementation of these concepts. To have your questions about this chapter answered by the author, browse to **www.syngress.com/solutions** and click on the **"Ask the Author"** form. You will also gain access to thousands of other FAQs at ITFAQnet.com.

Q: Can automation really minimize resource requirements?

A: Yes, as long as you don't over implement.

Q: Is over implementation really an issue?

A: Yes, if you lose sight of the business objectives and become engrossed in the open source applications and capabilities.

Q: Why shouldn't I use the template in this book?

A: You probably could if your environment mirrors either BuiltRight or NuStuff. However, we recommend that you use the process to develop your own template rather than use the ones in the book, but they can serve as a good place to start.

Q: Are there any open source tools that can assist me with Project Management?

A: Yes, some of these tools are included on the CD. Additionally, you might want to check out:

- **GanttProject** http://ganttproject.sf.net/
- **PHProjekt** www.phprojekt.com/
- **dotProject** www.dotproject.net/
- **Planner** http://developer.imendio.com/wiki/Planner

Q: Can I fully "take the people out of the process?"

A: No, as in BuiltRight, you can wrap automated processes around the functions, but you will not be able to completely take the people out of the process.

Q: Can tools that are not open source be used to assist with compliance?

A: Of course, but since this book is about open source, we focus our discussion there.

Q: This workflow stuff seems complicated. Does it add more time and effort in performing day-to-day operations?

A: As with any new procedure, you might experience some initial resistance to using the system. However, once this is ingrained in your internal procedures, you will find that it actually helps your efficiency as an IT group and gives you the ability to quantify your deliverables to the organization—not to mention the fact that your SOX auditors will be happy.

Chapter 7

Domain III: Delivery and Support

Solutions in this chapter:

- Overview
- What Do Delivery and Support Mean?
- Working the List
- Performance, Capacity, and SLAs
- System and Application Security
- Configuration and Data Management
- FastTrack CD

☑ Summary

☑ Solutions Fast Track

☑ Frequently Asked Questions

Overview

For this chapter we have decided on a quote by the author Michael Ferguson, who once said, "The first mark of good business is the ability to deliver. To deliver its product or service on time and in the condition which the client was led to expect. This dedication to provision and quality gives rise to corporate reliability. It makes friends and, in the end, is the reason why solvent companies remain solvent."

To illustrate the COBIT Delivery and Support Domain's impact, we will assume that as the chief financial officer (CFO), chief information officer (CIO), or information technology (IT) director, you have been asked the following questions: What do IT people do? What value does the IT department provide? Why not outsource the IT department? Some companies do not understand the importance of the IT department. How can an IT department add value? "To best describe the COBIT Delivery and Support Domain, we must amend Ferguson's quote slightly so that it refers to delivering IT "product or service on time and in the condition which the client was led to expect."

This part of the quote indicates how IT departments bring value to their companies. The inference of "on time" is self-explanatory. From a COBIT perspective, we would add criteria such as "within budget," "according to requirements," and so forth to "…in the condition which the client was led to expect." Including these additional elements encompasses the intent of the COBIT Delivery and Support Domain, whether your main objective is simply to comply with the Sarbanes-Oxley Act of 2002 (SOX) or you have elected to use SOX compliance as an opportunity to reposition your IT department.

This chapter looks at the numerous control objectives in the COBIT Delivery and Support Domain. It offers suggestions on how a small to medium-sized company might be able to reduce them to a manageable process, and suggests possible open source tools.

The Transparency Test...

The CFO Perspective

Let's repeat Michael Ferguson's quote from the introduction: "The first mark of good business is the ability to deliver."

Information technology departments will always be under pressure to deliver with limited resources. The only way to manage through the constant pressure is through the utilization of good processes and controls. The world of data integrity and security has taken on new levels of complexity. There often is a misconception in smaller businesses that strong control processes cost incrementally. Nowhere is this less true than in IT and financial controls.

As an IT director or CIO, you have a fiduciary responsibility first and foremost to protect the corporation's information. This may be difficult at times, but at the end of the day, the buck stops with you. Similarly, the CFO is ultimately responsible for protection of the company's assets. With that said, in order for the IT department to add value to the corporation, it must be efficient and support its customers. — *Steve Lanza*

What Do Delivery and Support Mean?

Chapter 2 established the following high-level definition of the COBIT Delivery and Support Domain: "This phase ensures that not only do systems perform as expected upon implementation, but that they continue to perform in accordance with expectations over time, usually managed via SLAs." This chapter looks at the specifics of each of the COBIT Delivery and Support Domain control objectives and attempts to summarize them so that they can lend themselves more to the structure of a small to medium-sized company.

The COBIT Domain III Delivery and Support Domain will cause the most concern for small to medium-sized companies because:

- Given the number of IT resources, can these activities be sustained?

- Do we really need all of this bureaucracy?

The answer to both questions is "yes." If the appropriate open source tools are implemented, the gain in efficiency, security, user satisfaction, and environmental stability will sufficiently mitigate the introduction of any bureaucracy. Similar to the "personal processes" discussed in Chapter 3, and the need to understand your company's culture, it is important to understand the normal perceptions of small to medium-sized companies, such as:

- It is easier and quicker to relay requests via phone or in person.

- People do not have time for processes and filling out forms.

As stated, the COBIT Delivery and Support Domain is where an IT department can gain the most benefit from a repositioning perspective. Therefore, the control objectives identified for our fictitious company have been designed to accomplish that goal. (For a complete list of the COBIT guidelines, please see Appendix A.)

1. Define and Manage Service Level Agreements

This section discusses the various elements and processes surrounding service level agreements (SLAs).

1.2 Aspects of SLAs (SOX and Repositioning)

SLAs should cover areas such as availability, reliability, performance, capacity, level of support provided to users, acceptable level of delivered system, and so forth.

1.3 Monitoring and Reporting (Repositioning)

If automation is leveraged and a quality control process is deployed, the burdening of an already taxed resource can be avoided.

1.4 Review of SLAs and Contracts (Repositioning)

The management of this activity can be automated through "eGroupware" via the workflow process.

2. Manage Third-Party Services

This section discusses third-party qualifications and management, an important area as it relates to the fictitious companies, because they elected to outsource their Oracle requirements.

2.4 Third-Party Qualifications (SOX and Repositioning)

Because the fictitious companies elected to outsource their Oracle requirements, they ensure that the selected outsourcer provided has the required SAS 70 certification for SOX compliance.

2.7 Security Relationships (SOX)

Processes and procedures to govern third-party service providers (i.e., nondisclosure agreements, contracts, and so forth) are established business processes, which can used to satisfy the SOX requirement.

2.8 Monitoring (Repositioning)

Monitoring processes should measure the delivery of service against the SLA contractual agreement. This should be included as part of the SLA, and managed via eGroupware.

3. Manage Performance and Capacity

This section gets to the heart of SLAs by way of performance and capacity management. [Bear in mind that areas identified as SOX pertain only to systems that are relevant in the process of reporting financial results.

3.2 Availability Plan (Repositioning)

This plan can be part of the SLA requirements, and documented via eGroupware.

3.3 Monitoring and Reporting (SOX and Repositioning)

This process should have reporting elements to ensure the timely resolution of issues. The key components for this objective could be Nagios, Quality Process, and eGroupware.

3.4 Proactive Performance Management (SOX and Repositioning)

Proactive performance management is the reason why establishing SLA monitoring criteria and setting a monitoring tool (Nagios) threshold is important. The threshold should be set in a manner that allows you to proactively correct any problems.

3.8 Resources Availability (SOX and Repositioning)

Although there is no stipulation to implement fault tolerance for SOX, you must be able to rationalize your architecture and plans if an outage occurs during a critical period (i.e., end-of-month financial reporting).

4. Ensure Continuous Service

This section discusses an IT department's ability to provide continuous service to their supported customer base. (For the purpose of SOX, the only COBIT control listed is 4.12 Off-Site Backup Storage [SOX]). It is worth mentioning that continuity planning will probably be critical during the next cycle of SOX audits.

4.12 Off-Site Backup Storage (SOX)

As described later in this chapter, business owners should be involved in establishing criteria for off-site storage. Certification is beneficial for this control objective.

5. Ensure Systems Security

This section discusses logical system security and resources. By reviewing the control objectives in this domain, we elected to leave several in that do not necessarily pertain to SOX.

5.2 Identification, Authentication, and Access (SOX)

Based on your own unique environment, this might be accomplished via Lightweight Directory Access Protocol (LDAP), Active Directory, and so forth. These control objectives or similar ones should be extended to remote access.

5.3 Security of Online Access to Data (SOX)

This control objective works in concert with the aforementioned control objective.

5.4 User Account Management (SOX)

This control objective should have a formal approval procedure that outlines the data or system owner who is granting access.

5.5 Management Review of User Accounts (SOX)

This control objective should include a reconciliation process, which can be as simple as comparing your authentication layer log against your user access request process logs.

5.8 Data Classification (SOX)

This is a good practice but a daunting one; therefore, it may be advantageous to limit this activity to financial data.

5.9 Central Identification and Access Rights Management

Although this control makes the administration of access/account information more efficient, it is not a SOX requirement. However, you must be able to demonstrate control over financial system access.

5.10 Violation and Security Activity Reports (SOX)

This control objective and any documented policies are important to demonstrate to auditors. It is important to enable logging and audit trails if you have the capability on your system.

5.19 Malicious Software Prevention, Detection, and Correction (SOX)

These processes and procedures should encompass clients and servers. When looking at virus detection software, consider the following capabilities:

- Centralized management
- Ability to record client virus activity
- Centralized and automated virus definition file distribution

5.20 Firewall Architectures and Connections with Public Networks (SOX)

It is important to ensure that your firewalls have logging capabilities and that there is a tracking method in place to capture any occurrences.

6. Identify and Allocate Costs

Although managing costs and allocating budgets is an important IT-related activity, it does not have a direct bearing on SOX compliance efforts. Therefore, this section can be skipped.

7. Educate and Train Users

This section discusses system security and resources. No matter what security measures are applied, if the end user is not aware of what constitutes good security practices, the security measures will likely fail.

7.3 Security Principles and Awareness Training (SOX)

This training can be done via policy statements on an intranet site, or by distributing these policies via employee handbook.

8. Assist and Advise Customers

This section discusses customers' experiences when dealing with an IT department; whether they have a dedicated Help Desk or a simple process of contacting IT personnel directly. The listed control objectives are fairly standard and, for the most part, are common sense.

8.2 Registration of Customer Queries (SOX and Repositioning)

This objective can be accomplished via eGroupware (the workflow process) or by putting a process in place to receive e-mail requests.

8.3 Customer Query Escalation

This can be accomplished via eGroupware in conjunction with Nagios. (Nagios is covered in detail in Chapter 8.)

8.4 Monitoring of Clearance (SOX and Repositioning)

The process described previously in "Customer Query Escalation" can be utilized for this control objective.

8.5 Trend Analysis and Reporting (SOX and Repositioning)

If you followed our suggestion regarding quality, the aforementioned elements will be part of your processes and procedures.

9. Manage the Configuration

This section discusses server and client configuration management to ensure that a process exists that does not allow standardized configurations and implemented configurations to be changed without going through the proper channels.

9.4 Configuration Control

There are many tools that provide configuration control for switches, routers, and firewalls, but we found Kiwi Cattools to be particularly good. It is not open source, but is relatively inexpensive.

9.5 Unauthorized Software (SOX)

All changes should follow the approved process, and procedures should be in place to detect deviations.

9.7 Configuration Management Procedures

This control can be satisfied by establishing processes that dictate where configuration files are stored and incorporating the backup of this location.

10. Manage Problems and Incidents

This section discusses server and client configuration management to ensure that a process exists that does not allow standardized configurations and implemented configurations to be changed without going through the proper channels.

10.1 Problem Management System (SOX)

This control objective is easily met with the correct implementation of eGroupware and Nagios.

10.2 Problem Escalation (SOX)

This control objective is easily met with the correct implementation of eGroupware and Nagios.

11. Manage Data

This section discusses what a SOX audit is (the ability to back up and restore data). In this area, you should focus on the systems that are important for reporting financial data.

11.23 Backup and Restoration (SOX)

The development of the necessary controls and processes are discussed in Chapter 6, "Domain 2: Acquisition and Implementation."

11.24 Backup Jobs (SOX)

This control objective is an ideal candidate for automation via eGroupware, because it is important to maintain verification for this activity.

12. Manage Facilities

This section, as it pertains to COBIT, deals with the control of physical access to and the control of environmentals for servers deemed to be critical or material in the process of reporting a company's financials.

12.1 Physical Security (SOX)

With a little creativity, this particular control objective can be met with Nagios. You will have to acquire an EM01B component, which will give you the capability to monitor temperature, relative humidity, illumination, and DC voltage. You will also be able to detect contact open/closure. If your facility does not have card key control for its doors, the above can still be utilized using a manual key process.

12.3 Visitor Escort (SOX)

This control objective can be accomplished via a visitor's log and reviews of the logs managed and captured by eGroupware.

12.5 Protection Against Environmental Factors

In conjunction with additional safeguards (fire suppressants, extinguishers, and so on) this control objective can be met with implementation of the Nagios EM01B component.

12.6 Uninterruptible Power Supply (SOX)

This control objective is traditionally part of standard IT audits; the main difference for SOX is the necessity for periodic testing and capturing the test result.

13. Manage Operations

We cover operational workflows as part of our discussion later in this chapter; however, from a SOX compliance perspective, this section discusses control objectives that auditors did not traditionally explore, but as part of Sarbanes-Oxley, will definitely want to see in place.

13.6 Operations Logs

COBIT suggests that you keep records of the day-to-day IT operations. This can be achieved using several facilities including an IT Help Desk, system logs, and workflows.

13.8 Remote Operations (SOX)

From a SOX perspective, you must include any remote function under the audit umbrella that touches the financial reporting chain, regardless of physical location.

Working the List

"Working the List" for the COBIT Domain of Delivery and Support follows the same process as the previous chapters, utilizing the fictitious companies as their environments. However, although not the primary objective of this book, we committed to noting areas where SOX compliance can be used to address previous IT issues and/or to reposition IT within a new department. The COBIT Domain of Delivery and Support presents such an opportunity.

While reviewing the control objectives, it was noted that the majority selected were defined by COBIT for domains related to SLAs. If the control objectives are stated and defined as part of your financial processes and procedures, the auditor expects you to show evidence. (Because the other focus of this book is SOX compliance utilizing open source, more specific tools that can be used to assist in this domain are provided later in this chapter.)

The control objectives in this chapter are a combination of SOX and COBIT, and each is clearly identified. Again, your particular environment should drive your customization activities, and you should work with your auditor prior to finalizing your efforts. For a complete list of the "COBIT Control Objectives of Delivery and Support," please see Appendix A.

Lessons Learned...

Don't Forget

COBIT requires a lot of documentation, and although your SOX effort does not require as much documentation, there is still a fair amount. To compound this, the Sabanes-Oxley Act requires that the audit firm rendering the test be independent of the compliance effort. This means that the audit firm will have their

Continued

own requirements for documentation, and that they will not be able to give any guidance regarding the necessary documentation.

Although the intent of the majority of the efforts listed in this book are focused on "taking the people out of the process," don't forget to update the "IT Department Role and Responsibilities" and the "Job Descriptions" based on how the department will look and what it will need to perform after all of the changes.

Performance, Capacity, and SLAs

Making your IT environment "available" is a large enough topic to justify its own book; therefore, we cover what we reasonably can in order to get you pointed in the right direction. One of the 404 section requirements is that your financial systems be available to end users, and that an explicit recovery plan be documented and executed in the event of a failure.

SLAs

Think of your IT group as being a "service department" for your company, with system and application end users as your "customers." The combination of policies and SLAs is what defines and articulates IT goals and the expected results of the delivery of those goals to the company. Executives may look at you and ask, "What am I paying for and what can I expect in return?" From the user's perspective, these goals define how they can expect to get their work done. From a SOX perspective, these goals provide a basis on which to establish how to test an environment and demonstrate compliance. We have provided some sample SLAs for you to consider. Even though they are simple and will not completely satisfy your departments' individual needs, they illustrate the sections that should be addressed when writing your own SLAs.

TIP

The sample SLAs provided are based on the standard templates available from *NextSLM.org*, which provides information concerning the strategies and practices surrounding IT service level management. In addition to templates, they provide tips, recommendations, and guidelines for managing IT as a service department. For more information, please visit http://www.nextslm.org/.

You have probably tried to implement SLAs from time to time. If your IT department is like most of those in small to medium-sized companies, those efforts probably yielded minimal results. Whether strictly for SOX compliance or for COBIT, there is no way to succeed if a clear and agreed-upon definition of success has not been developed. It is not necessary to articulate the value of SLAs beyond the establishment of success criteria; therefore, the processes and elements that derive a good SLA are our focus.

What Is an SLA?

In general, SLAs define the services and service levels that a department or company provides. As mentioned earlier in this chapter, SLAs that are defined and implemented correctly provide an effective method for measuring current performance levels and a way to anticipate future need. An SLA is basically a contract; therefore, it should address what the services and/or performances to be delivered are, and the resources and funding requirements that must be met. The addressing of resources and funding requirements and the agreement from management and customers will be a key strategy for establishing meaningful SLAs. This area may not have been successful in the past, but it is critical that SLAs be a part of the budget. It should be understood that if a budget or resource changes, the SLA is affected and must be renegotiated.

Key SLA Elements

SLAs include the following key elements:

- SLA metric levels should be driven by business objectives and meet user requirements, be agreed upon by the parties involved, and be attainable.

- Executive management should understand the correlation between IT funding and the ability to deliver agreed-upon services and service levels.

- SLA matrices should have performance cushions to allow for recovery from breaches.

- To avoid user dissatisfaction, it is essential that the service levels defined are achievable and measurable.

- Service level commitments should be monitored, managed, and measured on a continual basis. Monitoring and alerting should be done in a proactive manner, and should contain a performance cushion.

- Document, document, document. All performance matrices should be included in the appropriate documentation and, if feasible, contain sign-offs.

- Communicate, communicate, communicate. Communication is essential. If a problem arises or an SLA cannot be proactive, communication regarding the problem and a plan of action will go a long way toward establishing creditability for your department.

Template: Internal SLA

Internal SLAs include the following key sections.

1. Statement of Intent

This section defines exactly what you are agreeing to provide to the department; what you intend to do and why. However, it does not address how to meet your obligations.

1.1 Approvals

This section traditionally defines the key stakeholders who have participated and signed off on an agreement. However, in this case, a SLA workflow is applied to address this need.

1.2 Review Dates

Review dates are the dates the SLAs were reviewed by the stakeholders. This information is also captured via the workflow automation process.

1.3 Time and Percent Conventions

This section defines the conventions used in SLAs for describing service availability in terms of percentages, business hours, and time zones. This is typically consistent in all SLAs.

2. About the Service

This section defines the aspects of the service that should be considered for measurement and how they should be measured. It is important to maintain realistic commitments and to set achievable expectations. In an ideal environment, the SLA is defined before any infrastructure is implemented. It is important to consider the known limitations of any existing systems and applications when writing SLAs.

2.1 Description

This section provides a detailed description of the application or service, and defines who will provide support for the service.

2.2 User Environment

This section defines the environmental characteristics of the application or service, including the number of users, the geographical locations, and the supported platforms.

3. Service Availability

This section defines the normal availability of the application or service.

3.1 Normal Service Availability Schedule

This section describes the schedule (in terms of hours or days) when the application or service is available under normal circumstances

3.2 Scheduled Events That Impact Service Availability

This section describes the scheduled downtime of an application or service.

3.3 Change Management Process

This section discusses managing changes to the application or service (such as enhancement requests), which includes the procedures for requesting change, workflow approvals, implementation scheduling, and notification.

4. Roles and Responsibilities

This section defines who is responsible for providing support for the application or service, and how. It also addresses how new users are added, the request mechanism, who can make the request, who must approve the request, and the timeframe in which new users are added.

5. Service Measures

This section defines what is monitored and what thresholds of performance are acceptable (e.g., a SLA might describe storage availability in terms of percentage of disk space consumed before action is taken to reduce the current footprint or to acquire more capacity).

Fault Tolerance

Fault tolerance is the ability for a system or application to continue service without interruption in the event of a hardware or software failure. A *failure* is when the service delivered to users deviates from an agreed-upon specification for an agreed-upon period of time. To avoid any ambiguity, this concept should be tied directly to the SLAs. A *fault* is the condition or source that causes a failure. The distinction is that faults can exist without failures. For example, a design fault can exist on a bridge when a designer underestimates the amount of traffic to be supported, and the bridge ends up supporting more than the original specifications. Over time, the bridge would need to be reinforced as a preventative measure, because the extra traffic would cause stress fractures, which would ultimately lead to a failure.

The goal of fault tolerance is to prevent a fault from manifesting itself as a failure. There are several ways to approach this:

- **Fault Containment** Provides an automatic method for preventing failures by suppressing or limiting the original fault, and preventing faults in one subsystem from affecting other subsystems. Consider the role of a network firewall. Its job is to contain certain Transmission Control Protocol/Internet Protocol (TCP/IP) traffic from traversing to or from the connected networks based on a set of rules. In turn, the rules define faulty traffic and prevent failures (e.g., a network denial of service [DOS]), and also protects business policies by preventing employees from visiting non-work-related Web sites.

- **Fault Masking** Prevents the consumer or end user from knowing a fault has occurred. An example of this is the TCP/IP networking protocol, which has built-in error correction at the packet level, and the ability to request retransmission of corrupted packets, thus shielding the user from knowing a fault has occurred.

- **Fault Compensation** Provides an alternate method for the service to continue. One of the most common examples is a Redundant Array of Inexpensive Disks (RAID). Figure 7.1 presents an example of a RAID5 system that uses an n+1 disk configuration with a parity checksum "striped" across all of the disks. If any one disk experiences a failure, the system will continue to provide storage by generating the missing data from the parity information on the remaining disks.

Figure 7.1 RAID5 Fault Compensation

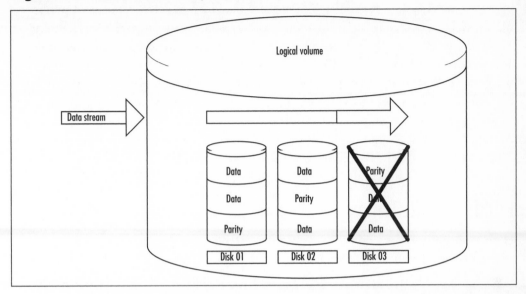

■ **Fault Repair** Automatically replaces or repairs the faulty item. Most modern RAID systems provide "hot spares," where a failed disk in an array is automatically removed and another unused disk is configured into the array. As illustrated in Figure 7.2, the information on the original disk is rebuilt on the fly, and the system returns to nominal operation without interruption.

Figure 7.2 RAID5 Fault Repair

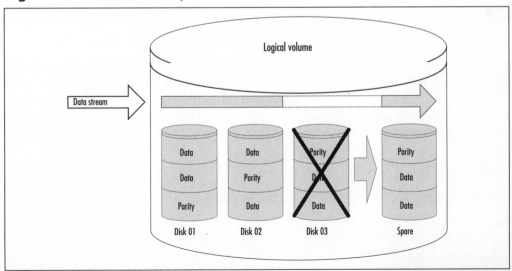

A typical computer system may deploy one or more of these methods to increase overall system reliability. While there may be a penalty in terms of performance, fault tolerance is the most robust way to achieve agreed-upon service levels. The main problem with fault tolerance, particularly in hardware, is cost. Fault tolerance is common in storage systems, because the cost for doing so boils down to how much each individual unit costs. Hard disks and other fully redundant hardware systems such as processors and memory, are typically difficult to deploy and expensive to acquire. With storage, you can simulate all of the recovery options with software. Although there are expensive hardware options, both Linux and Windows support RAID systems natively. By contrast, the design of redundant memory, processors, and application-specific integrated circuits (ASICs) can be more complex.

High Availability

High availability is the ability for a system or application to continue service in a reasonable amount of time (usually measured in small increments such a 30, 60, or 90 seconds) after a hardware or software failure. Because high availability uses off-the-shelf components and standard servers, it is typically far less expensive to achieve than fault tolerance. There are many high-availability products on the market; however, the approach is basically the same. One of the main differences is the number of failover hosts, whether it is an active/active or active/passive cluster, and what platforms are supported. The High-Availability Linux Project (*http://www.linux-ha.org*) provides the latest open source solution for high availability with its Heartbeat project. Figure 7.3 shows a typical heartbeat high-availability active/active cluster under normal operations and in failover mode.

There are typically four elements needed to make an application or service highly available:

- **Virtual IP Address** This is the IP address that clients query to utilize the service and that they must be able to migrate with the service. In the event of a failure and the application is started on an alternate node, the new box must respond to queries on the same IP address transparently to the clients. This is usually achieved by aliasing the IP address on the network interface connected to the production network, and sending the appropriate Address Resolution Protocol (ARP) broadcast to let clients know the physical Media Access Control (MAC) address has changed.

- **Daemon/Executable and Configuration** All of the potential failover candidates must have the application installed with an identical configuration, in order for a completely transparent failover to occur. In some instances, the application can be running on both boxes and fail just the IP. However, if the application has data, it is usually better not to have the secondary service running, because most applications will not run properly without its data being available. There may also be locking problems if the data is shared between the nodes at the same time. This is dependent on whether the application has been explicitly designed to share data.

Figure 7.3 High-Availability Cluster

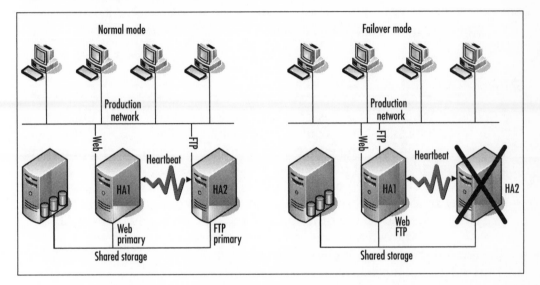

■ **Shared Storage** For applications such as Hypertext Markup Language (HTML) that serve static data, you might be able to replicate the data between the cluster nodes and avoid a shared storage system. The Linux Logical Volume Management (LVM) kernel module is an excellent solution, because it provides native snapshot capabilities, which can easily be copied to other nodes. If the primary system goes down, the secondary host can continue the service with its own copy of the data. In some cases, the application has replication or shared data capabilities of its own, thereby eliminating the need for shared storage. In cases where the data is dynamic, you need a shared storage mechanism such as a Storage Area Network (SAN) volume, a Network File Server (NFS), or a Server Message Block (SMB). In these cases the primary node reads and writes its data on the shared volume and in a failure situation the secondary takes over the data volume and resumes the application or service.

- **Heartbeat** This is the mechanism in which cluster nodes talk to each other to determine the up/down status of the applications being managed in the cluster. These heartbeat paths can be proprietary however more common devices include network interfaces and serial cables. If you are using a network interface, it should be a dedicated heartbeat device so that you do not introduce unnecessary traffic to your production network. You should have redundant devices to ensure that a failover does not occur if the heartbeat interface fails. Finally, you should have a peer device in the heartbeat mechanism external to the cluster, so that general network failures do not cause the application to failover.

NOTE

When a node fails in a cluster, it usually does not completely die. It may become unresponsive to your high-availability application, but still have files locked on your shared storage, or the application may be hung, but the IP address cannot be released. This is where a Shoot the Other Node in the Head (STONITH) device comes in handy. In this case, as part of the failover process, the node taking over the service sends a signal to a controller connected to the other system to completely power it off, thus ensuring that the new node can completely take control of the IP and data. NetReach remote power control (*http://www.wti.com/power.htm*) provides high-availability-compatible devices.

Load Balancing

Load balancing is similar to high availability in that multiple systems provide the same service. The difference is that these servers respond to queries either in a round-robin fashion or as a single virtual service (i.e., a cluster of Web servers appears as a single Web server to end users, or as a set of geographically dispersed Lightweight Directory Access Protocol (LDAP) servers that can respond to queries from clients in close proximity). The Linux Virtual Server project (http://www.linuxvirtualserver.org) provides mature load balancing software strategies on the Linux platform. Figures 7.4 and 7.5 illustrate these concepts.

Figure 7.4 Round-Robin Domain Name Service or Service Records

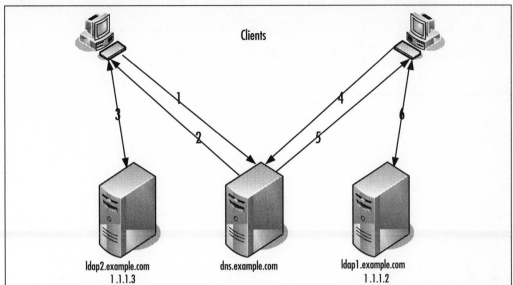

1. Client 1 requests the Domain Name Service (DNS) address for *ldap.example.com*.

2. The DNS returns 1.1.1.3.

3. Client 1 performs a LDAP query on 1.1.1.3, which is actually *ldap2.example.com*.

4. Client 2 requests the DNS address for *ldap.example.com*.

5. The DNS returns 1.1.1.2.

6. Client 2 performs a LDAP query on 1.1.1.2, which is actually *ldap1.example.com*.

Figure 7.5 Linux Virtual Server

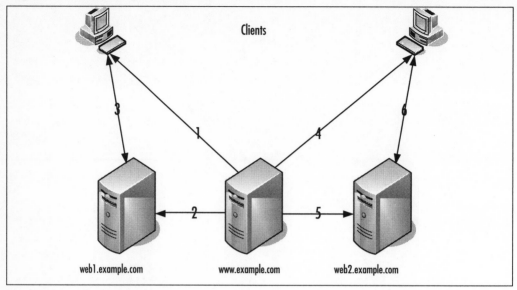

1. Client 1 requests the Domain Name Service (DNS) address for *www.example.com*.

2. *www.example.com* acts as a redirector and sends client requests to *web1.example.com*.

3. *web1.example.com* responds directly to Client 1 with the requested Web page.

4. Client 1 requests *www.example.com*.

5. *www.example.com* is a redirector and sends client requests to *web1.example.com*.

6. *web1.example.com* responds directly to Client 1 with the requested Web page.

In some cases, it is desirable to combine load balancing and fault tolerance into one service. If you use LDAP to perform authentication services for your environment, and the round-robin DNS method to spread the load between multiple LDAP servers, you must be sure that 100 percent of the client queries are handled successfully. If you just have load balancing and one out of two endpoint LDAP servers unexpectedly quits, 50 percent of your client LDAP requests will fail, because the DNS server is unaware that the service is unavailable. Service Records (SRV) add the ability to "weigh" the services so that you can send 75 percent of the requests to server one and the other 25 percent to server two; however, the client application must support SRV records. The solution is to make sure that all virtual IP's that can resolve to a mission-critical service are protected with a failover strategy. In Figure 7.6, *ldap.example.com* resolves to either *ldap1* or *ldap2*; however, since *ldap2* has failed, *ldap1* takes over the virtual IP address usually associated with *ldap2*, and responds to requests on both IPs. The Ultra Monkey Load Balancing and High-Availability project (*http://www.ultramonkey.org*) aims to combine the Heartbeat and Linux Virtual Server (LVS) projects into one managed framework.

Figure 7.6 High Availability with Load Balancing

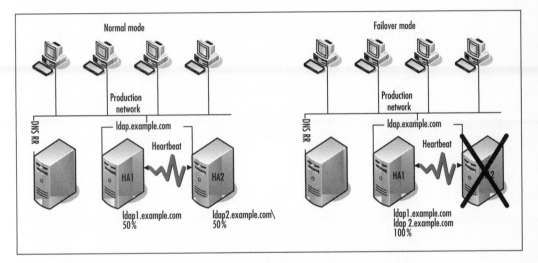

System and Application Security

The SOX auditors will take a comprehensive look at your corporate security footprint. They will look for prevention and detection controls at every point of your infrastructure, including network ingress and egress points, administrator roles, applications, and data security. The following section looks at the various open source tools that address these needs.

Network Security

A firewall is typically the first line of defense for a network. *Netfilter* and *iptables* are the building blocks for the Linux 2.4 and 2.6 kernel that provide a framework that enables packet filtering, network address, port translation, and stateless or stateful packet filtering. Because *iptables* can be challenging to configure, there are many high-quality open source "front ends" to assist in the definition and maintenance of the rule sets. Each of these firewalls has a different focus:

- **Shorewall** (*http://shorewall.net*) A general purpose, fully featured firewall that uses configuration files to set up and maintain the *netfilter/iptables* kernel module.

- **Smoothwall** (*http://smoothwall.org*) A complete firewall distribution that includes a hardened subset of the Linux operating system so that there is no separate operating system to install. It is designed for ease of use and is configured via a Web-based graphical user interface (GUI).

- **FireStarter** (*http://www.fs-security.com*) A visual firewall program with software that aims to combine ease of use with powerful features such as a wizard interface suitable for both desktop users and system administrators.

- **m0n0wall** (*http://www.m0n0.ch/wall*) A project aimed at creating a complete, embedded firewall software package that, when used together with an embedded PC, provides all of the important features of commercial firewall boxes based on a bare bones version of FreeBSD.

In the case of switches and routers, you are probably limited to the security provided by the individual devices. In any case, having Secure Shell (SSH) as an option for remote management is much more desirable than Telnet, because all communications via SSH are encrypted as opposed to Telnet where traffic is unencrypted. Most modern networking devices support the Remote Access Dial-in User Service (RADIUS), which provides centralized user authentication, authorization, and usage accounting for networking equipment. Open source FreeRADIUS (*http://www.freeradius.org*) is one of the most modular and feature-rich RADIUS servers available, and is used all over the world in large-scale installations comprising multiple radius servers with thousands of users.

Enterprise Identity Management

Three As identify management. *Authentication* is the process of verifying the identity, origin, or lack of modification of a subject or object. Authentication of a user is generally based on something the user knows (e.g., a password), is (e.g., eyes or fingerprints), or has (e.g., a key or ticket). *Authorization* is the process of determining (by evaluating applicable access control information) whether a user is allowed to have specified types of access to a particular resource. Authorization is usually in the context of authentication. *Auditing* is the capture of authentication and authorization attempts, which can be successes, failures, or both. Because authentication is central to your security, it should exhibit the following characteristics:

Security

An attacker should not discover that authentication is the weak link in your security footprint, nor should network sniffing reveal plaintext passwords on the network.

Transparency

Ideally, users should not be aware that authentication is taking place. They should only have to prove their identity once per session or period.

Reliability

The failure of an authentication system should force a failure to gain access to requested resource(s). The system should be designed to refuse authorization in the absence of authentication.

Scalability

The system should be able to handle 100 percent of expected client requests. It should not break because of a malformed authentication request.

Authentication Systems

When considering an identity management system from an open source perspective, you should be aware of how the authentication mechanisms that Linux uses stack up.

NOTE

It is best to use more than one factor for authentication, such as biometrics combined with a password, or keyfabs such as SecureID combined with a fingerprint. However, the implementation of these types of systems is typically very expensive, so we limit our discussion to the "over-the-counter" solutions that are available in all distributions.

Password and Shadow Text File System

This can be fairly secure if used exclusively via a local terminal, or remotely via SSH. The */etc/passwd* and */etc/shadow* system is time tested; however, this quickly becomes an administrative nightmare once more than one server or application comes into play. Consequently, it is not an ideal choice.

Network Information Systems

Network Information Systems (NIS') have built-in scalability where you can have multiple slave servers receive automatic updates from the master host. The main problem is that NIS is not secure because all passwords are transmitted in plaintext. Sun Microsystems, the inventors of NIS, addressed this security problem with NIS+, but unfortunately, it was very complex to implement and never gained much traction. In fact, Sun Microsystems has announced the end of life support for both NIS and NIS+.

LDAP

LDAP is a protocol that was derived from the old X500 DAP. Since it is optimized for "read" operations, it is particularly well-suited as an authentication mechanism, because it supports transport layer security on the wire, multiple password hashing algorithms, robust access control lists (ACLs), and multiple client replication, among other features. It is well supported in cross-platform applications. Many open source and proprietary software applications support LDAP authentication natively. OpenLDAP (*http://openldap.org*) is currently the premier open source LDAP server available. However, RedHat Corporation recently announced the release of the RedHat Directory Server (*http://directory.fedora.redhat.com*), which is an open source implementation of the popular Netscape Directory Server. It is too soon to tell how well this will be received and supported, but if past popularity and comparative features are any indication, it may surpass OpenLDAP in the number of installations worldwide. Currently, this is only supported on the open source Fedora version of Linux.

Kerberos

Kerberos is the state-of-the-art in enterprise authentication. It was developed by the Massachusetts Institute of Technology (MIT) and is freely available. The main goal of Kerberos is to provide security over an insecure connection between two parties via strong cryptography. This is accomplished via a trusted third-party scheme that allows users and services to prove their identity to each other while ensuring the integrity and confidentially of the data exchange, while only having to prove their identity to the Key Distribution Service once per session. A quick analogy is an amusement park pass that you purchase at the front gate, providing proof of your identity only once, and then using that same ticket to enjoy all of the rides at the park. Each operator examines your ticket rather than ask you for proof of identity (trusted third-party), and the ticket is only good for that particular day. Kerberos also has built-in support for replay detection so that no one can use a copy of your ticket to gain unauthorized access. Unfortunately, there is not much native support for

Kerberos from an application standpoint; however, interestingly enough, OpenLDAP supports Kerberos as the authentication layer, so you can deploy both and use either mechanism. (Visit MIT's Web site (*http://web.mit.edu/kerberos/www*) for more information.)

Microsoft Active Directory

Microsoft Active Directory is an amalgamation of Kerberos and LDAP, and a good choice for authentication. UNIX clients that support Kerberos V5 can authenticate; however, Windows clients cannot transparently authenticate to a standard Kerberos V5 KDC due to the use of proprietary bits in Microsoft's implementation. This can work, but it requires a lot of set up and is not ideal from an administrative standpoint, particularly if you have a large number of Windows clients. For Linux and UNIX, Microsoft provides AD4Unix (a plug-in extension for Microsoft's Active Directory Server), which enables UNIX-related authentication and user information to be stored in Active Directory. The main drawback is the requirement that sufficient client access licenses be available for authentication needs, which can quickly become costly. (See the Microsoft Web site [*http://www.microsoft.com/windowsserver2003/technologies/directory/activedirectory/default.mspx*] for more information.)

Data and Storage

Linux traditionally follows the UNIX *read (r)*, *write (w)*, and *execute (x)* file permissions for the three user groups: *owner*, *group*, and *world* or *other*. These 9 bits are used to determine the permission characteristics of all objects in the system. While usually adequate for most file access scenarios, some applications require a more complex and robust permissions structure, such as the assignment of permissions to individual users or groups even if they do not correspond to the primary user or group owner. In a mixed platform environment, it is particularly useful to be able to replicate the same access controls for both Linux and Windows clients. ACLs are a feature of the Linux 2.6 kernel and are currently supported by ReiserFS, Ext2, Ext3, JFS, and XFS file systems. ACLs are maintained by the *getfacl* and *setfacl* utilities, and provide the access methods shown in Table 7.1.

Table 7.1 Access Methods Provided by the *getfacl* and *setfacl* Utilities

Permission Type	Text Form
User Owner	user::rwx
Named User	user:name:rwx
Group Owner	group::rwx
Named Group	group:name:rwx
Mask	mask::rwx
Other	other::rwx

For securing sensitive file systems and data related to the financial reporting chain, you must fully document access controls by role. It is advised that you keep the permissions as simple as possible to keep the administration manageable, since you will be required to periodically review these permissions and document any changes.

This is also an appropriate time to mention antivirus and anti-spyware measures. If you are using Windows clients or servers, the audit team expects to see an antivirus solution in place that is scanning both the client and server files. They will expect to see automated virus definitions that do not require user interaction, and a regular scanning schedule. The following are some open source, low-cost tools:

- **ClamAV** (*http://www.clamav.net*) A command-line antivirus scanner for Linux that supports on-access scanning, detection of over 36000 viruses, worms, and Trojans, and built-in support for most standard compressed archive files.

- **ClamWin** (http://www.clamwin.com) A Windows-based antivirus scanner based on ClamAV.

- **Panda ActiveScan** (*http://www.pandasoftware.com/activescan*) A free online antivirus scanner for Windows.

- **AVG Anti-Virus** (*http://www.grisoft.com*) A low-cost antivirus scanner for Windows.

- **Spybot-SandD** (*http://www.safer-networking.org*) A free malware and spyware remover for Windows.

- **Ad-Aware** (*http://www.lavasoftusa.com/software/adaware*) A free malware and spyware remover for Windows.

Systems and Applications

The application and file servers that hold your financial applications and their supporting systems are scrutinized from both a "who currently has access" standpoint and a "how are you keeping unauthorized users out" standpoint. If your systems are running Windows, you can use Secure-It (*http://www.sniff-em.com/secureit.shtml*), which is a local Windows security hardening tool that secures Windows systems either by proactively disabling the intrusion and propagation vectors, or reducing the attack surface by disabling the underlying functionality that malware uses to execute itself. For systems running Linux, the Bastille Hardening Program (*http://www.bastille-linux.org*) is a script that helps lock down your operating system, configures the system for increased security, and decreases its susceptibility to compromise. Bastille can also assess a system's current state of hardening by granularly reporting on each security setting it works with. In addition to Linux, Bastille supports the HP-UX and Mac OS X operating systems. Other security considerations for systems and applications relate to administrator and user access.

TIP

All of the links provided in this book are on the enclosed CD and can also be accessed via the "Bookmarks" and "Links" sections of each portal site.

Account Management

One of the most important items you must demonstrate for your audit is the concept of "separation of duties." For access control, this means that the person approving access to sensitive information cannot be the same person who grants or reviews access. You must ensure that you have a system of obtaining the approval of the owners of the data or application. The workflow process is used to automate this. As you will see on the enclosed CD, system-level and application-level workflows are used to manage account requests for both activation and termination. The most important thing to the auditors is that the person creating the account or granting the access has someone (virtually) watching them, and ensuring that the proper people are aware of the changes being made.

Password Policy Enforcement

As seen in Chapter 5, a robust password policy is desirable for both security and auditing. Once you have clearly defined your parameters, you must make them compulsory. Unfortunately, you cannot trust end users to honor the password policy, so you must make the policy mandatory and have an automated mechanism for enforcement. If you are using Microsoft Windows and Active Directory, the policy is set in the Default Domain Group Policy and supports the following options:

- Maximum password age

- Enforce password history

- Minimum password age

- Minimum password length

- Passwords must meet complexity requirements

- Password is not based on the user's account name

- Contains at least six characters

- Contains characters from three of the following four categories:

  - Uppercase alphabet characters (A–Z)

  - Lowercase alphabet characters (a–z)

  - Arabic numerals (0–9)

  - Non–alphanumeric characters (e.g., !$#,%)

On the other hand, Linux uses the Pluggable Authentication Module (PAM) to handle the authentication stack for the system and for some applications. To enforce password policies you must load the appropriate PAM modules on the system. Following are the options typically supported by the native *shadow* and *pam_cracklib* PAM modules for password policies:

- Maximum password age

- Minimum password age

- Password expiration warning days

- Account Expiration

- **Palindrome** Is the new password a palindrome of the old one?

- **Case Change Only** Is the new password the old one with only a change of case?

- **Similar** Is the new password too much like the old one? This is primarily controlled by one argument (*difok*), which is a number of characters that, if different between the old and new, are enough to accept the new password. This defaults to 10 characters, or one-half the size of the new password, whichever is smaller. To avoid the lockup associated with trying to change a long, complicated password, *difignore* is available. This argument can be used to specify the minimum length a new password must be before the *difok* value is ignored. The default value for *difignore* is 23.

- **Simple** Is the new password too small? This is controlled by five arguments: *minlen*, *dcredit*, *ucredit*, *lcredit*, and *ocredit*.

    - **dcredit=N – (N >= 0)** The maximum credit for having digits in the new password. If you have less than or *N* digits, each digit will count *+1* towards meeting the current *minlen* value. The default for *dcredit* is *1*, which is the recommended value for *minlen* less than 10. *(N < 0)* is the minimum number of digits that must be met for a new password.

    - **ucredit=N – (N >= 0)** The maximum credit for having uppercase letters in the new password. If you have > or *N* in uppercase letters, each letter will count *+1* towards meeting the current minlen value. The default for *ucredit* is *1,* which is the recommended value for *minlen* less than 10. *(N < 0)* is the minimum number of uppercase letters that must be met for a new password.

    - **lcredit=N – (N >= 0)** The maximum credit for having lowercase letters in the new password. If you have > or *N* in lowercase letters, each letter will count *+1* towards meeting the current *minlen* value. The default for *lcredit*, which is the recommended value for *minlen* less than 10. *(N < 0)* is the minimum number of lowercase letters that must be met for a new password.

    - **ocredit=N – (N >= 0)** The maximum credit for having other characters in the new password. If you have > or *N* other characters, each character will count *+1* towards meeting the current *minlen* value. The default for *ocredit* is *1*, which is the recommended value for *minlen* less than 10. *(N < 0)* is the minimum number of other characters that must be met for a new password.

- **Rotated** Is the new password a rotated version of the old password?

- **Already Used** Was the password used in the past? Previously used passwords can be found in */etc/security/opasswd*.

Administrator Roles

System administrators can make it very difficult to track their activities, which is a necessary component of SOX. The number of staff with the *Administrator* or *Root* password should be limited, and the following measures should be considered to ensure that the proper audits are in place:

- Use a central *syslog* server with limited access for your Linux and UNIX hosts. This will ensure that all root activity is logged on a remote machine.

- Do not allow direct administrative logins. If using SSH as the primary method for remote access, require all administrators to login with a non-privileged account, and then switch to a privileged account. This activity will be captured and logged to the *syslog* server, and you will be able to audit who gained privileged access.

- Consider using the *sudo* facility to limit personnel to doing specified, pre-determined administrative activities.

- Use a managed framework such as *Webmin*, which allows users to login to a Web framework and perform administrative tasks using a non-administrative account. Webmin has a very robust access control and audit mechanism for tracking activities. (Webmin is demonstrated on the enclosed CD.)

- Exploit all available security and access control mechanisms afforded by the applications. For example, the eGroupware suite has very robust access control and audit mechanisms for limiting access to modules or restricting the activities that can be performed within the individual applications. (For more information on eGroupware access controls, see Chapter 8.)

Configuration and Data Management

In addition to change management, another important aspect of managing the operations is configuration management. The ability to roll back to a known good configuration or a previous set of values for your systems, network devices, and applications is essential to ensuring that you can recover from unexpected consequences as a result of intended or unintended changes to your environment.

Systems and Network Devices

In addition to the Wiki module of eGroupware where you have already seen automatic version control in action, there are a couple of open source version control systems available that can be used to save copies of configuration files and important data:

- **Concurrent Versions System (CVS)** (*https://www.cvshome.org*) CVS is the dominant Open Source, network-transparent version control system that uses a non-exclusive check-out model. Although CVS is typically used for software development, it can also be used to version control any types of files, and is suitable for storing configuration and system data.

- **Subversion** (*http://subversion.tigris.org*) Subversion is meant to be a CVS replacement, so it has most of the CVS' features but uses an *http/webdav* interface for checking files in and out.

The use of the aforementioned tools requires the administrator to check the in/out versions of the files you want to manage. The typical use of a model is to start with a baseline version as the initial check in, and then when a change is necessary, the baseline *config* is checked out and modified for the new configuration. If the new configuration successfully updates, tests, and deploys, the administrator makes the new configuration the latest version. This way you retain a full change history. When dealing with network devices, these configurations are typically designed to be remotely managed via the Simple Network Management Protocol (SNMP), so that you can take advantage of automatic collection tools such as Kiwi CatTools (*http://www.kiwisyslog.com*), which is a freeware tool designed to capture and manage network device configurations.

Application Data and Backups

Having no specific mention in the SOX as to methodology and/or architecture for backups, this is yet another nebulous area of SOX compliance. This being said, if your company has adopted industry standard retention periods for financial data, this stipulation will not be an issue. It will be up to you to determine which medium to use and the off-site storage rotation. You must make sure that the business owner agrees with your approach, frequency, off-site rotation, and so on.

Based on our experience, the following guidelines are generally accepted for the retention of financial data:

- Accounts Payable and Accounts Receivable – seven years
- Audit Reports – Permanent

- Bills of Lading – Five years

- Charts of Accounts – Permanent

- Fidelity and Surety Bonds – Three years

- Sales and Tax Returns – 10 years

- Tax Returns – Permanent

- Payroll Tax Returns – Seven years

- Expense Records – Seven years

NOTE

LDAP server logs can be used to support some of the user access control and auditing requirements of SOX. Therefore, it may be beneficial to include the appropriate logs with your backup process.

FastTrack CD

The COBIT Delivery and Support Domain is the "meat and potatoes" of the infrastructure. There are hundreds of open source tools available to help you meet your compliance goals. eGroupware was used heavily in this chapter; however, we have added sample configurations of several of the tools mentioned, to give you an idea of how they can be used.

SLAs

http://xfld/builtright/egw/Wiki/index.php
http://xfld/nustuff/egw/Wiki/index.php

http://xfld/builtright/egw/workflow/index.php
http://xfld/nustuff/egw/workflow/index.php

We have also provided the following sample SLAs, which are based on the format provided earlier in this chapter.

- **Finance Data Backups** This sample SLA covers the back up of all identified critical financial data. It is an agreement between the IT and Finance groups over what, how, and when IT will back up their files, and the roles and responsibilities surrounding this task. This relates back to the policy regarding data backups and retention.

- **Financial Systems Access** This sample SLA covers the authorization of users to see critical financial data. It covers the authentication of users and their passwords, and the availability of the LDAP identity management services. This SLA relates back to the password and access controls policies.

- **Financial Systems Environmental Protection** This sample SLA covers the physical building access management system. The IT group provides the agreement on the availability of the badge security system and the creation and termination of access cards to sensitive areas of the building that contain financial servers and storage. This SLA relates back to the physical access policy.

In addition, these sample SLAs are tied to an approval workflow process, similar to the policies covered in Chapter 5. Part of the SLA template is to capture the key stakeholders involved and obtain their approval. The SLA workflow is designed to be a generic process so that the IT Director can determine and route the SLAs to for approval from all key specified stakeholders. This workflow ensures that the IT Director is assigned the workflow instance, and either chooses a stakeholder to route for approval, denies the approval himself, or finishes and closes with final approval. Each loop to the stakeholder comes back to the IT Director for another cycle, until he or she decides there are no more stakeholders to send to. The Wiki page is then updated to reflect the disposition of the SLA workflow process.

Webmin

https://xfld:10000

Webmin is a Web-based interface designed for system administration for UNIX and Linux systems that can be used for managing user accounts, Apache, DNS, file sharing, and so on. Webmin consists of a simple Web server and a number of Common Gateway Interface (CGI) programs, which directly update system files such as */etc/inetd.conf* and */etc/passwd*. The Web server and all CGI programs are written in Perl version 5, and a significant number of third-party modules have been developed to administer a wide variety of applications and system devices. From a

SOX perspective, the best part of Webmin is that it provides a framework for authentication, authorization, and auditing of these administrative activities. It communicates over a Secure Sockets Layer (SSL)-encrypted port. The standard Webmin modules are installed on the enclosed CD. You can also visit http://www.webmin.com for more information and access to the third-party modules. The following server modules are included on the CD:

- **Apache** Used to can configure almost all Apache directives and features.

- **MySQL** Used to set up databases, tables, and permissions in your MySQL database server.

- **ProFTPd** Used to configure the powerful ProFTPD File Transfer Protocol (FTP) server. Supports all options in most of the standard modules.

- **Samba** Used to create and edit Samba Windows file and print shares for Server Message Block (SMB) file access to Linux hosts.

Security and Operations Workflows

http://xfld/builtright/egw/workflow/index.php

http://xfld/nustuff/egw/workflow/index.php

Account Activation Request

The Account Activation Request process is used to request the creation of a new account for an employee who has just been hired and needs a username and password so they can login to the network.

Workflow Roles

There are only two roles in the Account Activation Request process. The first role is of the Human Resources Administrator, who initiates the process of opening a new ticket when a new person is hired. The second role is of the IT Administrator, who is responsible for fulfilling the account request.

Workflow Activities

A four-step process is used for activities, which keeps the workflow simple and straightforward. The first step of the process occurs when the Human Resources Administrator opens a ticket and fills out the information needed to create an account. One of the variables that the Human Resources Administrator specifies is the Department Manager, who is the person in charge of hiring the new employee. After the creation of the ticket, the Department Manager is asked to approve the account request. The IT Administrator then creates the account in the "Fulfill Account Request" activity, and the Human Resources Administrator then closes the ticket.

Account Termination Request

This process is almost identical to the Account Activation Request process, but instead of creating an account, this process is used to request the deletion of one.

Workflow Roles

The roles of the Account Termination Request process are identical to the Account Activation Request process. Three people are needed to complete the process. The first two are the Human Resources Administrator, who opens the ticket, and the IT Administrator, who removes the account. Department Manager approval is also needed to complete the account removal.

Workflow Activities

All activities in this process are identical to the Account Activation Request process except that the information gathered within the activities is slightly different. There are four activities in the process, and with the exception of the Department Manager approval activity, the process follows the traditional three-step open, fulfill, and close layout.

Oracle Account Activation Request

When an employee needs an Oracle account, the Human Resources Administrator uses this process to grant access to the user. This process does not require the Human Resources Administrator to know exactly what type of account to grant, because the "Request Oracle Access" activity only requires a detailed description of what the account will be used for.

Workflow Roles

Oracle Account Activation Request tickets are opened by either the Human Resources Administrator or the IT Manager. The other users involved in the process are the IT Director, the Finance Controller, and the Business Analyst. The IT Director and the Finance Controller are used to get approval before the account is created. To fulfill the request, the Business Analyst is responsible for determining which rights the user needs on the database.

Workflow Activities

The process' flow is directed from the "Request Oracle Access" start activity to the "System Access Authorization Form." This is an important activity, because it is the stage where an accounts permissions are specified by the Business Analyst. After the Business Analyst completes the authorization form, the IT Director and the Finance Controller approve or deny the request, and the Business Analyst then creates the account and the ticket is closed.

Oracle Account Termination Request

The Oracle Account Termination Request workflow is very similar to the Oracle Account Creation Request, except that it removes accounts instead of creating them. All of the same approval steps exist, and the people involved are identical.

Workflow Roles

All of the same roles used for Oracle Account Creation Requests are used for Oracle Account Termination Requests. The Finance Controller and the IT Director approve the termination request, and the Business Analyst removes the account. The Human Resources Administrator opens the account termination request and closes the ticket when the request is complete.

Workflow Activities

Activities in this process remain unchanged from the creation workflow with one exception: the "System Access Authorization Form" activity is no longer required. The Business Analyst no longer needs to determine which rights to grant to an account, because the account is being removed. Therefore, after the termination request is made, the ticket is routed directly to the Finance Controller and IT Director for approval.

Data Access Request

This process is used to allow users access to data that is owned by someone else. For instance, if a user needs to read a network share to get specific documents off of a server, they would have to request access to the data. Regardless of the data permissions model you choose to implement, from a SOX perspective, once you have locked down your sensitive file systems or any data that is related to the financial reporting chain, you will need to quantify how people are granted access to this data, and who approves such access.

Workflow Roles

Only an IT Administrator role is needed for the Data Access Request process. Anyone within the company is allowed to request access to data, so the "All" role is used for the start activity, and the "Data Owner" role is determined dynamically when the ticket is already open.

Workflow Activities

The layout of this process is pretty straightforward. After a user requests access to data, the IT Administrator determines who currently owns the data, and the ticket is then routed to that data owner. Once the data owner approves the access request, the IT Administrator fulfills the access request and the ticket opener then closes the ticket to acknowledge that they have access to the data.

Data Restoration Request

When a user loses, accidentally removes, or somehow corrupts data, the Data Restoration Request process must be used to request that an IT Administrator restore the data.

Workflow Roles

The only role needed for this activity is the IT Administrator. Anyone can open a data restoration ticket, so the "All" role is used for the start activity. The layout of the process follows a simple three-step process. The ticket is opened, the IT Administrator restores the data, and the user closes the ticket.

Workflow Activities

This workflow captures the requested path to the data. It is up to the IT Administrator to determine how best to fulfill the request, either by restoring it from a recent snapshot of the data, or going back to the last full tape backup if necessary. This is a basic one-step workflow process.

Report a Virus or Spyware

If a user's computer is infected with spyware or a virus, the user must open a "Report a Virus or Spyware" ticket to alert the IT Department that their computer needs to be cleaned. This process is very simple and follows the General IT Request layout.

Workflow Roles

The only role in this process is the antivirus administrator. The start activity uses the "All" role so that anyone can report a virus or spyware, and the closure activity is automatically assigned to the person who opened the ticket.

Workflow Activities

When a virus or spyware is reported, the ticket is opened and routed to the IT Administrator in charge of cleaning computers. Once the IT Administrator cleans the computer, they log the results and specify whether their efforts ended in success or failure. After the IT Administrator has completed the cleaning, the person who opened the ticket must acknowledge the results and close it.

Virtual Private Network Access Request

Employees in remote locations may need to access the company's network. To do this, they must fill out a Virtual Private Network (VPN) Access Request so that IT Administrators can verify that they have protected their computers with firewall and virus scanner software.

Workflow Roles

The roles involved in this process are the IT Director and the IT Administrator. All users are allowed to request VPN access; therefore, the start activity uses the "All" role and the closure activity is automatically assigned to the person who opened the ticket.

Workflow Activities

When a user requests VPN access, they specify their manager. The Manager must then approve their request in the "Manager Approval" activity. Once the Manager signs off on the request, the IT Administrator approves the request. Finally, the IT Administrator fulfills the request in the "Fulfill VPN Access Request" activity. The requestor then closes the ticket and the process is complete.

Sample Configurations

http://xfld/builtright/?category_id=29
http://xfld/nustuff/?category_id=34

Because this chapter deals with operations, we have included sample configurations of some of the open source software that was discussed, to give you an idea of how to implement your own solutions. We have provided annotated examples of a short list of sample applications on the enclosed CD, which are geared toward the sample companies as appropriate. Although it is not an exhaustive list, it will give you an idea of the major open source projects and what it takes to set them up.

Authentication Cluster (NuStuff Electronics)

The following sample configurations illustrate how to build an LDAP+Samba authentication server for a cross platform environment (all of these run on the Linux platform):

- LDAP Master/Slave Authentication
- ISC Dynamic Host Configuration Protocol (DHCP)/Dynamic DNS with Bind 9
- Samba Primary Domain Controller/Backup Domain Controller (PDC)/(BDC)
- Heartbeat Cluster for LDAP/Samba

Web Server (BuiltRight Construction)

This sample configuration gives you everything you need to set up and run Apache and eGroupware on a Windows environment, including the following:

- Apache Web server and Hypertext Preprocessor (PHP)
- MySQ database
- eGroupware application

Summary

This chapter discussed the COBIT Delivery and Support Domain and why it is important, not only to SOX compliance activities, but also from an IT Department repositioning perspective. As part of this discussion, we identified the two biggest potential barriers to successfully executing the necessary control objectives identified in this chapter, which are:

- Given the number of IT resources, can these activities be sustained?

- Do we really need all of this bureaucracy?

We provided guidelines by which the control objectives in the COBIT Delivery and Support Domain can be minimized and customized. Finally, we discussed what constitutes an SLA, what are the key elements of an SLA, and the importance of SLAs as they relate to this chapter and the third domain of COBIT. The key elements of SLAs are:

- SLA metrics levels should be driven by business objectives and meet user requirements, be agreed upon by the parties involved, and be attainable.

- Executive management should understand the correlation between IT funding and the ability to deliver agreed-upon services and service levels.

- SLAs matrices should have performance cushions to allow for recovery from breaches.

- To avoid user dissatisfaction, it is essential that the service levels defined are achievable and measurable.

- Service levels should be monitored, managed, and measured on a continual basis. Monitoring and alerting should be done in a proactive manner and should contain a performance cushion.

- All performance matrices should be included in the appropriate documentation and, if feasible, contain sign offs.

- Communication is essential. If a problem arises or an SLA cannot be met, proactive communication regarding the problem and a plan of action goes a long way in establishing credibility for your department.

We looked at security and what it means to SOX compliance. We began with a look at network security in the context of open source solutions such as firewalls, intrusion detection and prevention systems, and then took a brief look at network devices. We continued with Enterprise identity management and how it affects your ability to prove provide the three aspects of identity: authentication, authorization, and auditing. We looked at the various open source authentication systems such as LDAP and Kerberos, and took a brief look at Active Directory. Our security discussion continued with data and storage permissions and access controls, and we finished with a look at application security and a revisit of password policies.

Configuration management is an important aspect of SOX compliance as it relates to both security availability concerns. We discussed how open source tools such as Webmin, Kiwi Cattools, and CVS can help establish a baseline for configurations and manage changes in a controlled and structured environment, while capturing the necessary audit trail via logs.

We then took a brief look at storage backups and data retention, to give you some ideas on what you may need to consider. Although SOX does not explicitly define what a data retention policy should be, it is important from an audit perspective that you have a policy in place.

Solutions Fast Track

Overview

- ☑ IT Departments can and should provide value to the company.
- ☑ The IT Department's main goal should be "To deliver **IT** product or service on time and in the condition which the client was led to expect."
- ☑ Most companies fail to see the value that IT Departments provide.

What Do Delivery and Support Mean?

- ☑ Systems should perform as expected upon implementation, and continue to perform in accordance with the expectations.
- ☑ COBIT Domain III Delivery and Support will probably cause the most concern in a small to medium size company.
- ☑ Open source tools can provide a gain in efficiency, security, user satisfaction, and environmental stability.

Working the List

- ☑ Establishment of good SLAs is critical to efforts to reposition an IT Department.

- ☑ eGroupware and Galaxia Workflow are key open source tools that can assist you in this COBIT III Delivery and Support Domain

Performance, Capacity, and SLAs

- ☑ SLA resources and services should be tied to IT funding, and executive management should understand the correlation between IT funding and the ability to deliver agreed-upon services and service levels/

- ☑ Documenting agreements should remove ambiguity and ease the reliance upon individual's recollections.

- ☑ Communication is essential when managing SLAs.

System and Application Security

- ☑ The three aspects of identity management are authentication, authorization, and auditing.

- ☑ Authentication must be secure (e.g., a network-sniffing program should not yield plaintext passwords on the wire).

- ☑ Authentication should be transparent. In an ideal world, the end user should not know that authentication is taking place and should only need to provide proof of identity once.

- ☑ Authentication systems need to be reliable. Failure of authentication should yield failure of authorization.

- ☑ Authentication systems need proper scalability and should be able to handle 100 percent of expected client requests.

- ☑ Kerberos and LDAP are two examples of robust and secure identity management mechanisms.

- ☑ Data permissions must be explicitly defined for both Windows and UNIX. These can be correlated as one overall policy with the use of UNIX ACLs.

- ☑ Password policies can be enforced on both Windows and Linux platforms.

Configuration and Data Management

☑ Applications and system configurations can be managed with open source revision control systems such as CVS and Subversion.

☑ Network devices can be managed via SNMP with Kiwi Cattools.

☑ Applications and Data should have a retention policy in place, although SOX does not explicitly define what that policy should be.

FastTrack CD

☑ Webmin is a great administrative tool that allows you to grant privileges to perform administrative functions. There are modules to manage virtually every major open source application available and provide an audit trail.

☑ Security and operations workflows perform an important data capture facility that auditors want to see, to make sure that the separation of duties is enforced and proper approval has been granted to security sensitive data and applications.

☑ Some sample configurations for popular open source application are provided on the enclosed CD.

Frequently Asked Questions

The following Frequently Asked Questions, answered by the authors of this book, are designed to both measure your understanding of the concepts presented in this chapter and to assist you with real-life implementation of these concepts. To have your questions about this chapter answered by the author, browse to **www.syngress.com/solutions** and click on the **"Ask the Author"** form. You will also gain access to thousands of other FAQs at ITFAQnet.com.

Q: What if an executive management or IT customer won't accept the changes need to comply with SOX?

A: Unfortunately, the odds will be great that your company will not obtain SOX compliance.

Q: Why is the Delivery and Support Domain so important?

A: From a SOX perspective, this domain affords the greatest opportunity to reposition an IT Department.

Q: Will my auditor require workflow diagrams?

A: No, but they will require documentation, and since workflows make great documentation and you will need to develop them for your processes anyway, you might as well use them for documentation purposes.

Q: The budget process at my company has been completed for this year. What should I do?

A: Ensure that funding for any additional resources is still stipulated in your SLA, and then negotiate with Executive Management or the customer for the additional funding.

Q: Are formal SLAs really necessary? Where can I find more information on writing effective SLAs?

A: The simple answer is yes. Keep in mind that SLAs are the criteria by which your success will be assessed. Here are a few Web sites that to get you started:

- http://www.nextslm.org/
- http://guide.darwinmag.com/technology/outsourcing/sla/
- http://www.nkarten.com/sla.html
- http://www.cio.com/archive/111598_sla.html

Q: Can a small- to medium-size company really stay on top of all of the SOX requirements?

A: Yes, if the right open source tools are selected and the right processes put in place.

Chapter 8

Domain IV: Monitoring

Solutions in this chapter:

- Overview
- What Does Monitoring Mean?
- Working the List
- Monitoring in Practice
- FastTrack CD
- Rolling Your Own Workflows

☑ Summary
☑ Solutions Fast Track
☑ Frequently Asked Questions

Overview

Harlow H. Curtice, president of General Motors from 1953 to 1958, once said, "Do it the hard way! Think ahead of your job. Then nothing in the world can keep the job ahead from reaching out for you. Do it better than it need be done. Next time doing it will be child's play. Let no one or anything stand between you and the difficult task, let nothing deny you this rich chance to gain strength by adversity, confidence by mastery, success by deserving it. Do it better each time. Do it better than anyone else can do it. I know this sounds old-fashioned. It is, but it has built the world."

COBIT is a closed-loop process, which means that the process itself never ends. Each additional domain is improved based on input from the previous domain. To illustrate this point, this chapter provides a summary of Deming's "Quality Cycle – PDCA." This chapter also examines the control objectives in the monitoring domain, and offers suggestions on how a small or medium-sized company might be able to reduce those objectives to a manageable process.

The Transparency Test...

The CFO Perspective

"Information technology plays a critical role in both the ongoing operations of a company and in its SOX compliance. Given the investment companies make in IT, and the reliance on IT for critical business processes - the quality and efficiency of IT support should be monitored and managed. Strong control processes are absolutely required to protect and maintain a company's information.

Utilization and efficiency metrics and service level agreements are important tools to the IT management team to ensure an effective organization."
— *Steve Lanza*

What Does Monitoring Mean?

Chapter 2 established the following high-level definition for the COBIT monitoring domain: "The monitoring phase uses the SLAs or baseline established in the subsequent phases to allow an IT organization to not only gauge how they are performing against expectation but also provides them with an opportunity to be proactive."

Previous chapters discussed good quality practices; Plan, Do, Check, Act (PDCA), and continuous improvement. This chapter attempts to accomplish three things:

- Give you more information on Deming and his quality system.

- Illustrate PDCA more clearly.

- Demonstrate, via Deming's PDCA cycle, that monitoring is not the end of the process, but rather the beginning.

Deming's PDCA Cycle

In the 1950s, W. Edwards Deming developed a quality system for the continuous improvement of business processes. Deming's quality system contended that business processes should be analyzed and measured to identify the sources of variations that cause products to deviate from customer requirements. He proposed that business processes be placed in a continuous feedback loop so that managers could identify and change the parts of the process that needed improvement. To illustrate his continuous improvement system, Deming developed a diagram using four arrows in a cyclical pattern. This diagram is commonly known as the PDCA cycle (see Figure 8.1).

Figure 8.1 Deming's PDCA

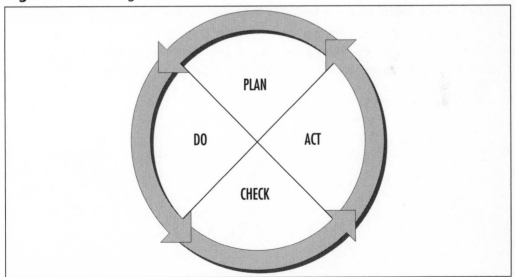

The sections of the diagram are defined as:

- **PLAN** Design or revise business-process components to improve results
- **DO** Implement the plan and measure its performance
- **CHECK** Assess the measurements and report the results to the decision makers
- **ACT** Decide on the changes that are needed to improve the process

Although Deming's focus was on industrial production processes, his method and philosophies just as easily applied to modern business practices. If you look carefully at the COBIT Guidelines, you will see a strong resemblance to the Deming PDCA model. Whether intentionally or by accident, these guidelines illustrate the point that good quality business practices endure the test of time.

How does this apply to the Sarbanes-Oxley Act of 2002 (SOX) and COBIT? Most monitoring activities in COBIT IV: Domain Monitoring come from service level agreements (SLAs). As much as possible, monitoring activities should be automated via Open Source tools such as Nagios and eGroupware. Keep in mind that when determining your thresholds, you may want to set them slightly below your SLA thresholds so that you have additional time to react and proactively correct problems prior to a service interruption.

This chapter looks at the specifics of each control objective, and attempts to summarize and distill those that lend themselves to small and medium-sized companies. If a particular control objective or an individual item is not applicable to BuiltRight or NuStuff, it generally does not apply to small to medium-sized companies. (For a complete list of the COBIT Guidelines, please see Appendix A.)

1. Monitor the Processes

This section discusses monitoring processes and activities associated with ensuring that previously defined systems and control objectives perform as expected.

1.2. Assessing Performance (SOX and Repositioning)

This process should include key performance indicators and critical success factors, and be performed on a continuous basis utilizing good quality practices and concepts. As discussed previously, these performance indicators must be SLA-based.

1.3. Assessing Customer Satisfaction (SOX and Repositioning)

Customer satisfaction should be measured at regular intervals, and any shortfalls should be addressed as part of a continuous improvement process. Again, the measurement criteria should be based on SLAs. As part of the normal course of operations, internal controls must be monitored for effectiveness through management and supervisory activities. As with Deming, any deviations must require analysis and corrective action plan(s). Also, these deviations must be reported to the individual responsible for their function and at least one level of management above. Any serious deviations should be immediately reported to executive management. This particular control objective is critical in the development of processes and procedures for SOX compliance.

2. Assess Internal Control Adequacy

Once you have implemented the various policies, processes, and procedures, and have obtained SOX compliance, you must sustain your new environment. This is where the various Open Source tools identified in this book pay off. Because the COBIT guidelines were developed in 1996, a lot of the recommended "Internal Control Adequacy" assessing activities appear to have been incorporated into the SOX compliance process.

3. Obtain Independent Assurance

Although the control objectives in this section have no bearing on Sarbanes–Oxley Compliance, they are noteworthy to review with regards to possibly adding credence to the effectiveness of an IT organization after obtaining Sarbanes–Oxley Compliance and/or any repositioning efforts.

4. Provide for Independent Audit

The control objectives in this section aren't required to comply with Sarbanes–Oxley, but because these control objectives are what Sarbanes–Oxley Compliance is all about, we felt compelled to list them and provide a few insights. As unfortunate as it is, most small to medium-sized companies can't afford the staffing on a full-time basis to comply with this COBIT section or periodically perform self-audits. However, what might be more feasible and realistic is to designate an audit team made up of existing employees. The main caveat to keep in mind is that the employee performing the audit of a department cannot work within the audited department. If the luxury of budgetary funding does exist at your organization, we would advise the periodic use of an independent audit firm, rather than one of the big four, to ensure your controls are still effective. The reason for using an independent audit firm is because the impartiality of the independent audit firm will lend more credence to the audit findings and your audit firm.

Working the List

By now we hope that as a result of the activities of the previous chapters, that it is clear that there is a difference between Sarbanes-Oxley compliance and the COBIT guidelines. That being said, the process for working the Control Objectives in the COBIT Monitoring Domain for Sarbanes-Oxley compliance is the same as the previous chapters. A fictitious company drives the process of customizing the control objectives in the COBIT monitoring domain.

From a SOX-compliance perspective, the monitoring domain has the least amount of control objectives identified. Imagine that the previous COBIT domains form the foundation, walls, doors, and windows of your compliance house, and the monitoring domain is the roof. The monitoring domain performs the vital role of ensuring that all unexpected results are kept off of the list. Therefore, use the following guidelines when you are customizing control objectives for your environment:

- The importance of the system, application, and infrastructure component should drive the frequency of monitoring and auditing.

- The monitoring process should be automated as much as possible.

- Monitoring capabilities should employ exception reporting.

- Above all, check, check, check.

NOTE

The question is not whether an IT department will change, but will it embrace change and derive additional benefits from its SOX compliance.

Monitoring in Practice

When discussing monitoring, there are three distinct steps to consider. The first step is health monitoring of the actual servers, services, and applications that comprise the infrastructure and the financial reporting chain. The second step is monitoring configurations and data points to ensure change management and security parameters are being captured. And finally, compliance monitoring makes sure that the two previous types are properly observed and reviewed and that any anomalies are corrected accordingly. This three-step process is critical to sustaining an ongoing healthy, managed SOX strategy that can be quantified at audit time.

Monitoring with Nagios

To accomplish the first step, we discuss Nagios, which is the premier open source network and host-monitoring application that runs on Linux and other UNIX operating systems. Nagios monitors hosts and services on the network, provides an overview of the status of the systems, notifies you know when things go wrong, and ultimately allows you to resolve problems that occur in a predefined manner. Nagios can also monitor historical reports and graphs of host and service down times, which can be used to support SLAs. More than 150,000 copies of the latest version have been downloaded, and many top installations monitor thousands of hosts and services.

Architecture

Nagios is designed in a modular fashion. A central daemon contains the monitoring logic and coordinates things such as escalations and scheduling downtime. Nagios executes external applications at regular intervals to handle the low-level monitoring of each individual item. Other external commands can be triggered to manage alerts, state changes, and monitor information. A Common Gateway Interface (CGI) is included, which allows users to view status information via any browser, respond to alerts, and manage schedules (see Figure 8.2).

Nagios Monitor Targets

Nagios can monitor anything that is essentially "reachable" by some kind of address. Although Transmission Control Protocol/Internet Protocol (TCP/IP) addresses are the most commonly used method, Nagios does not care about network protocols or addresses as long as the appropriate check command plug-in is written and can contact its intended host, appliance, or service target. Nagios has two classes of monitors: hosts and services.

Figure 8.2 Nagios Conceptual Design

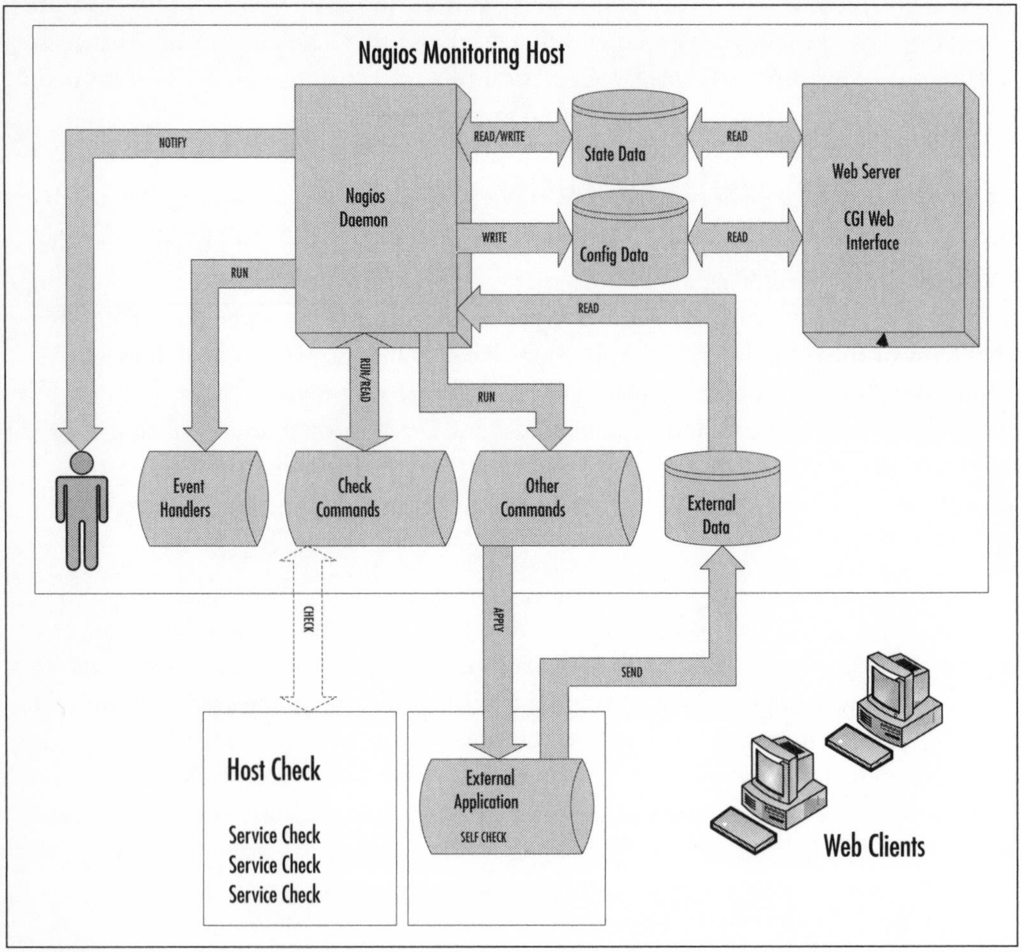

Hosts

These are usually physical objects such as servers, networking equipment, and printers. Monitored hosts can be arranged in parent/child relationships with other hosts, and hosts usually provide one or more services. Host checks are performed on-demand after the service state changes, and can return three possible states:

- Up
- Down
- Unreachable

A host is unreachable once a route verification is initiated to determine whether the host is dead or if there is a network or routing problem. Additionally, Nagios can detect "flapping," where hosts come up and go down in rapid succession, but only issue an alert for the first downtime.

Services

Services are usually associated with or provided by a host, and can include tangible items such as disk space, printer toner consumption, and memory usage, as well as intangible items or services such as Hypertext Transfer Protocol (HTTP), Simple Mail Transfer Protocol (SMTP), Domain Name System (DNS), and Lightweight Directory Access Protocol (LDAP). Services are the main reason for monitoring; if a host does not offer any useful services, there is no reason to monitor the host at all (see Figure 8.3).

Figure 8.3 Nagios View of Hosts and Services

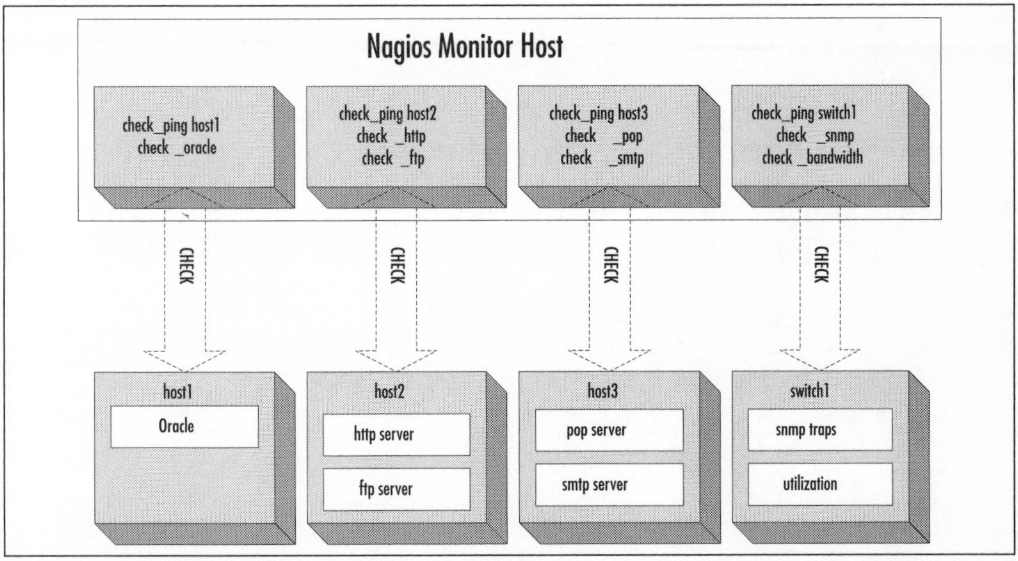

Nagios Plugins

Nagios plug-ins are the components that understand the network addresses, protocols, and services that must be checked. The Nagios daemon passes information about what needs to be checked to external plug-in commands, which then perform the actual checks of the hosts and services and then returns the information back to Nagios. Plug-ins can be simple shell or Perl scripts, or complex, compiled executables that perform "application-level" checks of services. Anything written for that a plug-in can be monitored, ranging from a simple HTTP service check to Web transactions and so forth. The information that is returned is a text description of the state of the application and one of the following error levels:

- 0 = OK
- 1 = WARNING
- 2 = CRITICAL
- 3 = UNKNOWN

In addition to proactively checking defined services, Nagios also has the ability to accept checks from other hosts in a predefined and secure manner. This is useful for localized checks on items such as CPU usage and disk space consumption, which cannot usually be measured remotely.

Nagios Escalations

When a state change occurs (such as OK to WARNING), Nagios can be configured to take specific actions based on the transition that has occurred. Nagios can send pages of e-mail and run external commands to escalate the problem or notify when recovery takes place (see Figure 8.4).

Figure 8.4 Nagios Escalation Process

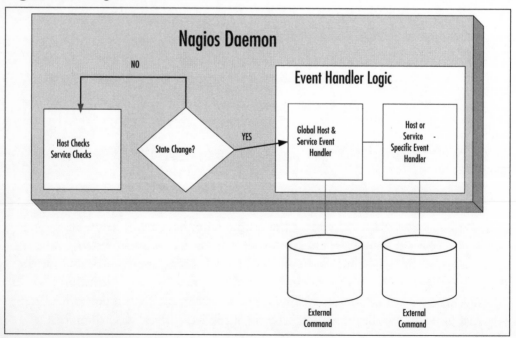

Configuration Monitoring

Other tools are available that can assist with SOX compliance monitoring requirements. The following three examples were each designed to capture and monitor a different type of resource, system, or application.

Syslog

Log files are the central place to find information regarding system event errors. With most Linux and UNIX services, when anything significant happens a message is reported to the syslogd facility. The problem is that this creates thousands of events for each server, and is impossible for an administrator to review manually. Therefore, log checkers are needed as time savers and to make sure that any important indication of trouble is not missed. Analysis tools such as Swatch (**http://swatch.source-forge.net**), scan the logs periodically and take action when it encounters certain log messages such as "send e-mail" or "execute a predefined command or script." The key is to identify the anomalous log traffic, such as root access attempts, account password failures, or hardware problems on critical financial systems.

A centralized syslog server is also desirable from a security standpoint, because potential attackers cannot clean up the evidence of their penetration into the local system. It would take more compromise for the syslog server to cover their tracks. Centralizing your syslogs and integrating them with Nagios so that you have a common capture and escalation footprint for your IT infrastructure, largely solves your SOX compliance monitoring and data capture requirements.

Tripwire and Advanced Intrusion Detection Environment (AIDE)

For security and availability purposes, once a baseline is established for critical financial servers in terms of the installation footprint, it is important to demonstrate that the files will not change without a corresponding "Change Management Request." This is where tools such as Tripwire and AIDE can help.

Tripwire (**http://sourceforge.net/projects/tripwire**) is a system integrity checker, a utility that compares the properties of designated files and directories against information stored in a previously generated database. Any changes to these files are flagged and logged, including those that were added or deleted with optional e-mail reporting. Additionally, support files (databases, reports, and so forth) can be cryptographically signed.

Advanced Intrusion Detection Environment (AIDE) (**http://sourceforge.net/projects/aide**) is another tool, which is similar to Tripwire in that it creates a database from a set of regular expression rules that are defined in a *config* file. Once this database is initialized, it can be used to verify file integrity using several message digest algorithms such as Message Digest 5 (MD5) and Secure Hash Algorithm Version 1.0 (SHA1).

Both of these tools can be configured to specify which files and directories to keep track of and the level of detail to watch for (e.g., changes in size, access time, modification time, inode creation time, content). Additionally, you can check for changes to the permissions and file mode, the inode, the number of links, the file owner, and the file group. These tools can be used to verify, monitor, and, most importantly, prove at audit time that your security-sensitive systems have not been tampered with.

Kiwi CatTools

Kiwi CatTools is a freeware application designed to run on a Windows platform, which provides automated device configuration management on routers, switches, and firewalls. It supports most major vendor network equipment such as Cisco, 3Com, Extreme, Foundry and HP. Kiwi CatTools can perform configuration backups and alert you of any differences via e-mail. It can also issue commands to devices via Telnet or Secure Shell (SSH), change all of your device passwords in one session, and change configurations according to a user-defined schedule. Change management is an important aspect of SOX compliance, and CatTools can help you achieve it. The free version of Kiwi CatTools is limited to five devices, five scheduled activities, and two simultaneous Trivial File Transfer Protocol (TFTP) sessions. See **http://www.kiwisyslog. com** for more information and a complete list of supported devices.

Compliance Monitoring

Here are a few examples of Nagios that can be configured to assist in your compliance monitoring efforts to meet your compliance obligations.

FastTrack CD

Nagios by Example

 http://xfld/nagios

Nagios is a powerful and flexible enterprise-worthy monitoring system. On the enclosed CD, there are working examples of Nagios together with sample configurations to help get you started in setting up your own organization. Nagios can be obtained from the **http://nagios.org/**. The *check_command* plug-ins are a separate project, which can be downloaded from **http://sourceforge.net/projects/ nagiosplug**. Also, valuable community and third-party tools can be found at **http://www.nagiosexchange.org**.

> **NOTE**
>
> You must have a working CGI-compliant Web server in order for Nagios' CGI's to work. Apache is the most popular server; however, the Webmin *miniserv.pl* Web server was also successful in using Nagios' CGI's by writing a custom Webmin module. The Webmin module can be found in the "Others" category. The *cgi.cfg* access controls are still enforced in either case.

Nagios Configuration

This section provides an overview of the Nagios configuration files, which are located (by default) in */usr/local/nagios/etc* and */etc/nagios* on RedHat systems. They are included on the enclosed CD under the "Sample Configurations" section of each portal site. Also included is a working example of Nagios' CGIs, which monitor the *xfld* host, the Apache Web server, and the MySQL database.

- *nagios.cfg* The main configuration file that defines how Nagios operates in general; read by both the Nagios process and the CGIs. A sample main configuration file comes with each out-of-the-box distribution that works.

- *cgi.cfg* The configuration file used by the Web CGI interface; contains directives such as path information and access controls.

- *resource.cfg* Used to store custom configuration information such as macros and database settings. The main reason for having resource files is to use them to store sensitive configuration information.

The object definition files are used to define hosts, services, host groups, contacts, contact groups, and *check_command* plug-in definitions. This is where you define what you want to monitor and how you want to monitor it, and is generally made up of these following types:

- **Services and Service Groups** The actual services you want to monitor and the hosts they reside on.

- **Hosts and Host Groups** The hosts that contain services.

- **Contacts and Contact Groups** The people or processes you want to notify of state changes.

- **Time Periods** The definitions of when to execute **check** commands for hosts and services.

- **Commands** The actual *check_command* plug-ins that can be used and how they can be used.

- **Host and Service Escalations** The actions to take in the event of state changes; contacts are notified and event handlers are fired.

- **Host and Service Dependencies** Lists any dependencies that a service might have so that you can organize checks into parent/child relationships.

- **Extended Host and Service Information** Defines some of the CGI options and behaviors for individual hosts and services.

Nagios Monitoring of Windows Hosts

Although Nagios is designed to run on a Linux platform, there is no limitation to the *check_command* plug-ins that can be performed on certain operating systems, including the Windows platform. There are two main approaches to integrating Windows host and service checks. The first is the NSClient, which runs on Windows NT4 and higher. The items that can be monitored include CPU load, disk usage, uptime, service states, process states, memory usage, file age, and most perflib counters. The latest copy is available from **http://nsclient.ready2run.nl/**. In order to configure this you must:

- Copy *pNSClient.exe*, *pdh.dll*, *psapi.dll*, and *counters.defs* in any directory on the machine you want to monitor (i.e., *c:\nsclient*).

- Run the following *pNSClient.exe /install* command.

- Type **net start nsclient** on the command line, or start the Nagios Agent service in the services applet on the control panel.

- Configure the *check_nt* plug-in on the Nagios server to monitor your desired items.

The second approach is to trap Simple Network Management Protocol (SNMP) data. Windows has a lot of performance data that can be monitored; however, it is usually difficult to monitor remotely. The best approach is to install SNMP services on all of your Windows servers. To expose the performance counters, you must also install any necessary performance Management Information Bases (MIBs) for the services you want to monitor. Web site **http://snmpboy.msft.net** contains valuable information to assist in your setup.

Nagios Integration with syslog

This integration can be easily accomplished by making the Nagios host the central syslog server, and configuring Swatch to monitor the master logs for anomalies. Any Linux host running syslogd can be a central syslog server. On each Linux or UNIX host, configure the local *syslogd.cfg* to route traffic to the central syslog server. Following are some configuration examples. (Do not forget to restart syslogd after making any changes to your */etc/syslogd.conf* file):

- **Mail.*** **@mysyslogserver** Redirects all mail messages to the mysyslogserver host.

- **Kern.*** **@mysyslogserver** Redirects all kernel messages to the mysyslogserver host.

- ***.*** **@mysyslogserver** Redirects all messages to the mysyslogserver host.

Windows hosts can also take advantage of the central syslog facility by using the Windows syslog client (available at **http://ntsyslog.sourceforge.net**). The basic installation procedure is:

- Unzip files to *%windir%*.

- Run *ntsyslog –install*.

- Launch *ntsyslogctrl.exe* for configuration.

Once you have centralized your log files, set up and use the *check_log* Nagios plug-in to scan for items. On the first run of the plug-in, it will return an **OK** state with the message "Log check data initialized." On successive runs, it will return an **OK** state if any ***no*** pattern matches have been found between the most recent log file and an older copy of the log file. If the plug-in detects any pattern matches in the log, it returns a **CRITICAL** state and prints a message with the following format: *(x) last_match*, where *x* is the total number of pattern matches found in the file, and *last_match* is the last entry in the log file that matches the pattern. The following is an example of trapping authentication failures that you can try from the command line: (This check is set up for Nagios on the enclosed CD.)

```
/usr/local/lib/nagios/check_log -F /var/log/messages -O
./check_log.badlogins.old -q "authentication failure"
```

Compliance Workflows

 http://xfld/builtright/egw/workflow/index.php
http://xfld/nustuff/egw/workflow/index.php

The following are examples of the monitoring workflows that can help you sustain your compliance obligations.

Annual Oracle Admin Review

The Annual Oracle Admin Review process reminds IT management to review all Oracle administration accounts. To maintain a secure database, the business analyst must periodically make sure that there are no expired administration accounts and that only those users with access are valid.

Workflow Roles

There are two roles in this process. The Business Analyst is the main administrator of the Oracle database system, and is in charge of reviewing all current active administrative accounts. The IT Director closes the ticket.

Workflow Activities

There are three activities in this process: 1) a ticket is created by a timed service such as Command Run On (CRON); 2) the Business Analyst reviews the administration accounts for the Oracle database; and 3) the IT Director closes the ticket.

Bi-annual IT Policy Review

The Bi-annual IT Policy Review process is used to remind the IT Director to review the policies. If the policies are stored in a Wiki such as eGroupWare's Wiki application, any modifications made since the last review must be checked and validated.

Workflow Roles

There are three roles in this process: 1) the IT Administrator reviews the policies; 2) the IT Administrator notes any changes made since the last review; and 3) the IT Director closes the ticket.

Workflow Activities

There are three activities in this process. First, a ticket is automatically created on a timed interval. Next, the IT Administrator reviews the IT policy documents." The IT Director then closes the ticket.

Monthly Data Restoration Test

To be prepared in the event of a system failure, it is necessary to run a Monthly Data Restoration Test from a back up mechanism. This process reminds the IT Administrator to run the test and to notify management that all back up devices are functioning properly.

Workflow Roles

There are two roles in this process. The IT Administrator fulfills the back up test and verifies that all data is restored and reading as expected. The IT Infrastructure Manager then closes the ticket.

Workflow Activities

There are three activities in this process: 1) the ticket is opened by a timed service; 2) the IT Administrator completes the data restoration test; and 3) the ticket is closed in the "Close Data Restoration Ticket" activity.

Monthly Off-site Backup

Monthly off-site backups are required to be sure that data and software are secure. This process is used to remind the IT Director to back up any new software and any data or serial numbers that must be stored offsite.

Workflow Roles

There is one role for this process. The IT Administrator must gather all of the data that needs to be backed up, and then complete the process.

Workflow Activities

There is one activity in this process. The IT Administrator makes note of what is being backed up and marks the data as "shipped off site" in the "Backup Software" activity.

Monthly Oracle Active User Review

This Monthly Oracle Active User Review workflow is used to review all accounts for the Oracle databases, and is also a way for management to specify any changes that they want to implement in the account list.

Workflow Roles

There are three roles in this process. The Business Analyst administers the Oracle database and supplies the account list. The IT Director reviews it and recommends changes. The Finance Controller reviews it and recommends changes.

Workflow Activities

There are five activities in this process: 1) once the ticket is opened, the Business Analyst must convert the Oracle account list to text form and store it in the workflow; 2), once the list is stored, the IT Director and the Finance Controller must approve it; 3) if either of the two managers do not approve the list, the ticket is routed to the "Make Requested Changes" activity where the Business Analyst implements the requested changes and resubmits the user list; 4) once all users have signed off on the list, the ticket arrives at the "Review and Print" activity; and 5) the ticket is closed once the Business Analyst prints the user list.

Quarterly AV Inventory Report

This ticket is a reminder for the IT department to review all audio and video devices that they have in inventory. Any missing inventory must be located and accounted for before the ticket can be closed.

Workflow Roles

There are two roles in this process. The IT Administrator is in charge of reviewing the inventory and locating any lost items, and the IT Manager must sign off on the ticket before closing it.

Workflow Activities

There are three activities in this process: 1) The ticket is automatically opened, and the IT Administrator runs a review; 2) the ticket is routed to the "Close AV Inventory Report" activity; and 3) the IT Manager reviews and closes the ticket.

Quarterly File Permissions Review

The Quarterly File Permissions Review workflow is used to verify that all data is secure. When the process is run, the IT department must check to make sure that any access that was granted to users on a temporary basis has been removed. It must also verify that users have access to data that they need, and that all data is secure.

Workflow Roles

There are two roles in this process. Both the IT Administrator and the IT Manager are responsible for handling Quarterly File Permissions Review tickets.

Workflow Activities

There are two activities in this process: 1) After the ticket is opened, the IT Administrator reviews the file permissions on any important or recently changed files, and then logs his review; and 2) before the ticket closes, the IT Manager double checks the ticket and then closes it.

Quarterly Infrastructure Change Review

All Infrastructure Change Requests submitted over the past quarter must be reviewed. All changes that have been made must be double checked to ensure that policies are not being violated and no changes have expired.

Workflow Roles

There are two roles in this process. The IT Administrator reviews any Infrastructure Change Requests that have been submitted since the last quarter. The IT Manager double checks the review and then closes the ticket.

Workflow Activities

There are two activities in this process: 1) The IT Administrator reviews the activity; 2) the IT Manager handles the closure activity; and 3) once the IT Manager closes the ticket, no further action is needed and the ticket is complete.

Quarterly Oracle DBA Review

The Quarterly Oracle DBA Review is identical to the Monthly Oracle Active User Review. The only difference is that this workflow is meant to review the Oracle DBA rather than the active users for the database.

Workflow Roles

There are three roles in this process: 1) The Business Analyst reviews the Oracle DBA; 2) the IT Director approves the review and suggests changes; and 3) the Finance Controller approves the review and suggests changes.

Workflow Activities

There are four activities in this process: 1) Once the ticket is automatically created, the Business Analyst conducts the Oracle DBA review and logs any required information into the workflow; 2) after the logs are reviewed, the IT Director and Finance Controller are responsible for making suggested changes; 3) changes are handled by the Business Analyst and the review re-approved; and 4) the ticket is printed and closed.

Quarterly Oracle System Defaults Review

All Oracle System Defaults must be reviewed periodically to maintain the database and ensure that it is secure. This process is created once per quarter, and serves as a reminder to the Oracle Business Analyst in charge to review the system defaults.

Workflow Roles

There are two roles in this process. The manager verifies the review, and the Business Analyst logs and reviews the Oracle System Defaults.

Workflow Activities

There are two activities in this process: 1) The ticket is created automatically by a timed service, and the process is routed straight to the "Review Oracle System Defaults" activity; and 2) once the defaults are reviewed, the IT Manager receives and closes the ticket.

Quarterly Security and Monitoring Review

A Quarterly Security and Monitoring Review must be done to ensure that all monitoring devices and security implementations are reviewed and that they are running properly. This process reminds the IT Department to review the network and make sure that all security measures are functioning properly.

Workflow Roles

There are two roles in this process. The IT Manager approves the review and closes the ticket, and the IT Administrator conducts the review itself.

Workflow Activities

There are two activities in this process: 1) The IT Administrator creates the review; and 2) the IT Manager approves the review.

Quarterly VPN Access Review

A Quarterly VPN Access Review must be done in order to keep a company's intranet secure. The IT department should periodically review all VPN access to ensure that terminated employees do not have access, and that nothing has expired.

Workflow Roles

There are two roles in this process. The IT Administrator reviews the VPN Access list and verifies that all users are keeping their firewall and anti-virus software up-to-date. The IT Manager closes the ticket and verifies that a review has taken place.

Workflow Activities

There are two activities in this process: 1) Once the ticket is created, the IT Administrator completes an activity to verify that a VPN Access Review has been conducted; and 2) the IT Manager closes the ticket and verifies that a review has taken place.

Gluing Nagios and Workflow Together

Workflow apparatus offer a valuable tool for capturing data. A Nagios monitoring solution is a robust automation and capture tool for workflows (developed specifically for SOX). When considering how to make these processes more efficient, we decided to combine the two so that alert data could be captured, approved, and reviewed in the same manner as the other compliance workflows. (A Hypertext Preprocessor (PHP) script written to submit a workflow instance from Nagios is on the enclosed CD.)

TIP

The Nagios workflow submitter script is fairly large, so it is not listed it here. This script can be found on the enclosed CD in the /etc/nagios/egw_workflow_submitter.php directory, or downloaded from the portal Web sites under the "Sample Configurations" section.

Following are the appropriate sections of code that you must place into your Nagios configurations in order to take advantage of the *egw_workflow_submitter.php* script:

/etc/nagios/escalations.cfg

```
define serviceescalation {
service_description              *
hostgroup_name                  egw_workflow-notifiers
first_notification              2
```

```
last_notification              2
contact_groups                  egw_workflow-contacts
notification_interval          0
}
```

/etc/nagios/misccommands.cfg

```
define command {
name              submit-itworkflow-servicealert
command_name      submit-itworkflow-servicealert
command_line      /usr/bin/php /etc/nagios/egw_workflow_submitter.php \
    --user=nagios \
    --process_id=5 \
    --priority=1 \
    --ticket_note=$SERVICESTATE$ alert for $HOSTALIAS$/$SERVICEDESC$: \
    $OUTPUT$
}
```

```
define command {
name              submit-itworkflow-hostalert
command_name      submit-itworkflow-hostalert
command_line      /usr/bin/php /etc/nagios/egw_workflow_submitter.php \
    --user=nagios \
    --process_id=5 \
    --priority=1 \
    ---ticket_note=$OUTPUT$
}
```

You must define the following parameters in your code to send this to the correct workflow type.

- **--user** This is the requestor of the workflow; this would normally be Nagios.

- **--process** This is the process ID of the workflow type; this information can be determined from the workflow process list.

- **--ticket_note** This is the summary posted to the workflow instance (e.g., Host *$HOSTNAME$* is *$HOSTSTATE$!*).

- **--priority** The priority in which you want the Nagios alert to be submitted.

Rolling Your Own Workflows

Once the application is installed, you must give users access to the application. To do this, login using an account with administrative rights such as "bjohnson," and select the "Admin" application. Under the "Admin" header, there are two links of importance: User Accounts and User Groups. Use these two links to grant groups and users access to the workflow application by browsing the list of users or groups and selecting **Edit** on the account you want to change. The "Edit User" page presents a list of applications. To activate the workflow application for the user or group selected, check the **Workflow** check box and select **Save**.

Workflow Configuration

The workflow application also uses Access Control Lists (ACLs) to control access to the monitor or to develop the workflow. Workflow monitors can view, edit, and delete all workflow instances, and also track the activity of any open instances. Workflow developers can edit, create, and delete workflow processes. Essentially, workflow monitors are in charge of controlling the operation of workflow, and workflow developers are in charge of designing, coding, and maintaining actual workflow processes. To make a user a workflow monitor or developer, login using an administrator account. Select the **Admin** icon, and then select **User Accounts**. Browse to the account you want to give monitor or developer access to and click on **Edit**. A page with application names will be presented. Click on the **ACL Rights** link located on the left side of the "Edit User" page. Under the "Workflow" header is an option to grant or revoke access to develop or monitor workflows. Use these two links to give developer or monitor rights to accounts.

If e-mail is set up for an eGroupware install base, the workflow application can send e-mail alerts to users when they are assigned to an activity, or if a user requests information. This feature is disabled by default, but can be enabled by accessing the workflow application with a developer account (see "Access Rights"). Click on the **Workflow** application icon and locate the "Workflow Developer" menu. Click the **Admin E-Mail** link and a page will load that allows you to enable workflow e-mails.

To enable e-mail, select **Enable E-Mail Alert** and fill out the "Workflow From Address" (e.g., *workflow@yourdomain.com*). Next, fill out the "Workflow From Name" (e.g., *Workflow* or *eGroupWare Workflow*). When these fields are filled out, select **Save**; the workflow application will now send e-mail alerts.

Basic Workflow Example: General IT Request

This section focuses on the development of a simple workflow process for handling Help requests for an IT Department. The name of the process is "General IT

Request," and is broken down into four activities: "Request IT Help," "Handle IT Request," "Close IT Request," and "End." These activities operate as follows:

- **Request IT Help** When a user wants to open a ticket for the "General IT Request" process, they go to the "Request IT Help" activity and fill out a basic description of the problem and then submit the ticket.

- **Handle IT Request** Once a user opens a ticket for the "General IT Request" process, it is routed to this activity. Any users with access to the "Handle IT Request" activity can then either view and resolve the user's problem, request additional information, or re-assign the ticket to another user.

- **Close IT Request** After the IT Department handles the ticket, the original user must acknowledge the response of the IT Department and write any final comments before closing the ticket.

- **End** The last activity in the process is "End," which is the only non-interactive activity in the process. "End" changes the ticket status from "active" to "completed," and does not require any input from the user.

Creating the Process

To create the "General IT Request" process, login to eGroupware using an account with developer rights to the workflow application (see "Access Rights"). Click **Admin Processes** and type **General IT Request** into the "Process Name" field. In the "Description" field, type a short description of the process (in this case, "Get help from the IT Department)." Finally, select **Active** and click **Create**. The workflow application then creates the process and sends out an alert message that the process is incomplete. The next step is to make the process a complete and valid workflow (see Figure 8.5).

Figure 8.5 Workflow Creation

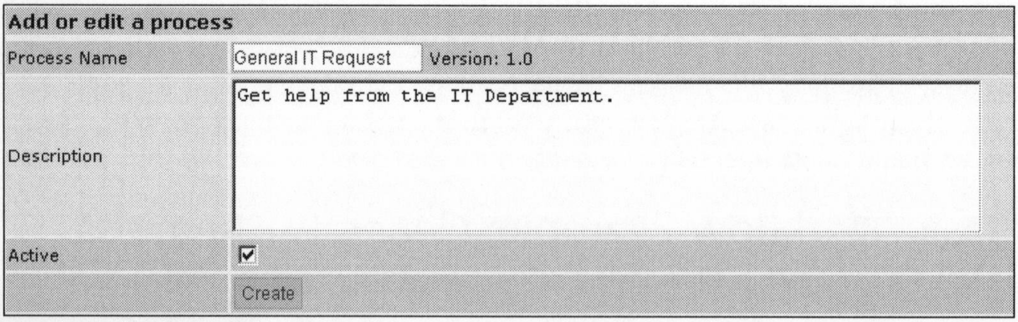

Creating Roles

The "General IT Request" activity has only one role associated with it, the "IT Help Desk" role. "IT Help Desk" contains all of the people that can take care of the IT requests made by users. The role will be assigned at the "Handle IT Request" activity. (See Figure 8.6.)

Figure 8.6 Workflow Roles Creation

Add or edit a role
Name
IT Help Desk
Description
Save

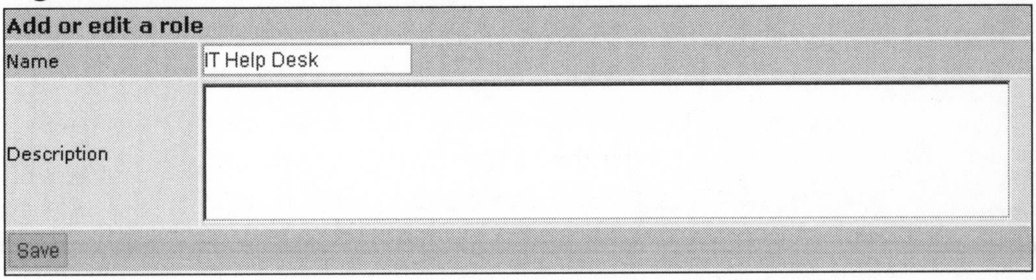

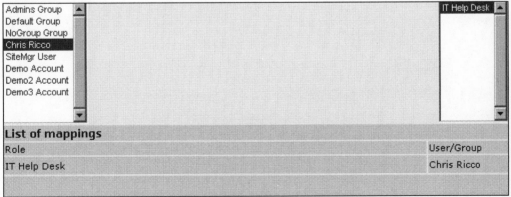

To create an "IT Help Desk" from the "Admin Processes" page, locate "General IT Request" and click on the red and blue people icons. The role page will appear. Find the "Add or edit a role" table and type **IT Help Desk** in the "Name" field. Click **Save** to add the role. Once the role is added, eGroupware users must be mapped to the role. In the "Map users/groups to roles" field, press **CTRL-CLICK**. Select "IT Help Desk" in the "Roles" field and select the users or groups you want to map to the role. Finally, click **Map** so that the users are mapped to the "IT Help Desk" role (see Figure 8.7).

Figure 8.7 Workflow Roles Assignment

Admins Group
Default Group
NoGroup Group
Chris Ricco
SiteMgr User
Demo Account
Demo2 Account
Demo3 Account
IT Help Desk
List of mappings
Role
User/Group
IT Help Desk
Chris Ricco

Creating Activities

After creating the "IT Help Desk" role, the next step is to add activities to the process. Return to the "Admin Processes" page. Find the "General IT Request" process in the list of processes and click the green circle that says **ACT**.

The "Admin Process Activities" page will load. By default, all processes create a "Start" and "End" activity, which can be seen in the "Process Activities" list. To create the activities for "General IT Request," do the following:

- **Request IT Help** This is the "Start" activity, which the workflow application creates by default. Click the "Start" activity located in the "Process Activities" section. Once **Start** is clicked, you can edit the "Start" activity in the "Add or Edit an Activity" table. Change the "Name" field from **Start** to **Request IT Help**. Finally, all users must be able to request help from the IT Department, therefore, select the **Add New** drop down box in the "Add Role" section and change it to **All**. This will allow all users to access the "Start" activity. Click **Save** to update the changes (see Figure 8.8).

Figure 8.8 Workflow Activities Definition

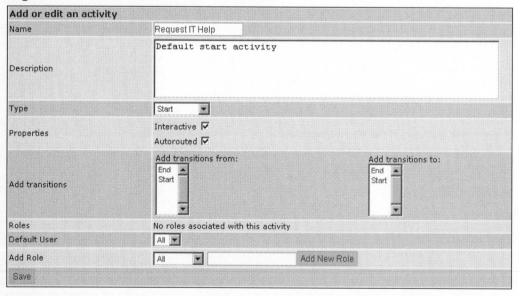

- **Handle IT Request** After the "Start" activity is updated, you must create the "Handle IT Request" activity. Notice that the "Add or Edit an Activity" field is still editing the "Request IT Help" activity. To create a new activity, click **New** and type **Handle IT Request** into the "Name"

field. Leave the "Type" field as "Activity." In "Properties," make sure both **Interactive** and **Autorouted** are checked. This ensures that the activity will stop to allow users to input data, and also ensures that once the activity is completed, it will move on to the next activity (i.e., the "Close IT Request" activity). The "Close IT Request" activity should be connected to the "Start" activity, so that once a ticket is opened, it moves to the "Handle IT Request" activity. To link the activities, find the "Add Transitions From" box in "Add Transitions" and click **Request IT Help**. Finally, assign the "IT Help Desk" role to this activity, so that all users in that role can handle tickets. Find "Add Role" and change "Add New" to **IT Help Desk**. Click **Save** to update the changes.

- **Close IT Request** The last interactive activity is the "Close IT Request" activity. Click **New** and change the "Name" field to **Close IT Request**. Check **Interactive** and **Autorouted**. Add a transition from "Handle IT Request." Make sure the "Add Role" drop down is set to **Add New** because you do not want any roles mapped to this activity. Only the ticket opener has access to "Close IT Request" activity; therefore, only users who opened a ticket will see the activity. Click **Save** to create the activity. Now that the activity is saved, change the default user to the ticket opener. Under "Default User," select **Ticket Opener** and click **Save**. Now, whenever the workflow reaches the "Close IT Request" activity, it automatically designates the ticket opener the owner of the activity, thereby ensuring that the person who opened the ticket is the one who will close it.

- **End** The "End" activity requires adding a transition from the "Close IT Request" activity to the "End" activity. Under "Process Transitions," locate the "Add a Transition" box. In the "From:" section, select **Close IT Request**, and in the "To:" select box, select **End**. Click **Add Transition** to update the changes (see Figure 8.9).

Figure 8.9 Workflow Activities with Transition Detail

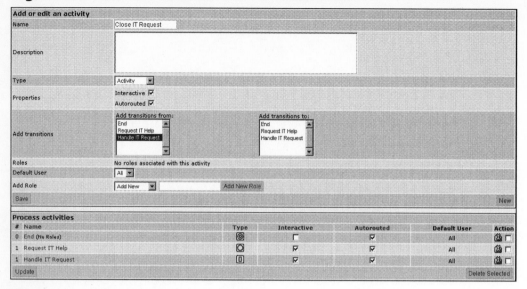

Code and Templates

Now that the activities are created, they must be programmed to function. To access the code and template forms, click **re-enter** on the "Admin Process Activities" page. In the activities page, find the name of the activity you want to edit in "Process Activities" and click on the icon of the folder with the wrench. The page that loads allows you to edit the source code and template for any activity in the workflow process. In the "Select Sources" drop down box, select **Request IT Help**.

Request IT Help

In the "Request IT Help" box, input the following code and click **Save**:

```
01 <?php
02
03 $GLOBALS['workflow']['submit_array'] = Array(
04     'Request' => Array('problem_summary'),
05 );
06
07 if (isset($_REQUEST['request'])) {
08     $summary      = $_REQUEST['problem_summary'];
09     $priority     = $_REQUEST['priority_level'];
10
```

```
11      $instance->create($summary, $priority);
12 }
13 ?>
```

Lines 03 through 05 draw the submit button on the activity, which have the word "Request" written on it. *Array('problem_summary')* is used to force the user to enter text into a form field with the name *problem_summary*. The workflow application will not allow the "Request" button to be clicked if the *problem_summary* field is empty. Lines 07 through 12 are used to create the ticket in the database. This code will not run unless the "request" variable is posted to the Web page, where "request" corresponds to the "Request" on line 04. If the submit button is named "Click Here," all spaces are converted to underscores, and the variable name is entirely lowercase (e.g., line 07 would read: if (*isset($_REQUEST['click_here'])*)). Lines 08 through 09 take the *problem_summary* and *priority_level* form fields and put them into variables. Line 11 creates the ticket. $instance->create() must be called on all Start activities in order for the workflow to be valid. The "Create" function also supports two other parameters: *$nextUser* and *$activityId*. *$nextUser* is used to assign the owner to the next activity, and *$activityId* is used internally only.

Click **Show Template** to display the template form field. Enter the following code and click **Save**:

```
01 Problem Summary:<br>
02 <textarea style="width: 100%;" name="problem_summary" rows="7" \
   cols="45"></textarea>
```

Line 2 contains the form field *problem_summary*, which, in this case, is a text area where users can enter details about their "General IT Request" problems.

NOTE

There is no "Priority" form field in the template, because workflow automatically draws a priority box in the header of all start activities. It is up to the developer whether to use it or not.

The templates are stored using Hypertext Markup Language (HTML) and eGroupWare's internal template engine, which is complex and powerful. For more information on eGroupWare's template engine, consult the *eGroupWare.org* knowledgebase and developer documents.

Handle IT Request

Next, go to the "Handle IT Request" code page, and input the following text:

```
01 <?php
02
03 $parser->parse_history($instance);
04 $parser->parse_report($instance);
05 $parser->parse_reassign($instance, $activity);
06
07 $GLOBALS['workflow']['submit_array'] = Array(
08      'Fulfilled' => '',
09      'Could Not Fix' => Array('action_note')
10 );
11
12 if(isset($_REQUEST['submit_option'])) {
13      $summary      = $_REQUEST['action_note'];
14      $problem_type = $_REQUEST['problem_type'];
15
16      if($_REQUEST['submit_option'] == 'fulfilled') {
17             $action      = "Fulfilled";
18      } else if($_REQUEST['submit_option'] == 'could_not_fix') {
19             $action      = "Could Not Fix";
20      }
21
22      if($instance->complete($action, $summary))
23      {
24             $instance->set('Problem Type', $problem_type);
25      }
26 }
27
28 ?>
```

Lines 03 through 05 draw special tables on this activity's page. The *parse_history()* function outputs information about past activities. In this case, *parse_history* shows information about the "Request IT Help" activity. The *parse_report* function is used to output information about the ticket itself, such as priority, creation date, and ticket opener. Finally, *parse_reassign* allows the current activity to be reassigned to new users. Omitting any of these functions will remove their respective table from the page.

Lines 07 through 10 draw another submit button. Because there is more than one submit option, the output is handled in a different manner than the "Request IT Help" submit button. Instead of checking for *fulfilled* or *could_not_fix* on line 12, simply check for *submit_option* to see if the form was submitted.

Lines 16 through 20 are used to determine what type of action was taken on the activity. The *$action* variable is a string that can contain any information. The *if* statement is used to find out whether the current user could fix the problem, or whether the user's request was fulfilled.

Line 22 marks this activity as complete so that the workflow can continue routing the ticket. The *complete()* function uses *$action* and *$summary* to keep track of what was done to the ticket on this activity. All non-start activities that are interactive must have the *complete()* function in their code.

Line 24 creates a variable for the workflow process. The *set()* function takes two parameters: a variable name and the value of the variable. Variables stored using the *set()* function are persistent across all future activities, and all variables appear in a ticket's history so that viewers can see what variables were set and when. Later activities can also retrieve variable information using the *get()* function. In this case, we want to store the type of problem that the user reported so that it can be displayed in the future using the *parse_history()* function.

```
01 Problem Type:
02 <select name="problem_type">
03     <option value="Software">Software
04     <option value="Hardware">Hardware
05     <option value="Not Applicable">Not Applicable
06 </select>
07
08 Note:<br><textarea name="action_note" rows="7" cols="45" \
   style="width: 100%;"></textarea><br>
```

The "Handle IT Request" template is similar to the "Request IT Help" template. The only difference is that "Handle IT Request" uses a supplement variable, *problem_type*, to store additional information.

Close IT Request

The last interactive activity is "Close IT Request," which is close to the two previous activities. Copy this code into the "Close IT Request" section:

```
01 <?php
02
```

```
03 $parser->parse_history($instance);
04 $parser->parse_report($instance);
05
06 $GLOBALS['workflow']['submit_array'] = Array(
07     'Done' => ''
08 );
09
10 if(isset($_REQUEST['done'])) {
11     $summary       = $_REQUEST['action_note'];
12     $satisfaction = (isset($_REQUEST['satisfied']))? \
         'Satisfied':'Unsatisfied';
13     $action        = "Closed";
14
15     if($instance->complete($action, $summary)) {
16             $instance->set("Satisfaction", $satisfaction);
17     }
18 }
19
20 ?>
```

This code is almost identical to the "Handle IT Request" code. As in the previous activity, "Close IT Request" stores *$satisfaction* as a supplement using the *set()* function. This activity does not include the *parse_reassign()* function, because we want to force the ticket opener to close this ticket, and not allow anyone else to be reassigned to the closing activity.

```
01 I am satisfied with this outcome:<input type="checkbox" \
   name="satisfied" checked=true><br><br>
02 Final Comment:<br>
03 <textarea name="action_note" rows="7" cols="45" \
   style="width: 100%;"></textarea>
```

End

The "End" activity does not require any code or template editing. The final activity can be used to do things such as make final changes to *$instance*, make database changes, write logs to disk, or e-mail other users. For these purposes, the "End" code can be left blank; however, there must be an "End" activity in all workflows.

Testing

Once the code from the previous section is in the proper activity's section, there should not be any more errors listed at the top of the workflow application. After the final code and template updates, from the "Edit Source" page, click the green circle with **ACT** written on it. This brings you back to the "Admin Process Activities" page. Notice that there is now a new icon at the top with a circle with two arrows inside of it. The arrow-circle icon means that your workflow process is valid and can now be activated. Click on the icon, and a red circle with an X will replace it. You can now toggle your workflow process on and off; however, leave it activated so that it can be tested.

To test the process, click the **Open Ticket** link under "Work-Flow Menu." Under "Open Ticket" you will see a link for the "General IT Request" process. Click on it to bring up the "Start" activity. In the "Start" activity, fill out a problem summary, select a priority, and click **Request**. At this stage, a ticket is opened for the "General IT Request" process, and the workflow is routed to the "Handle IT Request" activity. Login to eGroupware using one of the accounts mapped to the "IT Help Desk" activity. After logging in using one of the proper accounts, enter the workflow application and click on **My Tickets** under the "Work-Flow Menu" box. The ticket should now be visible under "My Tickets" along with two options: "View" and "Finish." Your workflow may say "Take Control" instead of "Finish." This means that more than one account has been mapped to the "IT Help Desk," so you must take control before running the activity. Click on **Finish** or **Take Control** (depending on which option you are given). You will now see the "Handle IT Request" activity. From here you can re-assign the activity to other users, or simply complete the form. To complete the form, enter text into the "Note" field and change the "Software" drop-down menu to read **Hardware**. Finally, click **Submit**.

Log back in to the account that was used to open the ticket so that the ticket can be closed. Once logged in, open the workflow application and click on the **My Tickets** link in the "Work-Flow Menu" table. Click the **Finish** link under "My Tickets," complete the form, and click **Done**. The ticket should now be closed. Click on **My Ticket History**, locate the ticket you have been working on, and click **View**. The next page should present a complete summary of the ticket you just created. The "Instance History" activity should show the supplement variables that were set, who operated on the ticket, and the actions taken.

Advanced Topics

The workflow application contains more features than the ones illustrated in the preceding example. Some additional features include a basic external scripting interface, many more activity types, and scheduled processes using CRON.

Switches

Switches are an integral part of almost all workflow processes. A switch is an activity that allows you to have multiple paths. At runtime, based on user input, a specific path is chosen and the workflow proceeds down the specified path. This is practical in situations that require approval, or where a process may not be able to continue without specific information.

To use a switch in an activity, when creating the activity, change the "Type" field to **Switch**. The code for a switch is standard activity code, except that switches require the developer to specify which activity to go to before calling the *complete()* function. For instance, in the basic workflow example, we could have used the following code in the "Handle IT Request" activity:

```
01 if($_REQUEST['submit_option'] == 'fulfilled') {
02     $action       = "Fulfilled";
03     $instance->setNextActivityByID(13);
04 } else if($_REQUEST['submit_option'] == 'could_not_fix') {
05     $action       = "Closed";
06     $instance->setNextActivityByName('Close IT Request');
07 }
```

This example code uses the *setNextActivityByID* and *setNextActivityByName* functions to tell the workflow engine which activity it should move to. If there is an activity with the primary key value of 13 or the name "Close IT Request," then, depending on the input from the user, the workflow would be routed to different activities. The *setNextActivityByName* function uses the activity name to decide where to move to next, and *setNextActivityByID* function uses the activity's primary key in order to route the workflow.

In order to use the *setNextActivity* functions, it is important to set the transitions between any activities that the code could potentially route to.

File Uploading

The workflow application also supports file uploads so that developers can allow users to post files or store binary data on the server. Any activity can store files using the *set()* function:

```
01 function set_upload_file($file_array, $supplement_name, &$instance)
02 {
03     $filename = $file_array['tmp_name'];
04
05     if(is_uploaded_file($filename) && filesize($filename) > 0)
06     {
07             $fhandle = fopen($filename, r);
08             $fcontent = fread($fhandle, filesize($filename));
09             fclose($fhandle);
10
11             if(count($fcontent) > 0)
12             {
13                     return $instance->set($supplement_name,
   $file_array['type'], $fcontent, 'file', $file_array['name']);
14             }
15     }
16
17     return false;
18 }
```

This code should be placed in the shared code section so that any activity that needs to post files can access it. This function can be used to convert a file posted from a form field into a binary array. Once the bytes are read in, the data is stored using the *set()* on line 13.

In the activity that wants to post a file, use the following code:

```
01 if($instance->complete($action, $summary))
02 {
03     set_upload_file($_FILES['test_upload'], 'Test Upload', $instance);
04 }
```

In the template field, add an input field such as:

```
01 <input type="file" name="test_upload">
```

Users should then be able to post a file to the database, which will be viewable in the same way that all other supplements are.

Wiki Integration

Workflow processes can also be integrated into the Wiki so that users can open a workflow that is associated with a Wiki. To do this, open the Wiki application and select the **Work-Flow** link in the "Wiki Administration" menu. On the "Work-Flow" page, select any workflow processes that you may want to submit via Wiki.

To open a workflow process via Wiki, select the **Work-Flow** link located at the bottom of any Wiki page. A generic ticket opener page will appear that allows the user to open a workflow ticket. All tickets opened in this manner have a "Wiki" supplement, which contains the name of the Wiki page that opened the workflow ticket. It is up to the workflow developers whether or not to use that supplement.

Schedule Processes (CRON)

If the "Asynchronous Timed Services" (see *http://www.egroupware.org/index.php?page_name=&category_id=38&domain=developers&wikipage=TimedAsyncServices*) function has been enabled for an eGroupware installation, workflow can open tickets automatically over a given interval of time using eGroupware's built-in timed service function. This is useful remembering maintenance, backups, or other jobs. To make a workflow process automatically open at a specific time, go to the "Admin Processes" panel and click on the clock icon for the process you wish to automate. Using the "Schedule Process" table, can schedule the process to open at any rate of time (see Figure 8.10).

Figure 8.10 Workflow CRON Schedule Process

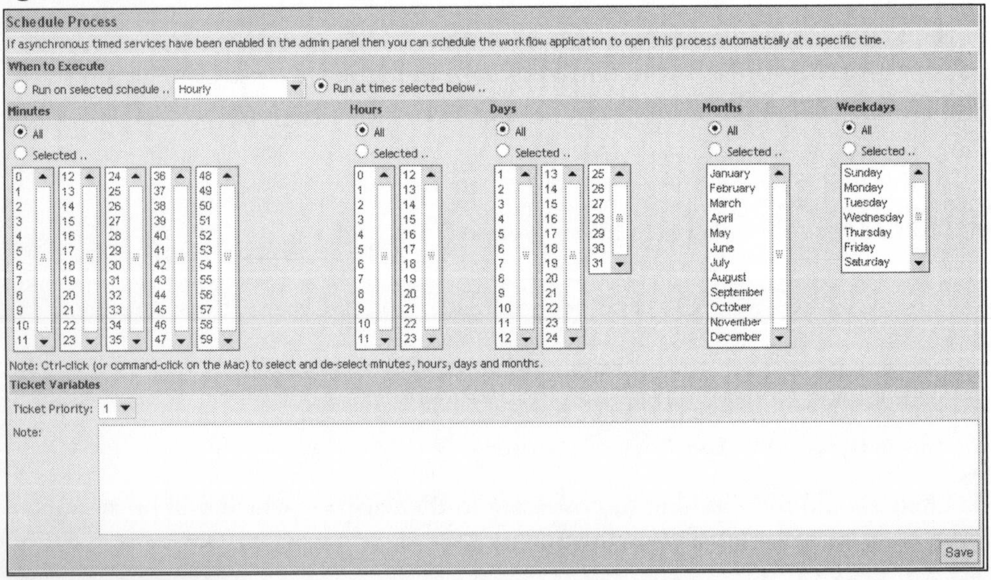

Summary

This chapter discussed Deming's continuous quality improvement process, specifically how it was predicated on a closed-loop process. It examined how the COBIT Guidelines have a surprising resemblance to Deming quality cycle. This resemblance should crystallize the point that if an IT Department has been following and implementing good sound quality practices all along, then they are already half-way to SOX compliance. Utilizing the Open Source tools listed in this chapter, should enable users to obtain the remaining practices required for SOX compliance.

The various control objectives of the "Monitoring Domain" were discussed, and the items that relate specifically to SOX compliance were illustrated in the context of the sample companies. We then looked at monitoring in practice and some of the Open Source tools that can be leveraged to meet your compliance goals. One important tool is Nagios, which is an enterprise-ready monitoring and escalation tool. Others that can be useful are centralized dyslog (that can be scanned for security anomalies and system problems), Tripwire, AIDE, which can help establish a baseline of files on your critical systems and report any unauthorized changes, and Kiwi CatTools, which can monitor and manage changes made to the networking devices.

Monitoring is not limited to hosts and services; there are quite a few ongoing compliance objectives to meet and maintain over time. This is where compliance monitoring workflows can be of great assistance, as they remind you of important recurring compliance activities that you may need to perform, combined with review routing to make sure the proper management team keeps up with their requirements.

This chapter closed with a look at some of the samples provided on the enclosed CD, which includes working examples of Webmin and Nagios, as well as a complete tutorial on how to roll your own workflow processes by creating a simple "General IT Request" workflow.

Solutions Fast Track

Overview

- ☑ The monitoring process should be close-looped
- ☑ Deming developed the PDCA quality cycle
- ☑ SOX compliance drives a closed loop process
- ☑ COBIT Guidelines resemblance the Deming PDCA model

What Does Monitoring Mean?

- ☑ SLA thresholds so that you may have additional time to react and proactively correct prior to a service interruption.

- ☑ In the 1950s, W. Edwards Deming developed a quality system for continuous improvement of business processes

- ☑ Deming's quality system contended that business processes should be analyzed and measured to identify sources of variations that cause products to deviate from customer requirements.

- ☑ Deming stated that business processes should be placed in a continuous feedback loop so that managers can identify and change the parts of the process that need improvement.

Working the List

- ☑ SOX compliance is different from COBIT.

- ☑ Do not trivialize the importance of "Monitoring."

- ☑ Keep an eye on the ability to sustain compliance.

Monitoring in Practice

- ☑ The thrree types of monitoring are services, configuration, and compliance.

- ☑ Service and host monitoring can be accomplished by Nagios, which is an enterprise-worthy monitoring and escalation tool.

- ☑ Configuration monitoring can be achieved using centralized syslog, Tripwire, and AIDE.

- ☑ The eGroupware workflow application can assist with compliance monitoring.

FastTrack CD

- ☑ Nagios is a powerful tool; however, it can be complex to set up. To get you started, a working example is provided on the enclosed CD.

☑ Workflows can be created for nearly any type of processes, including compliance monitoring. Several examples are provided on the enclosed CD.

Rolling Your Own Workflows

☑ Workflows are made up of Roles and Activities.

☑ A feature-rich API is provided for your use.

☑ Some code is required to capture information at activities and to determine and execute transitions.

☑ SOX is different from compliance COBIT.

Frequently Asked Questions

The following Frequently Asked Questions, answered by the authors of this book, are designed to both measure your understanding of the concepts presented in this chapter and to assist you with real-life implementation of these concepts. To have your questions about this chapter answered by the author, browse to **www.syngress.com/solutions** and click on the **"Ask the Author"** form. You will also gain access to thousands of other FAQs at ITFAQnet.com.

Q: If my company does not have a top-down quality methodology in place, can I still use Deming?

A: Yes, although it would be more beneficial if it were top-down. Deming can be used within any organization.

Q: My company has implemented another quality methodology. Can I use the one already implemented at my company?

A: Yes, as long as it drives continuous improvement.

Q: My organization already performs Customer surveys. Can I use these for SOX compliance?

A: Yes, as long as you have history that captures the results and any actions.

Q: Are there any other quality systems?

A: Yes, Taguchi, Six Sigma, and ISO.

Q: What monitoring thresholds should I set?

A: Monitoring thresholds should be based on the criticality of the systems or applications that are being monitored.

Q: Is it really necessary to strive for continuous improvement?

A: Yes, not only for SOX but also as a customer satisfaction tool.

Chapter 9

Putting It All Together

Solutions in this chapter:

- Overview

- Organization—Repositioning

- Policies, Processes, and SLAs

- Control Matrices, Test Plan, and Components

- Return on Investment (ROI)

☑ Summary

☑ Solutions Fast Track

☑ Frequently Asked Questions

Overview

H. W. Andrews once said, "While an open mind is priceless, it is priceless only when its owner has the courage to make a final decision which closes the mind for action after the process of viewing all sides of the question has been completed. Failure to make a decision after due consideration of all the facts will quickly brand a man as unfit for a position of responsibility. Not all of your decisions will be correct. None of us is perfect. But if you get into the habit of making decisions, experience will develop your judgment to a point where more and more of your decisions will be right. After all, it is better to be right 51% of the time and get something done, than it is to get nothing done because you fear to reach a decision."

This quote applies to this chapter for three fundamental reasons:

- An inordinate amount of decisions must be made as part of the Sarbanes-Oxley Act of 2002 (SOX) compliance process.

- As the quote states, "None of us is perfect"; it is inevitable that mistakes will be made.

- The auditors are still unclear of what truly constitutes SOX compliance.

Based on the preceding points, some people would wonder if SOX compliance was actually achievable, and some would say, "Why bother?" The following is a summary of the major reasons why you should obtain SOX compliance:

- Exposure to the possibility of lawsuits and negative publicity.

- If a corporate officer unintentionally files an inaccurate certification, they are subject to a fine of up to $1 million and 10 years in prison.

- If a corporate officer intentionally files an inaccurate certification, they are subject to a fine of up to $5 million and 20 years in prison.

This chapter attempts to "Put It All Together" by delving into areas such as "Repositioning and Policies" and "Processes and SLAs." A sample "Test Plan and Components" is studied in detail, and the concept of Return on Investment (ROI) and whether it is applicable to SOX is looked at.

The Transparency Test...

The CFO Perspective

"With any program, the implementation process is key. For smaller companies, as we mentioned earlier, the cost of 404 compliance is often overwhelming. It is up to management to tackle 404 head on. This requires establishing an effective, controlled implementation methodology. I recommend adopting the author's viewpoint of utilizing software tools to aid in the implementation. In addition establishing a control matrix, keeping a gap analysis up to date at all times and using a well thought out comprehensive test plan should increase your probability of success. While I have not met a CFO who claims any ROI from 404 compliance, hopefully industry is some better off from its implementation."
– *Steve Lanza*

Organization—Repositioning

In general, most Chief Financial Officers (CFOs), Chief Information Officers (CIOs), and Information Technology (IT) Directors have been confronted with these questions: "What do IT people do? What value does the IT Department provide? Why not outsource the IT Department? As discussed earlier, as part of SOX compliance you can choose to reposition your IT Department using COBIT. The majority of this book discusses the innumerable problems involved and how much work it takes to obtain SOX compliance.

You must assess your own individual needs and priorities when making the choice to reposition your IT Department. If you take on this challenge, take comfort in the knowledge that the majority of the repositioning activities you must undertake are ones you must accomplish to obtain SOX compliance.

The remaining task is just "old fashioned marketing." In this aspect, the mantra should be leverage, leverage, and leverage. Once you determine your performance matrices, post them, distribute them, do whatever it takes to make your customers and management aware of what you are doing. Your awareness effort, however, may require that you produce separate reports for the executive management and separate reports for the customers.

The following list includes traditional marketing items (with no exceptions, they either match or can be aligned to SOX compliance objectives):

- Executive Summary

- Situation Assessment

- Competition Assessment—Benchmark Services

- Statement of Objectives

- Develop Action Plan

- Develop Budget

Along with your awareness activities, you will want to ensure that you continually update executive management. By sharing your plans, activities, and accomplishments, this session can be used as an opportunity to build credibility with Executive Management.

Policies, Processes, and Service Level Agreements (SLAs)

In previous chapters, COBIT was correlated to "A Good Quality Process," and Deming's Plan Do Check Act (PDCA) quality cycle. This section illustrates this concept and provides some practical guidelines and recommendations.

It is imperative that you remember that your first priority is to pass the SOX audit. The intent of SOX is to ensure that public companies maintain auditable business processes and effective internal controls over their financial systems. SOX also requires that public companies have an *ongoing* process to identify, evaluate, and correct control deficiencies. So if you cannot sustain an activity, do not, by any means, state it as a process or one of your Control Objectives—this is one of the surest ways to fail your audit.

Ideally, as you look at your environment and start to develop and implement processes for SOX compliance, the best approach is to take a holistic view. The value of taking a holistic view is the ability to build sustainability into your processes, and to minimize the amount of work required for your next audit. Conversely, you can approach SOX compliance as a point-in-time event and merely perform spot correction or develop short-term processes.

> **NOTE**
>
> Although we strongly advise against the latter approach for complying with Sarbanes-Oxley, it will not preclude you from using the methods described in this book.

As with Deming's PDCA quality model, each phase of the SOX process work-flow model feeds into an ensuing phase and is fed from the preceding phase. The SOX Process Flow model is straightforward and simple to follow. However, if after following the flow of the model you find that your process did not yield the desired results (i.e., did not produce evidence or produced the wrong evidence), look at the preceding phase to ensure that the correct output was generated and received as input by the ensuing phase. This is a tedious but necessary process if you want to determine why the process did not yield the expected results.

SOX Process Flow

Figure 9.1 represents the flow for SOX compliance as it relates to Deming's PDCA quality model. By substituting the various categories of PDCA with terminology more suited toward SOX and COBIT, you can see that COBIT and SOX are additional quality processes. You will also see that SLAs play an important role in SOX compliance efforts.

Figure 9.1 SOX Process Flow

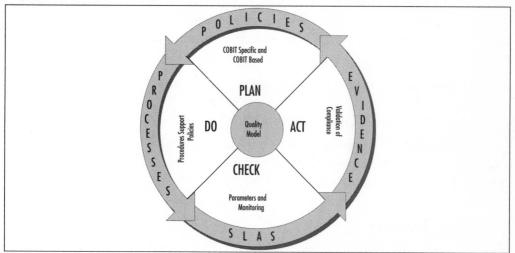

As you proceed with the process of identifying, documenting, and ulti-mately implementing your processes for SOX compliance, you should pay particular attention to areas such as the following:

- The change management process

- Data integrity

- Disaster recovery practices: not critical for initial SOX compliance; how-ever, BCP will probably be critical in subsequent audits

- Electronic records retention policy

- Patch management

- Process/workflows internals and partners

- Security policies and practices: these policies and practices pertain to user access and data security

Control Matrices, Test Plan, and Components

This section examines three of the fundamental forms you will utilize to capture your control objectives in order to prepare for your SOX audit. The forms used were created in Excel, but there is no requirement for you to do so; as long as you have the required fields, you can use whatever application you choose.

- **Control Matrix** The intent of the "Control Matrix" form is to summarize your processes and controls for your auditor. Beyond documenting or developing control processes, you must be sure that what is stated in your documentation matches what is described in this form.

- **Gap and Remediation** The intent of the "Gap and Remediation" form is to capture and track any identified deficiencies within your documented control objectives. You will probably use this form as part of your internal discovery process, and to capture the results of your audit activities.

- **Test Plan** The intent of the "Test Plan" form is to validate that a control is in place to mitigate a known risk, and to validate the methodology for testing that control.

Control Matrix

Table 9.1 represents an example of a form you might use to capture and represent the information contained in your documented processes. Although this form may appear to be daunting, it really is not. The category that will require the most amount of thought and may provide the most difficulty is determining the correct Control Activity. As you have probably gathered the Control Activity should be derived from your documentation and/or narratives. What may not be so intuitive is that the Control Activity should address the *Control Objective*, which in turn mitigates the Business Risk.

Table 9.1 Control Matrix

Windows & Unix Authentication Password Controls

CobiT Ref	Key Ctrl	Ctrl Pt.	Business Risk	Control Objective	Control Activity	Control Performer	Control Evidence	Application/IT Depend/Manual	Prevent/Detect	Frequency
SDS 5.4	X	01	Unauthorized user access may lead to unauthorized access to financial data.	Procedures exist and are followed to maintain the effectiveness of authentication and access mechanisms (e.g., regular password changes).	Authentication to the NuStuff Windows domain is required to obtain access to any NuStuff files stored on any of the file servers.	System Administrator	Server Configuration	Application	Prevent	Real-time
SDS 5.4	X	02			Corporate Domain (Active Directory) Password Policy. Windows passwords must comply with the following standards, which are automatically enforced: (a) Minimum length of 8 characters; (b) Multiple character sets; (c) History verification of three;	System Administrator	Server Configuration	Application	Prevent	Real-time
SDS 5.4	X	03			When a new user's system is prepared by Client Services, they expire the initial password, which forces the user to change their password on first login.	Help Desk Manager	User password history log	Manual	Prevent	Upon Demand
SDS 5.4	X	04			Unix Server, Local Password Policy. Unix must comply with the following standards, which are automatically enforced: (a) Minimum length of six characters; (b) Multiple character sets; (c) Expiration of 13 weeks;	System Administrator	Server Configuration	Application	Prevent	Real-time
SDS 5.4	X	05			Oracle DB Password Policy. Oracle DB passwords are automatically enforced: (a) Minimum length of six characters; (b) Multiple character sets; (c) Expiration of 13 weeks;	Oracle DBA	Database Configuration	Application	Prevent	Real-time

The following are the categories utilized on the Control Matrix form and a brief definition:

- **COBIT Ref**. - relates to the COBIT Domain that the Control Objective is contained

- **Key Ctrl** – is this considered to be a key Control Objective

- **Ctrl Pt.** – the Ctrl Pt. merely enumerates the items

- **Business Risk** - represents the risk to the business in the absence of effective controls as defined by COBIT

- **Control Objective** Represents the control objective as defined by COBIT.

- **Control Activity** Should be verbiage gleaned from your narratives as to what processes are in place in your organization to mitigate the defined risk.

- **Control Performer** Denotes who or what performs the stated control.

- **Control Evidence** Denotes what evidence is produced to demonstrate that the control works. It is important to keep in mind that auditors' preference is to have system-generated evidence.

- **Application/IT Depend/Manual** Denotes what performs the control. As with Control Evidence, the auditors' preference is to have as many application-driven processes as possible.

- **Prevent/Detect** Denotes the type of the process. The control objectives will utilize one of two categories: Prevent or Detect. Auditors generally like it when there are multiple Prevent and Detect Controls in place for a control objective.

- **Frequency** Denotes when the control is executed.

Gap and Remediation

The "Gap and Remediation" form represents an example of a form that can be used to capture any deficiencies that result from your initial testing or the auditor's testing. This form is relatively straightforward regarding the information that should be contained in the respective fields. The main thing to remember is that the auditor will monitor how well you manage the actions and due dates of the items captured. Therefore, be sure that you adhere to the actions and due dates that you have committed to (see Table 9.2.)

Table 9.2 The Gap and Remediation Form

NuStuff
21 Windows & Unix Authentication Password Controls

Ref	Control Pt.	Gap	Action	Resp	Due Date
1		None			
2					
3					
4					

- **Ref**. Enumerates the number of items

- **Control Pt**. Enumerates the items; should match your "Control Matrix and Test Plan."

- **Gap** Denotes any identified deficiencies in the control objectives.

- **Action** Denotes the actions to be taken to remediate identified deficiencies in the control objectives.

- **Resp** Denotes the person responsible for resolution of the identified deficiencies in the control objectives.

- **Due Date** Denotes the date that the deficiencies identified in the control objectives must be resolved.

Test Plan

Table 9.3 represents an example of a form you might use to capture and represent the information contained in your documented processes.

Table 9.3 The Test Plan

NuStuff
21 - Windows & Unix Authentication Password Controls

Key Ctl	Ctl Pt	Control Activity	Control Performer	Control Evidence	Application/ IT Depend/ Manual	Frequency	Test Period Start	Pop Size	Sample Size	Test Plans	Tester	Test Date
X	01	Authentication to the NuStuff Windows domain is required to obtain access to any NuStuff files stored on any of the file servers.	System Administrator	Server Configuration	Application	Real-time	1/1/2004	1	1	Browse to Windows file server without connecting to the Company Corporate Domain. Verify it is not possible to connect to Windows file server.		
X	02	Corporate Domain (Active Directory), Password Policy Windows passwords must comply with the following standards, which are automatically enforced: (a) Minimum length of 8 characters; (b) Multiple character sets; (c) History verification of three;	System Administrator	Server Configuration	Application	Real-time	1/1/2004	1	1	1. Verify the Windows password configuration point that automatically enforces these standards. 2. Attempt to change an existing password to a password which for each of the rules (a)-(c) complies with the other standards but not that particular standard. Verify this is not possible.		
X	03	When a new user's system is prepared by Client Services, they expire the initial password, which forces the user to change their password on first login.	Help Desk Manager	User password history log	Manual	Upon Demand (add freq)	1/1/2004	1	1	Select a sample of users who have recently been assigned new accounts. BA to view password file and verify that all pass words are not the initial password granted at initial login. Note: Only the BA may conduct this test and sight this data. No record of user passwords is to be printed.		
X	04	Unix Server, Local Password Policy Unix must comply with the following standards, which are automatically enforced: (a) Minimum length of six characters; (b) Multiple character sets; (c) Expiration of 13 weeks;	System Administrator	Server Configuration	Application	Real-time	1/1/2004	1	1	1. Verify the Unix password configuration point that automatically enforces these standards. 2. Attempt to change an existing password to a password which for each of the rules (a)-(c) complies with the other standards but not that particular standard.		
X	05	Oracle DB Password Policy Oracle DB passwords are automatically enforced: (a) Minimum length of six characters; (b) Multiple character sets; (c) Expiration of 13 weeks;	Oracle DBA	Database Configuration	Application	Real-time	1/1/2004	1	1	1. Verify the Oracle DB password configuration point that automatically enforces these standards. 2. Attempt to change an existing password to a password which for each of the rules (a)-(c) complies with the other standards but not that particular standard.		

The following are the categories utilized on the Test Plan form and a brief definition:

- **Key Ctrl** Considered to be a key control objective.

- **Ctrl Pt.** Enumerates the items.

- **Control Activity** Should be verbiage gleaned from your narratives as to what processes are in place to mitigate the defined risk.

- **Control Performer** Denotes who or what performs the stated control objective.

- **Control Evidence** Denotes what evidence exists to demonstrate that the control objective works. It is important to keep in mind that auditors' preference is to have system-generated evidence.

- **Application/IT Depend/Manual** Denotes what performs the control. As with Control Evidence, the auditors' preference would be to have as many application-driven processes as possible.

- **Frequency** Denotes when the control is executed.

- **Test Period Start** Denotes the date that the control was implemented.

- **Pop Size** Denotes the total number of auditable evidence.

- **Sample Size** Denotes the number of Pop Sizes selected to audit.

- **Test Plan** Denotes the actions and/or steps that must be taken to demonstrate the effectiveness of the control.

- **Tester** Denotes the person or persons responsible for performing and documenting the test results.

- **Test Date** Denotes the date that the test was performed.

What Makes a Good Test Plan

Since there is no specific format for performing SOX tests and capturing the results, you can elect to develop a format that suits your particular company better than the examples provided in this book. If you elect to develop your own form and format for control objective testing, the following criteria are key elements that you should keep in mind:

- Documented test plan

- Appropriate controls identify

- Appropriate test for control

- Selection of correct sample size

- Rational of sample size

- Method to capture test results

Return on Investment (ROI)

There are countless periodicals and Internet-based articles concerning SOX compliance and ROI. To frame the discussion for this section, we have selected some excerpts from various articles.

The following is an excerpt from an article published in the March 2005 edition of "The BizNet Brief":

> "The cost implications are even more troubling for smaller public companies, most of which are slogging through their Section 404 compliance initiatives this year. A February report from the American Electronics Association (AeA), based in part on previous FEI data, found that Section 404 compliance costs (as a percentage of revenue) are four times greater for companies with less than $100 million in annual revenue than they are for companies with $5 billion or more in annual revenue."

Table 9.4 shows Section 404 Compliance Costs for Companies with $5 Billion in Average Annual Revenue.

Table 9.4 Section 404 Compliance Costs for Companies with $5 Billion in Average Annual Revenue

	March 2005	Estimated in July 2004	Estimated in January 2004
Internal costs*	$1,337,935	$1,283,385	$613,250
External costs	$1,716,987	$1,037,100	$732,100
Auditor attestation fees	$1,301,050	$823,200	$590,100
Total	$4,355,972	$3,143,685	$1,935,450

Source: Financial Executives International (FEI).
*"Internal costs" assume that full-time professionals (at 2,000 hours per year) are compensated $100,000 per year (salary plus benefits).

The following statistics were summarized from an article in Business Performance Management titled "Managing the Next Phase of Compliance":

- Of participants surveyed, 31 percent implemented software to assist with SOX compliance.

- Of participants surveyed, 69 percent believe they will need software to manage ongoing SOX compliance.

According to a survey by the American Institute of Certified Public Accounts, 28 percent of Total SOX compliance costs were spent on technology.

By summarizing the above information into concise statements, we can conclude that:

- SOX compliance costs for businesses are significant.

- SOX compliance costs for small businesses is significantly more

- Almost 70 percent of companies required to comply with SOX believe that they will have to acquire software to sustain their compliance.

We define ROI as a change that requires funding that over time, by cost savings or avoidance, will pay for itself. Looking at the data in the preceding list, you can conclude that there is no quantitative way to do any kind of realistic ROI for SOX compliance. Based on a recent Computerworld article entitled "Sarb-Ox Adds To Cost, Length Of IT Projects," one could conclude that not only is there no realistic way to calculate ROI for SOX compliance, but if there were, there would be no positive ROI for SOX. The value of SOX compliance is qualitative and not quantitative.

If there is no way to justify SOX compliance, how do I answer questions about how my company's compliance activities affect the bottom line? By shifting the ROI from SOX and the cost savings to Open Source and cost avoidance. As stated previously, a decision point of whether to comply with SOX or not does not exist. What you can decide is how much software acquisition cost you are willing to accept and whether you will need to add additional headcount to sustain your environment after compliance. The next logical question would be how much savings could a small company reasonably be expected to save in cost avoidance by utilizing Open Source? The answer depends on various factors at a particular company; however, based on what we have seen at our fictitious company, the savings could start at approximately $300,000.00 the first year (see Table 9.5).

Table 9.5 Cost Avoidance

Area	Open Source	Commercial
Nagios	$0.00	$4,000.00
eGroupware	$0.00	$250,000.00
SubTotal	$0.00	$254,000.00
H/C Avoidance	$45,000.00	$45,000.00
Total Cost Avoidance	$299,000.00	$209,000.00

Lessons Learned...

There Is Life After SOX

The journey to SOX compliance is probably one of the most difficult challenges you will face in your career, not necessarily due to the technical aspect of the activity, but rather as a result of the amorphous nature of the requirements and the professional challenges of dealing with auditors, customers, and management.

Summary

This chapter discussed the how and what of repositioning an IT Department utilizing COBIT for SOX. We attempted to illustrate quality processes and the tie between Policies, Processes, and SLAs. As a subset of quality, we reviewed an example test plan and its components.

The following criteria are key elements that you should keep in mind when testing control objectives:

- Documented test plan
- Appropriate controls identity
- Appropriate test for control
- Selection of correct sample size
- Rational of sample size
- Method to capture test results

This chapter also discussed SOX and Open Source ROI, and why SOX does not lend itself to a traditional ROI format.

Solutions Fast Track

Overview

☑ An inordinate amount of decisions must be made as part of the process of obtaining SOX compliance.

☑ As the quote states" None of us is perfect." Therefore, it is inevitable that mistakes will be made.

☑ The auditors are still unclear on what truly constitutes SOX compliance.

Organization – Repositioning

☑ Repositioning requires only a few additional activities beyond SOX.

☑ Repositioning is just "old fashion marketing."

☑ The mantra for repositioning should be leverage, leverage, leverage.

Policies, Processes and SLAs

- ☑ SOX compliance can be approached as a point-in-time activity, but this is not recommended.
- ☑ The best approach for SOX compliance is holistic.
- ☑ SLAs can provide evidence of compliance.

Control Matrices, Test Plan, and Components

- ☑ **Control Matrix** The intent of the "Control Matrix" form is to summarize your processes and control for your auditors. Beyond documenting or developing your control processes, it is absolutely critical that what is stated in your documentation matches what is described in this form.
- ☑ **Gap and Remediation** The intent of the "Gap and Remediation" form is to capture and track any identified deficiencies within your documented control objectives. You will probably use this form as part of your internal discovery process and as a result of your auditor's activities.
- ☑ **Test Plan** The intent of the "Test Plan" form is to identify what controls are in place to mitigate the known risk and the methodology for testing the control.

Return on Investment (ROI)

- ☑ SOX compliance costs for businesses will be significant.
- ☑ SOX compliance costs for small businesses will be significantly more.

Frequently Asked Questions

The following Frequently Asked Questions, answered by the authors of this book, are designed to both measure your understanding of the concepts presented in this chapter and to assist you with real-life implementation of these concepts. To have your questions about this chapter answered by the author, browse to **www.syngress.com/solutions** and click on the **"Ask the Author"** form. You will also gain access to thousands of other FAQs at ITFAQnet.com.

☑ Almost 70 percent of companies required to comply with SOX believe they will have to acquire software to sustain their compliance.

Q: Can SOX compliance be obtained even if deficiencies are found in my environment?

A: Yes, you can almost count on deficiencies being found. Your objective should be to not have any material weaknesses, significant deficiencies, or too many deficiencies.

Q: Considering the cost of compliance to businesses is there anything being done to lessen the impact?

A: Yes, but not from the Securities and Exchange Commission (SEC). If any relief from SOX is given it will probably come from Capital Hill.

Q: Can I use the test plan examples?

A: Yes, or you can develop your own. Just keep in mind the component that we covered.

Q: Can SOX compliance really be accomplished as a point-in-time project?

A: Yes, but that is not the question to ask. The question is, do you want to do it all over again?

Q: Quality seems to be a major theme in the majority of the chapters. Is it really that important?

A: Yes, quality and processes will either make or break your compliance activities.

Q: Can I really achieve cost avoidance utilizing Open Source?

A: Yes. Recently, a lot of major companies have started to realize the ROI on Linux and Open Source, including Goggle, e-bay, IBM, and SUN.

COBIT
Control Objectives

Planning and Organization

1.   Define a Strategic IT Plan

- IT as part of the organization's long- and short-range plan
- IT long-range plan
- IT long-range planning—approach and structure
- IT long-range plan changes
- Short-range planning for the IT function
- Communication of IT plans
- Monitoring and evaluating of IT plans
- Assessment of existing systems

2.   Define the Information Architecture

- Information architecture model
- Corporate data dictionary and data syntax rules
- Data classification scheme
- Security levels

3.   Determine Technological Direction

- Technological infrastructure planning
- Monitor future trends and regulations
- Technological infrastructure contingency
- Hardware and software acquisition plans
- Technology standards

4. Define the IT Organization and Relationships

- IT planning or steering committee
- Organizational placement of the IT function
- Review of organizational achievements
- Roles and responsibilities
- Responsibility for quality assurance
- Responsibility for logical and physical security
- Ownership and custodianship
- Data and system ownership
- Supervision
- Segregation of duties
- IT staffing
- Job or position descriptions for IT staff
- Key IT personnel
- Contracted staff policies and procedures
- Relationships

5. Manage the IT Investment

- Annual IT operating budget
- Cost and benefit monitoring
- Cost and benefit justification

6. Communicate Management Aims and Direction

- Positive information control environment
- Management's responsibility for policies

- Communication of organization policies
- Policy implementation resources
- Maintenance of policies
- Compliance with policies, procedures, and standards
- Quality commitment
- Security and internal control framework policy
- Intellectual property rights
- Issue-specific policies
- Communication of IT security awareness

7.   Manage Human Resources

- Personnel recruitment and promotion
- Personnel qualifications
- Roles and responsibilities
- Personnel training
- Cross-training or staff backup
- Personnel clearance procedures
- Employee job performance evaluation
- Job change and termination

8.   Ensure Compliance with External Requirements

- External requirements review
- Practices and procedures for complying with external requirements
- Safety and ergonomic compliance
- Privacy, intellectual property, and data flow
- Electronic commerce
- Compliance with insurance contracts

9. Assess Risks

- Business risk assessment
- Risk assessment approach
- Risk identification
- Risk measurement
- Risk action plan
- Risk acceptance
- Safeguard selection
- Risk assessment commitment

10. Manage Projects

- Project management framework
- User department participation in project initiation
- Project team membership and responsibilities
- Project definition
- Project approval
- Project phase approval
- Project master plan
- System quality assurance plan
- Planning of assurance methods
- Formal project risk management
- Test plan
- Training plan
- Post-implementation review plan

11. Manage Quality

- General quality plan
- Quality assurance approach

- Quality assurance planning
- Quality assurance review of adherence to IT standards and procedures
- System development life cycle methodology
- System development life cycle methodology for major changes to existing technology
- Updating of the system development life cycle methodology
- Coordination and communication
- Acquisition and maintenance framework for the technology infrastructure
- Third-party implementer relationships
- Program documentation standards
- Program testing standards
- System testing standards
- Parallel/pilot testing
- System testing documentation
- Quality assurance evaluation of adherence to development standards
- Quality assurance review of the achievement of IT objectives
- Quality metrics
- Reports of quality assurance reviews

Acquisition and Implementation

1. Identify Automated Solutions

- Definition of information requirements
- Formulation of alternative courses of action
- Formulation of acquisition strategy
- Third-party service requirements
- Technological feasibility study
- Economic feasibility study

- Information architecture
- Risk analysis report
- Cost-effective security controls
- Audit trails design
- Ergonomics
- Selection of system software
- Procurement control
- Software product acquisition
- Third-party software maintenance
- Contract application programming
- Acceptance of facilities
- Acceptance of technology

2.   Acquire and Maintain Application Software

- Design methods
- Major changes to existing systems
- Design approval
- File requirements definition and documentation
- Program specifications
- Source data collection design
- Input requirements definition and documentation
- Definition of interfaces
- User-machine interface
- Processing requirements definition and documentation
- Output requirements definition and documentation
- Controllability
- Availability as a key design factor
- IT integrity provisions in application program software

- Application software testing
- User reference and support materials
- Reassessment of system design

3. Acquire and Maintain Technology Infrastructure

- Assessment of new hardware and software
- Preventive maintenance for hardware
- System software security
- System software installation
- System software maintenance
- System software change controls
- Use and monitoring of system utilities

4. Develop and Maintain Procedures

- Operational requirements and service levels
- User procedures manual
- Operations manual
- Training materials

5. Install and Accredit Systems

- Training
- Application software performance sizing
- Implementation plan
- System conversion
- Data conversion
- Testing strategies and plans
- Testing of changes

- Parallel/pilot testing criteria and performance
- Final acceptance test
- Security testing and accreditation
- Operational test
- Promotion to production
- Evaluation of meeting user requirements
- Management's post-implementation review

6.   Manage Changes

- Change request initiation and control
- Control of changes
- Emergency changes
- Documentation and procedures
- Authorized maintenance
- Software release policy
- Distribution of software

Delivery and Support

1.   Define and Manage Service Levels

- Service level agreement framework
- Aspects of service level agreements
- Performance procedures
- Monitoring and reporting
- Review of service level agreements and contracts
- Chargeable items
- Service improvement program

2.   Manage Third-Party Services

- Supplier interfaces
- Owner relationships
- Third-party contracts
- Third-party qualifications
- Outsourcing contracts
- Continuity of services
- Security relationships
- Monitoring

3.   Manage Performance and Capacity

- Availability and performance requirements
- Monitoring and reporting
- Modeling tools
- Proactive performance management
- Workload forecasting
- Capacity management of resources
- Resources availability
- Resources schedule

4.   Ensure Continuous Service

- IT continuity framework
- IT continuity plan strategy and philosophy
- IT continuity plan contents
- Minimizing IT continuity requirements
- Maintaining the IT continuity plan
- Testing the IT continuity plan

- IT continuity plan training
- IT continuity plan distribution
- User department alternative processing backup procedures
- Critical IT resources
- Backup site and hardware
- Off-site backup storage
- Wrap-up procedures

5.   Ensure Systems Security

- Manage security measures
- Identification, authentication, and access
- Security of online access to data
- User account management
- Management review of user accounts
- User control of user accounts
- Security surveillance
- Data classification
- Central identification and access rights management
- Violation and security activity reports
- Incident handling
- Reaccredidation
- Counterparty trust
- Transaction authorization
- Nonrepudiation
- Trusted path
- Protection of security functions
- Cryptographic key management
- Malicious software prevention, detection, and correction

- Firewall architectures and connections with public networks
- Protection of electronic value

6.   Identify and Allocate Costs

- Chargeable items
- Costing procedures
- User billing and chargeback procedures

7.   Educate and Train Users

- Identification of training needs
- Training organization
- Security principles and awareness training

8.   Assist and Advise Customers

- Help desk
- Registration of customer queries
- Customer query escalation
- Monitoring of clearance
- Trend analysis and reporting

9.   Manage the Configuration

- Configuration recording
- Configuration baseline
- Status accounting
- Configuration control
- Unauthorized software
- Software storage

- Configuration management procedures
- Software accountability

10. Manage Problems and Incidents

- Problem management system
- Problem escalation
- Problem tracking and audit trail
- Emergency and temporary access authorizations
- Emergency processing priorities

11. Manage Data

- Data preparation procedures
- Source document authorization procedures
- Source document data collection
- Source document error handling
- Source document retention
- Data input authorization procedures
- Accuracy, completeness and authorization checks
- Data input error handling
- Data processing integrity
- Data processing validation and editing
- Data processing error handling
- Output handling and retention
- Output distribution
- Output balancing and reconciliation
- Output review and error handling
- Security provision for output reports
- Protection of sensitive information during transmission and transport

- Protection of disposed sensitive information
- Storage management
- Retention periods and storage terms
- Media library management system
- Media library management responsibilities
- Backup and restoration
- Backup jobs
- Backup storage
- Archiving
- Protection of sensitive messages
- Authentication and integrity
- Electronic transaction integrity
- Continued integrity of stored data

12. Manage Facilities

- Physical security
- Low profile of the IT site
- Visitor escort
- Personnel health and safety
- Protection against environmental factors
- Uninterruptible power supply

13. Manage Operations

- Processing operations procedures and instructions manual
- Startup process and other operations documentation
- Job scheduling
- Departures from standard job schedules
- Processing continuity

- Operations logs
- Safeguard special forms and output devices
- Remote operations

Monitoring

1.   Monitor the Processes

- Collecting monitoring data
- Assessing performance
- Assessing customer satisfaction
- Management reporting

2.   Assess Internal Control Adequacy

- Internal control monitoring
- Timely operation of internal controls
- Internal control level reporting
- Operational security and internal control assurance

3.   Obtain Independent Assurance

- Independent security and internal control certification/accreditation of IT services
- Independent security and internal control certification/accreditation of third-party service providers
- Independent effectiveness evaluation of IT services
- Independent effectiveness evaluation of third-party service providers
- Independent assurance of compliance with laws and regulatory requirements and contractual commitments
- Independent assurance of compliance with laws and regulatory requirements and contractual commitments by third-party service providers

- Competence of independent assurance function
- Proactive audit involvement

4.   Provide for Independent Audit

- Audit charter
- Independence
- Professional ethics and standards
- Competence
- Planning
- Performance of audit work
- Reporting
- Follow-up activities

KNOPPIX Live CD Parameters

Cheat Codes

lang=bg|be|ch|cn|cs|cz|da|de|dk| es|fi|fr|ie|it|ja|nl|pl|ru|sk|tr|tw|uk|us

Specify language/keyboard.

keyboard=us

Specify only *console* keyboard.

xkeyboard=us

Specify [Xfree86 X] keyboard.

atapicd

Do *not* use SCSI-Emulation for IDE CD-ROMs—Knoppix V3.4 and later.

screen=1280x1024

Use specified screen resolution for X.

xvrefresh=60 or vsync=60

Use 60Hz vertical refresh rate for X.

xhrefresh=80 or hsync=80

Use 80kHz horizontal refresh rate for X.

xserver=XFree86|XF86_SVGA

Use specified X Server.

xmodule=ati|radeon|fbdev|vesa|savage|s3|nv |i810|mga|svga|tseng

Use specified XFree4 module.

2

Runlevel 2, textmode only.

myconfig=scan|floppyconfig|floppyconf

Run knoppix.sh from a floppy. The "floppyconfig" option allows you to reconfigure the system after autoconfig, or install your own config files, by mounting a floppy disk and running a Bourne shell script called knoppix.sh from the root directory on this floppy. There is a GUI to create such a configuration floppy disk called "save-config" (also located in the KDE menu under "KNOPPIX," but experts also know how to do this by creating their own shell scripts. The configuration with network and graphics setup are stored in configs.tbz. A file called *knoppix.sh*, if located in the top-level KNOPPIX directory on the CD, will also be executed at startup. This makes it easier to create customized versions without having to change anything on the compressed filesystem KNOPPIX/KNOPPIX.

myconf=/dev/sda1

Run "knoppix.sh" from a partition—Knoppix V3.4.

myconf=scan (or config=scan)

Try to find "knoppix.sh" automatically—Knoppix V3.4.

noapic noagp noapm nodma nomce nofirewire nopcmcia noscsi noswap nousb nosmp noaudio

Skip parts of Hardware-detection, In case of a failing hardware autodetection, try booting with any of the previously listed "no-" options, as in knoppix noagp noapm noapic nodma nopcmcia noscsi nousb to skip some critical parts of the autodetection system. The "noswap" option is useful for a forensic analysis without touching existing swap partitions.

pci=irqmask=0x0e98

Notebook if PS/2 mouse doesn't work. Try "knoppix pci=irqmask=0x0e98" if (you have a notebook and) your PS/2 mouse doesn't work. (Possibly caused by a BIOS-flaw on your board.)

ide2=0x180 nopcmia

Boot from PCMIA-CD (Transmeta notebooks).

pci=biosirq

Will force the use of the BIOS assigned **I**nterrupt **ReQ**uests on the PCI bus. Possible cure for nonfunctioning hardware. Very handy for unruly IRQ conflicts. Look at **dmesg** and **cat /proc/pci** to find out if you have any such troubles.

mem=128M

Specify memory size in MBytes; some boards apparently don't pass the proper memory size to the Linux kernel. It may cause the message "Panic cannot mount root file system" and the system hangs. Use "knoppix mem=128M" to solve that problem if your system has 128MByte memory, for example (caution: you *must* use an uppercase "M" here). Stuff like mem=16320K also works.

noeject

Do *not* eject CD after halt.

noprompt

It's especially useful in combination with **noeject**. With **noprompt**, Knoppix won't eject the CD and ask for a keypress. It was a much-requested feature some time ago. Version 2003-09-22 and later.

nodhcp

Skip dhcp/network broadcast detection.

splash

Shows the upper half of the KDE splash screen, while booting up. You can press **Esc** anytime to see all the messages. Ever wanted to hide those cryptic messages? Version 2003-09-22 and later.

New in 3.4: Animations (see for yourself) and the ability to press *any* key.

modules-disk

This cheatcode allows you to insert a floppy disk with additional modules; for example, USB-stick or similar. Yes, its also possible with "expert," but there you lose the automatic configuration afterwards. Version 2003-09-22 and later.

toram

Copy CD to RAM and run from there. Version 2003-09-05 and later.

tohd

You can now do a "poor mans install" on vfat and EXT2 partitions with **knoppix tohd=/dev/hda1** Version 2003-09-22 and later.

fromhd

With this cheatcode, the CD-ROMs are ignored, so you can finally boot your "poor man's install" with just the original CD-ROM—Version 2003-09-05 and later. Note: cheatcode "toram" and "fromhd" now work together. Usage fromhd=/dev/hda1.

bootfrom=/dev/hda1

Access image and then boot from previously copied CD-Image (enables booting from NTFS/ReiserFS)—Knoppix V3.4.

bootfrom=/dev/hda1/KNX.iso

Access image, boot from ISO-Image—Knoppix V3.4. Note: **bootfrom** needs access to a running Knoppix system with the same kernel as the Boot kernel, before it is able to mount the partition/ISO image. This should allow a poor man's install from NTFS partitions and makes it possible to boot an ISO image directly. You can also use wildcards in the ISO-Filename, but it must be unique. Therefore, if you have just one KNOPPIX.iso on /dev/hda1, you can access it as bootfrom=/dev/hda1/K*.iso, but if there are several, you need to make clear which one you want. (Feature added by Fabian Franz.)

Caution: The 2.4 kernel that is on the KNOPPIX 3.4 CD does not support the ext3 filesystem, so make sure that the ISO is stored in an ext2 filesystem.

gmt|uce

Hardware clock is set to GMT/UCE.

vga=normal

No-framebuffer mode, but X.

vga=ext

50-line TEXT mode.

dma

Enable DMA for all IDE drives.

home=scan

Set home directory. 'scan' will search for knoppix.img in the root of all partitions. To create a home directory, go to **K-menu -> Knoppix -> Configure -> Create persistent home directory**. Be careful when creating the home-dir; do *not* use the entire partition unless you know what you are doing. Other options could be home=/dev/hda1/knoppix.img home=/mnt/hda1/knoppix.img. If you are using a USB memory stick, typing **home=/dev/sda1/knoppix.img but home=scan** will probably do.

blind

Start Braille-Terminal (no X).

brltty=type,port,table

Parameters for Braille device. For more information on brltty parameters, see http://mielke.cc/brltty/guidelines.html.

alsa

Autoconfigure alsa for a PCI sound card.

alsa=es1938

Configure alsa for the snd-es1938.o-module PCI sound card.

testcd

Check CD data integrity. If your KNOPPIX CD makes strange noises during boot, or you see frequent errors like "cloop read error" or programs on your KDE desktop keep crashing randomly, your CD image is probably defective or incomplete, or your CD burner created a defective CD due to wrong writing speed or bad media. This is the most common error reported. Please boot with "knoppix testcd" to check if the CD is OK, and/or even better, verify the MD5 checksums that are present on the mirrors before writing the CD. Also, please read the KNOPPIX FAQ.

pnpbios=off

No PnP BIOS initialization.

acpi=off

Disable ACPI BIOS completely.

pci=bios

Workaround for bad PCI controllers.

knoppix_dir=KNOPPIX

Directory to search for on the CD.

knoppix_name=KNOPPIX

Cloop-File to search for on the CD.

Kernels

knoppix or linux

Default settings.

knoppix26 or linux26

Boot the 2.6 kernel for use with the new Knoppix 3.4 Edition.

knoppix26 acpi=off or linux26 acpi=off

Disable ACPI configuration in kernel 2.6.

knoppix-txt

No framebuffer at startup.

fb1280x1024 or fb1024x768 or fb800x600

Use fixed framebuffer graphics.

failsafe

Boot with (almost) no hardware detection.

expert

Interactive setup for experts. The "expert" mode provides a very simple and not yet well tested interface to loading additional Kernel modules from floppy disks (ext2 or vfat), plus interactive configuration of mouse/keyboard/soundcard/xserver. "Expert" mode supports the same boot options as "knoppix."

expert26

The same as for expert,   only with 2.6 kernel—Knoppix V3.4.

knoppix -b

Quick-and-dirty boot, almost no HW detection, only 1 VT; press **Enter** at root-password prompt and start typing commands. Good if you just need to fdisk IDE devices, activate a different partition for booting, DD stuff, and you are planning to reboot **Real Fast** after you're done. You can actually Alt-SysRQ-B safely (i.e., imme-diate reboot without worrying about shutting down nicely or anything else), because nothing is mounted r/w—not even swap. Also works on other Linux distros.

memtest

Run memtest86 instead of Linux—Knoppix V3.4.

The GNU General Public License

Version 2, June 1991

Copyright (C) 1989, 1991 Free Software Foundation, Inc.
59 Temple Place, Suite 330, Boston, MA 02111-1307 USA

Preamble

The licenses for most software are designed to take away your freedom to share and change it. By contrast, the GNU General Public License is intended to guarantee your freedom to share and change free software—to make sure the software is free for all its users. This General Public License applies to most of the Free Software Foundation's software and to any other program whose authors commit to using it. (Some other Free Software Foundation software is covered by the GNU Library General Public License instead.) You can apply it to your programs, too.

When we speak of free software, we are referring to freedom, not price. Our General Public Licenses are designed to make sure that you have the freedom to distribute copies of free software (and charge for this service if you wish), that you receive source code or can get it if you want it, that you can change the software or use pieces of it in new free programs; and that you know you can do these things.

To protect your rights, we need to make restrictions that forbid anyone to deny you these rights or to ask you to surrender the rights. These restrictions translate to certain responsibilities for you if you distribute copies of the software, or if you modify it.

For example, if you distribute copies of such a program, whether gratis or for a fee, you must give the recipients all the rights that you have. You must make sure that they, too, receive or can get the source code. And you must show them these terms so they know their rights.

We protect your rights with two steps: (1) copyright the software, and (2) offer you this license which gives you legal permission to copy, distribute and/or modify the software.

Also, for each author's protection and ours, we want to make certain that everyone understands that there is no warranty for this free software. If the software is modified by someone else and passed on, we want its recipients to know that what they have is not the original, so that any problems introduced by others will not reflect on the original authors' reputations.

Finally, any free program is threatened constantly by software patents. We wish to avoid the danger that redistributors of a free program will individually obtain patent licenses, in effect making the program proprietary. To prevent this, we have made it clear that any patent must be licensed for everyone's free use or not licensed at all.

The precise terms and conditions for copying, distribution and modification follow.

Terms and Conditions for Copying, Distribution and Modification

0. This License applies to any program or other work which contains a notice placed by the copyright holder saying it may be distributed under the terms of this General Public License. The "Program", below, refers to any such program or work, and a "work based on the Program" means either the Program or any derivative work under copyright law: that is to say, a work containing the Program or a portion of it, either verbatim or with modifications and/or translated into another language. (Hereinafter, translation is included without limitation in the term "modification".) Each licensee is addressed as "you".

    Activities other than copying, distribution and modification are not covered by this License; they are outside its scope. The act of running the Program is not restricted, and the output from the Program is covered only if its contents constitute a work based on the Program (independent of having been made by running the Program). Whether that is true depends on what the Program does.

1. You may copy and distribute verbatim copies of the Program's source code as you receive it, in any medium, provided that you conspicuously and appropriately publish on each copy an appropriate copyright notice and disclaimer of warranty; keep intact all the notices that refer to this License and to the absence of any warranty; and give any other recipients of the Program a copy of this License along with the Program.

    You may charge a fee for the physical act of transferring a copy, and you may at your option offer warranty protection in exchange for a fee.

2. You may modify your copy or copies of the Program or any portion of it, thus forming a work based on the Program, and copy and distribute such modifications or work under the terms of Section 1 above, provided that you also meet all of these conditions:

a) You must cause the modified files to carry prominent notices stating that you changed the files and the date of any change.

b) You must cause any work that you distribute or publish, that in whole or in part contains or is derived from the Program or any part thereof, to be licensed as a whole at no charge to all third parties under the terms of this License.

c) If the modified program normally reads commands interactively when run, you must cause it, when started running for such interactive use in the most ordinary way, to print or display an announcement including an appropriate copyright notice and a notice that there is no warranty (or else, saying that you provide a warranty) and that users may redistribute the program under these conditions, and telling the user how to view a copy of this License. (Exception: if the Program itself is interactive but does not normally print such an announcement, your work based on the Program is not required to print an announcement.)

These requirements apply to the modified work as a whole. If identifiable sections of that work are not derived from the Program, and can be reasonably considered independent and separate works in themselves, then this License, and its terms, do not apply to those sections when you distribute them as separate works. But when you distribute the same sections as part of a whole which is a work based on the Program, the distribution of the whole must be on the terms of this License, whose permissions for other licensees extend to the entire whole, and thus to each and every part regardless of who wrote it.

Thus, it is not the intent of this section to claim rights or contest your rights to work written entirely by you; rather, the intent is to exercise the right to control the distribution of derivative or collective works based on the Program.

In addition, mere aggregation of another work not based on the Program with the Program (or with a work based on the Program) on a volume of a storage or distribution medium does not bring the other work under the scope of this License.

3. You may copy and distribute the Program (or a work based on it, under Section 2) in object code or executable form under the terms of Sections 1 and 2 above provided that you also do one of the following:

a) Accompany it with the complete corresponding machine-readable source code, which must be distributed under the terms of Sections 1 and 2 above on a medium customarily used for software interchange; or,

b) Accompany it with a written offer, valid for at least three years, to give any third party, for a charge no more than your cost of physically per-forming source distribution, a complete machine-readable copy of the cor-responding source code, to be distributed under the terms of Sections 1 and 2 above on a medium customarily used for software interchange; or,

c) Accompany it with the information you received as to the offer to dis-tribute corresponding source code. (This alternative is allowed only for noncommercial distribution and only if you received the program in object code or executable form with such an offer, in accord with Subsection b above.)

The source code for a work means the preferred form of the work for making modifications to it. For an executable work, complete source code means all the source code for all modules it contains, plus any associated interface definition files, plus the scripts used to control compilation and installation of the executable. However, as a special exception, the source code distributed need not include anything that is normally distributed (in either source or binary form) with the major components (compiler, kernel, and so on) of the operating system on which the executable runs, unless that component itself accompanies the executable.

If distribution of executable or object code is made by offering access to copy from a designated place, then offering equivalent access to copy the source code from the same place counts as distribution of the source code, even though third parties are not compelled to copy the source along with the object code.

4. You may not copy, modify, sublicense, or distribute the Program except as expressly provided under this License. Any attempt otherwise to copy, modify, sublicense or distribute the Program is void, and will automatically terminate your rights under this License. However, parties who have received copies, or rights, from you under this License will not have their licenses terminated so long as such parties remain in full compliance.

5. You are not required to accept this License, since you have not signed it. However, nothing else grants you permission to modify or distribute the Program or its derivative works. These actions are prohibited by law if you do not accept this License. Therefore, by modifying or distributing the Program (or any work based on the Program), you indicate your acceptance of this License to do so, and all its terms and conditions for copying, distributing or modifying the Program or works based on it.

6. Each time you redistribute the Program (or any work based on the Program), the recipient automatically receives a license from the original licensor to copy, distribute or modify the Program subject to these terms and conditions. You may not impose any further restrictions on the recipients' exercise of the rights granted herein. You are not responsible for enforcing compliance by third parties to this License.

7. If, as a consequence of a court judgment or allegation of patent infringement or for any other reason (not limited to patent issues), conditions are imposed on you (whether by court order, agreement or otherwise) that contradict the conditions of this License, they do not excuse you from the conditions of this License. If you cannot distribute so as to satisfy simultaneously your obligations under this License and any other pertinent obligations, then as a consequence you may not distribute the Program at all. For example, if a patent license would not permit royalty-free redistribution of the Program by all those who receive copies directly or indirectly through you, then the only way you could satisfy both it and this License would be to refrain entirely from distribution of the Program.

    If any portion of this section is held invalid or unenforceable under any particular circumstance, the balance of the section is intended to apply and the section as a whole is intended to apply in other circumstances.

It is not the purpose of this section to induce you to infringe any patents or other property right claims or to contest validity of any such claims; this section has the sole purpose of protecting the integrity of the free software distribution system, which is implemented by public license practices. Many people have made generous contributions to the wide range of software distributed through that system in reliance on consistent application of that system; it is up to the author/donor to decide if he or she is willing to distribute software through any other system and a licensee cannot impose that choice.

This section is intended to make thoroughly clear what is believed to be a consequence of the rest of this License.

8. If the distribution and/or use of the Program is restricted in certain countries either by patents or by copyrighted interfaces, the original copyright holder who places the Program under this License may add an explicit geographical distribution limitation excluding those countries, so that distribution is permitted only in or among countries not thus excluded. In such case, this License incorporates the limitation as if written in the body of this License.

9. The Free Software Foundation may publish revised and/or new versions of the General Public License from time to time. Such new versions will be similar in spirit to the present version, but may differ in detail to address new problems or concerns.

Each version is given a distinguishing version number. If the Program specifies a version number of this License which applies to it and "any later version", you have the option of following the terms and conditions either of that version or of any later version published by the Free Software Foundation. If the Program does not specify a version number of this License, you may choose any version ever published by the Free Software Foundation.

10. If you wish to incorporate parts of the Program into other free programs whose distribution conditions are different, write to the author to ask for permission. For software which is copyrighted by the Free Software Foundation, write to the Free Software Foundation; we sometimes make exceptions for this. Our decision will be guided by the two goals of preserving the free status of all derivatives of our free software and of promoting the sharing and reuse of software generally.

NO WARRANTY

11.   BECAUSE THE PROGRAM IS LICENSED FREE OF CHARGE, THERE IS NO WARRANTY FOR THE PROGRAM, TO THE EXTENT PERMITTED BY APPLICABLE LAW. EXCEPT WHEN OTHERWISE STATED IN WRITING THE COPYRIGHT HOLDERS AND/OR OTHER PARTIES PROVIDE THE PROGRAM "AS IS" WITHOUT WARRANTY OF ANY KIND, EITHER EXPRESSED OR IMPLIED, INCLUDING, BUT NOT LIMITED TO, THE IMPLIED WARRANTIES OF MERCHANTABILITY AND FITNESS FOR A PARTICULAR PURPOSE. THE ENTIRE RISK AS TO THE QUALITY AND PERFORMANCE OF THE PROGRAM IS WITH YOU. SHOULD THE PROGRAM PROVE DEFECTIVE, YOU ASSUME THE COST OF ALL NECESSARY SERVICING, REPAIR OR CORRECTION.

12.   IN NO EVENT UNLESS REQUIRED BY APPLICABLE LAW OR AGREED TO IN WRITING WILL ANY COPYRIGHT HOLDER, OR ANY OTHER PARTY WHO MAY MODIFY AND/OR REDIS-TRIBUTE THE PROGRAM AS PERMITTED ABOVE, BE LIABLE TO YOU FOR DAMAGES, INCLUDING ANY GENERAL, SPECIAL, INCIDENTAL OR CONSEQUENTIAL DAMAGES ARISING OUT OF THE USE OR INABILITY TO USE THE PROGRAM (INCLUDING BUT NOT LIMITED TO LOSS OF DATA OR DATA BEING RENDERED INACCURATE OR LOSSES SUSTAINED BY YOU OR THIRD PARTIES OR A FAILURE OF THE PROGRAM TO OPERATE WITH ANY OTHER PROGRAMS), EVEN IF SUCH HOLDER OR OTHER PARTY HAS BEEN ADVISED OF THE POS-SIBILITY OF SUCH DAMAGES.

END OF TERMS AND CONDITIONS

How to Apply These Terms to Your New Programs

If you develop a new program, and you want it to be of the greatest possible use to the public, the best way to achieve this is to make it free software which everyone can redistribute and change under these terms.

To do so, attach the following notices to the program. It is safest to attach them to the start of each source file to most effectively convey the exclusion of warranty; and each file should have at least the "copyright" line and a pointer to where the full notice is found.

One line to give the program's name and a brief idea of what it does.
Copyright (C) <year> <name of author>

This program is free software; you can redistribute it and/or modify it under the terms of the GNU General Public License as published by the Free Software Foundation; either version 2 of the License, or (at your option) any later version.

This program is distributed in the hope that it will be useful, but WITHOUT ANY WARRANTY; without even the implied warranty of MERCHANTABILITY or FITNESS FOR A PARTICULAR PURPOSE. See the GNU General Public License for more details.

You should have received a copy of the GNU General Public License along with this program; if not, write to the Free Software Foundation, Inc., 59 Temple Place, Suite 330, Boston, MA 02111-1307 USA

Also add information on how to contact you by electronic and paper mail.

If the program is interactive, make it output a short notice like this when it starts in an interactive mode:

Gnomovision version 69, Copyright (C) year name of author Gnomovision comes with ABSOLUTELY NO WARRANTY; for details type `show w'. This is free software, and you are welcome to redistribute it under certain conditions; type `show c' for details.

The hypothetical commands `show w' and `show c' should show the appropriate parts of the General Public License. Of course, the commands you use may be called something other than `show w' and `show c'; they could even be mouse-clicks or menu items—whatever suits your program.

You should also get your employer (if you work as a programmer) or your school, if any, to sign a "copyright disclaimer" for the program, if necessary. Here is a sample; alter the names:

> Yoyodyne, Inc., hereby disclaims all copyright interest in the program `Gnomovision' (which makes passes at compilers) written by James Hacker. signature of Ty Coon, 1 April 1989
> Ty Coon, President of Vice

This General Public License does not permit incorporating your program into proprietary programs. If your program is a subroutine library, you may consider it more useful to permit linking proprietary applications with the library. If this is what you want to do, use the GNU Library General Public License instead of this License.

Appendix D

CD Contents at a Glance

Main Toolbar

Figure D.1 illustrates the main toolbar that appears when you boot the enclosed Live CD. The first five functions are outlined to help get you started.

Figure D.1 Main Toolbar

 This icon launches the Main Menu, giving you access to all of the features and applications on the Live CD.

 This icon launches a "bash" terminal. From this shell, you can launch applications and obtain or set other system information.

 This icon launches the Risc OS on x (ROX) filer, an explorer–style file navigator and manager.

 This icon launches the Firefox Web browser, which is used to view the portal sites listed in this appendix.

 This icon launches the XFLD-Welcome application, which provides shortcuts to the main features of the Live CD. This is a great place to start exploring the CD examples.

NOTE

There are four main applications that must be running on the Live CD in order for the examples to be available. They should start automatically at boot time; however, you might need to start them manually. These applications are:

- Apache Web Server
- Webmin Administration Server
- MySQL Database Server
- Nagios Monitoring Server

To start these applications, select the terminal icon to launch a bash shell. You must have administrative privileges (root rights) to perform the following tasks. You can "switch user" to root, as illustrated in the following example, followed by the command. You should choose the appropriate option from the list provided for what you wish to do:

- *su – root*
- */etc/init.d/apache2 [start | stop | restart]*
- */etc/init.d/webmin [start | stop | restart]*
- */etc/init.d/mysql [start | stop | restart]*
- */etc/init.d/nagios [start | stop | restart]*

BuiltRight Construction Site Index

This is the main site for the first sample company, accessed via the Firefox browser at *http://xfld/builtright.*

Main

The main category

Home Page

The main page and index

Portal

Access to the portal site; requires login

Launch Pad

This section launches applications that are not directly related to the BuiltRight Construction portal site.

The Other Side

Goes to the NuStuff Electronics portal site

Webmin Admin

Goes to the Webmin login page *https://xfld:10000*; login with *root/letmein*

Nagios Monitoring

Goes to the Nagios login page *http://xfld/nagios*; login with *nagios/letmein*

Reference

This section references the examples and links given in the book.

Bookmarks and Links

Links to all Web resources provided in the book

Knowledge Base

Sample Configurations

Sample configurations and code examples

Sample Workflow Diagrams

Workflow diagrams of activities and transitions:

- Account Setup Request
- Request Virtual Private Network (VPN) Access
- Policy Approval
- Oracle Change Request
- Infrastructure Change Request
- Firewall Change Request
- Data Access Request
- Bi-annual Information Technology (IT) Policy Review
- Annual Oracle Admin Review
- Account Termination Request
- Service Level Agreement (SLA) Approval

Wiki Templates

Wiki templates for portal examples:

- Policy template
- SLA template

Apache Webserver Example

Sample configurations for an Apache Webserver and Hypertext Preprocessor (PHP):

- Apache configuration file
- PHP configuration file

Nagios Configuration Files

- **apache.conf** Apache file
- **cgi.cfg** CGI script configurations
- **check_nagios_db** Checks the Nagios MySQL database
- **checkcommands.cfg** Commands that execute Nagios plug-ins
- **contactgroups.cfg** Groups of persons for notifications
- **contacts.cfg** Individual contact details for notifications
- **dependencies.cfg** Nagios-dependency relationships
- **escalations.cfg** Actions taken by Nagios in an exception state
- **hostgroups.cfg** Logical groups of hosts
- **hosts.cfg** Hosts that contain items to be monitored
- **htpasswd.users** Apache access file for simple logins
- **misccommands.cfg** Miscellaneous commands that are not plug-ins
- **nagios.cfg** Nagios main configuration file
- **resource.cfg** Resources available to Nagios
- **services.cfg** Items on hosts to be monitored
- **timeperiods.cfg** Time period definitions for escalations

NuStuff Electronics Site Index

This is the main site for the second sample company, accessed via the Firefox browser at *http://xfld/builtright*.

Main

The main category

Home Page

Main page and index

Portal

Access to the portal site; requires login

Launch Pad

This section launches other applications not directly related to the NuStuff Electronics portal site.

The Other Side

Takes you to the BuiltRight Construction portal site

Webmin Admin

Takes you to the Webmin login page *https://xfld:10000*; login with *root/letmein*

Nagios Monitoring

Takes you to the Nagios login page *http://xfld/nagios*; login with *root/letmein*

Reference

This is the reference section for examples and links given in the book.

Bookmarks and Links

Links to all Web resources provided in the book

Knowledge Base

Sample Configurations

Sample configurations and code examples

Sample Workflow Diagrams

Workflow diagrams of activities and transitions

- Account Setup Request
- Request VPN Access
- Policy Approval
- Oracle Change Request
- Infrastructure Change Request
- Firewall Change Request
- Data Access Request
- Bi-Annual IT Policy Review
- Annual Oracle Admin Review
- Account Termination Request
- SLA Approval

Wiki Templates

Wiki templates for portal examples:

- Policy template
- SLA template

LDAP Authentication Cluster Example

adminhost.nustuff.com – administration host

- *named.conf* Domain Name System (DNS) master configuration file
- *example.hosts* DNS Master Zone file
- *slapd.conf* Lightweight Directory Access Protocol (LDAP) master file
- *smb.conf* Samba Primary Domain Controller (PDC)

node1.nustuff.com – node1 of authentication cluster

- *ha.cf* Heartbeat main configuration file
- *haresources* Heartbeat resource file
- *authkeys* Heartbeat authentication configuration

- *slapd.conf* LDAP1 slave configuration
- *ldap1* LDAP1 init.d script
- *start.sh* LDAP1 start script
- *stop.sh* LDAP1 stop script
- *status.sh* LDAP1 status script
- *smb.conf* Samba domain Backup Domain Controller (BDC) configuration
- *smb* Samba init.d script
- *start.sh* Samba start script
- *stop.sh* Samba stop script
- *status.sh* Samba status script
- *dhcpd.conf* Dynamic Host Control Protocol (DHCP) with Dynamic DNS configuration file
- *dhcpd* DHCP init.d script
- *start.sh* DHCP start script
- *stop.sh* DHCP stop script
- *status.sh* DHCP status script

node2.nustuff.com – node2 of authentication cluster

- *ha.cf* Heartbeat main configuration file
- *haresources* Heartbeat resource file
- *authkeys* Heartbeat authentication configuration
- *slapd.conf* LDAP2 slave configuration
- *ldap2* LDAP2 *init.d* script
- *start.sh* LDAP2 *start* script
- *stop.sh* LDAP2 *stop* script
- *status.sh* LDAP2 *status* script
- *named.conf* DNS slave configuration file
- *named* DNS *init* script

- ***start*** - DNS *start* script
- ***stop*** - DNS *start* script
- ***status*** - DNS *status* script

Nagios Configuration Files

- ***apache.conf*** Apache file
- ***cgi.cfg*** CGI script configurations
- ***check_nagios_db*** Checks the Nagios MySQL database
- ***checkcommands.cfg*** Commands that execute Nagios plug-ins
- ***contactgroups.cfg*** Groups of persons for notifications
- ***contacts.cfg*** Individual contact details for notifications
- ***dependencies.cfg*** Nagios dependency relationships
- ***escalations.cfg*** Actions taken by Nagios in an exception state
- ***hostgroups.cfg*** Logical groups of hosts
- ***hosts.cfg*** Hosts that contain items to be monitored
- ***htpasswd.users*** Apache access file for simple logins
- ***misccommands.cfg*** Miscellaneous commands that are not plug-ins
- ***nagios.cfg*** Nagios main configuration file
- ***resource.cfg*** Resources available to Nagios
- ***services.cfg*** Items on hosts to be monitored
- ***timeperiods.cfg*** Time period definitions for escalations

Index

Numerals

404 Section, 3, 60–61, 95–96, 265, 275

A

Acceptance, 220
Account creation and maintenance policy, 129, 131
Account management, 203
Account request processes, 210–213
Acquisition for COBIT, 37, 147–148
Active Directory (Microsoft), 201
Ad-Aware malware and spyware remover, 202
Address Book application, 20
Addresses, virtual, 192
Admin application, 19
Administrative access control policy, 128, 130
Administrator roles, 206
Administrators, Sarbanes–Oxley effect on, 7
AMANDA (Advanced Maryland Automatic Network Disk Archiver) backup system, 67–68
Antivirus scanners, 202
Application development
  closed source, 83–87
  open source, 87–96
Application requirements
  closed source, 84–85
  open source, 88–89
Applications, 19–24
Applications and tools, 62–69, 79–80
Architecture, information, 115–116
Architecture, platform-agnostic, 94

Assessing risk, 118
Astaro Security Linux, 65
Audit trails design, 148–149
Authentication, 198–201
Automation
  categories, 155
  identifying, 148–149
  monitoring, 226
  need for, 60–61, 146
Availability, high, 192–194
AVG antivirus scanner, 202
Avoiding COBIT controls, 112

B

Backup and restore policy, 128, 130–131
Bacula network-based backup program, 68
Badging policy, 129, 131
Beta testing, 86
Big Brother host and service monitor, 66
Bookmarks application, 23
BSD license, 83
Bug fixes
  closed source, 86–87
  open source, 90–91
Building access and badging policy, 129, 131
BuiltRight Construction example
  access by auditor, 70–71
  compliance policy, 73–76
  corporate policy documents, 128–130
  description, 99–100
  employees, auditors, and IT consultants, 126

password, 127
portal, 16
web server migration, 155–156,
    160–161
see also Policy management
Business case for open source, 91–96

C

Calendar application, 20
Capacity management, 179
Categories of COBIT controls, 63
CD. *see* FastTrack CD
CEOs, Sarbanes-Oxley effect on, 7
CFOs
  in example companies, 134–135
  perspectives, 4, 32, 61, 120, 147,
    224, 265
  review of evidence, 72
Change management
  approval workflow, 157–160
  control objectives, 63, 80
  firewall change request, 165–166
  Oracle change request, 166–168
  policy, 128, 130
Changing the Live CD, 10
"Cheat Code" parameter, 9–10,
    298–304
Chief executive officers. *see* CEOs
Chief financial officers. *see* CFOs
CIOs (chief information officers)
  origins of, 33–34
  Sarbanes-Oxley effect on, 7
ClamAV antivirus scanner, 202
ClamWin antivirus scanner, 202
Closed-loop process, 224
Closed source application
    development
  application requirements, 84–85
  bug fixes, 86–87

customer beta testing, 86
debugging, 86
diagram, 84
regression testing, 86
release, 86
support cycle, 86–87
system design, 85–86
"Closed" Wiki page state, 133
COBIT (Control Objectives for
    Information and Related
    Technology)
  components, 35–36
  controls, full list of, 282–296
  controls, partial list of, 38–45
  customizing, 139
  description, 34–35
  domains, 37
  information sources, 57
  reasons for using, 140
  Sarbanes-Oxley, distinction from,
    113, 120, 153
  scope, review, and enforcement, 72
  see also Controls, COBIT
Communicating management goals,
    117–118
Compensating for faults, 190–191
Compliance
  reasons for, 61–62, 79, 264
  requirements, 51
  resistance to, 69–70, 220
  workflows, 237–243
Configuration
  backup policy, 129, 131
  executables and daemons, 192–193
  management, 182–183, 206–207
  monitoring, 232–234
  Nagios, 235–236
  samples, 214–215
  workflows, 245

Containment of faults, 190
Control matrix, 268–270
Control Objectives for Information
    and Related Technology. *see*
    COBIT
Controls, COBIT
    avoiding, 112
    categories, 63
    choosing among, 45–50
    full list, 282–296
    objectives, 36
    partial list, 38–45
    simplicity, 50
    small and medium-sized companies,
        226
    working the list, 120–121, 153, 185,
        227–228
Cost of open source application
    development, 91–92, 93
CRON scheduling, 258
Customer assistance, 182
Customer beta testing, 86
Customer satisfaction, 226–227
Cycles
    Deming, 225–226, 261
    PDCA (plan, do, check, and act),
        225–226
    quality control process, 77
    support, 86–87

D

Daemon configuration, 192–193
Data and storage security, 201–202
Data backup and restore policy, 128,
    130–131
Data management, 183–184, 206–208
Data restoration process, 213
Debugging
    closed source, 86

open source, 90–91
Deficiencies
    addressing, 145–146
    not uncommon, 280
Delivery for COBIT, 37, 177–178
Deming, W. Edwards, 225
Deming cycle, 225–226, 261
Disclaimer, 5–6
Distribution vendors, 92
Documentation, 164
Domain name service, round-robin,
    194–195

E

Education, 181–182
eGroupWare, 16–19, 21, 23
Email application, 20
Enforcement in COBIT, 72
Entity level controls, 36
Environmental factors, 184
Environmental policy, 130, 132
Examples. *see* BuiltRight
        Construction example; NuStuff
        Electronics example; XYZ
        Sprockets example
Executables, configuration of,
        192–193
Expertise, in-house. *see* In-house
        expertise
External requirements, 118

F

Facilities management, 184
FastTrack CD
    changing, 10
    "Cheat Code" parameter, 10
    description, 8–9
    documentation, 164

employees, auditors, and IT
    consultants, 126
firewall change request, 165–166
General Public License (GPL), 28
hard-disk safety, 125
installing, 11–16
intrusion detection implementation,
    156–157
list of other Live CDs, 29
Oracle change request, 166–168
passwords, 18, 127
project management, 153–154
running, 9
sample configurations, 214–215
security and operations workflows,
    210–214
service level agreements (SLAs),
    208–209
test environment, 162–163
web server migration, 155–156
Webmin interface, 209–210
Fault tolerance, 189–192
Finance directors, Sarbanes-Oxley
    effect on, 7
FireStarter firewall, 198
Firewall and intrusion detection
    policy, 128, 131
Firewall change request, 165–166
Firewalls, 198
Forms, 139
    control matrix, 268–270
    "Gap and Remediation," 268–272
    test plan, 272–275
Fud Forum application, 21

G

"Gap and Remediation" form,
    268–272
General Public License (GPL), 28, 82,
    305–314

getfacl utility, 201–202
GNU General Public License (GPL),
    28, 82, 305–314
Goals of Sarbanes-Oxley Act, 32–33
GPL (General Public License), 28, 82,
    305–314

H

Heartbeat, Linux-HA, 66–67
Heartbeat mechanism, 194
Heartbeat project, 192
High availability, 192–194
High-Availability Linux Project, 192
History of Sarbanes-Oxley Act, 32
Home application, 19
Human resources, 118
Hydra backup system, 68

I

Implementation, excessive, 172
Implementation for COBIT, 37
In-house expertise
    deficiencies, addressing, 145–146
    deployment and support
        proficiency, 143–145
    development, 92
    evaluating, 142–143
InfoLog application, 20
Information architecture, 115–116
Information resources
    financial aspects of compliance, 28
    open source development, 109
    Wiki collaboration, 140
Infrastructure, technological, 116
Infrastructure assessment, 96
Installing the Live CD, 11–16
Internal control adequacy, 227
Intrusion detection

implementation, 156–157, 161–163
policy, 128, 131
Investment, IT, 117
IP addresses, virtual, 192
IT consultants, Sarbanes-Oxley effect on, 7
IT directors, Sarbanes-Oxley effect on, 7
IT investment, 117
IT organization and relationships, 116–117
IT planning, strategic, 115
ITIL (IT Infrastructure Library), 34

K

Kerberos authentication protocol, 69, 200–201
Kiwi CatTools application, 234
Knoppix Live CD project. *see* Live CD
Knowledge Base application, 23

L

Launch Pad application, 18
LDAP (Lightweight Directory Access Protocol)
description, 200
flexibility, 131
load balancing, 194–197
logs, 208
security, 180
Lesser GNU Public License (LPGL), 83
Licenses, 28, 82–83
Lightweight Directory Access Protocol. *see* LDAP
Linux
distributions, 96–97
ease of use, 110

return on investment (ROI), 280
Linux-HA Heartbeat, 66–67
Linux Logical Volume Management (LVM) kernel module, 193
Linux Virtual Server project, 194, 196
List, working the, 120–121, 153, 185, 227–228
Live CD. *see* FastTrack CD
Load balancing, 194–197
Logical access, control objectives for, 63
LPGL (Lesser GNU Public License), 83
LVM (Linux Logical Volume Management) kernel module, 193

M

m0n0wall firewall, 198
Malicious software policy, 129, 131, 181
Malware removers, 202
Management
accounts, 203
configuration, 182–183, 206–207
data, 183–184, 206–208
facilities, 184
goals, communicating, 117–118
operations, 184–185
performance and capacity, 179
problems and incidents, 183
projects, 118–119, 153–154, 172
quality, 119
Marketing items, 265–266
Masking of faults, 190
Metasploit, 162
Metzman, Gustav, 112
Microsoft Active Directory, 201
Migration

Section 404, 95–96
web server, 155–156, 160–161
Modified BSD license, 83
Monitoring
  automating, 226
  COBIT domain description, 37, 224
  configuration, 232–234
  control objectives for, 63, 66–68
  Nagios, 66, 228–232, 234–237, 243–244
  policy, 129, 131
  thresholds, 262

N

Nagios monitoring application, 66, 228–232, 234–237, 243–244
Network device configuration backup policy, 129, 131
Network Information Systems (NIS), 200
Network security, 197–198
Network security monitoring and controls policy, 129, 131
New-user account creation and maintenance policy, 129, 131
New-user password policy, 129, 131
News Admin application, 23
NIS (Network Information Systems), 200
"Not Submitted" Wiki page state, 133
NuStuff Electronics example
  corporate policy documents, 130–132
  description, 101–104
  employees, auditors, and IT consultants, 126
  financial summary, 122

intrusion detection implementation, 156–157, 161–163
IT functional chart, 124
IT organizational chart, 123
password, 127
single-page strategy, 121
see also Policy management

O

Open source application development
  application requirements, 88–89
  attackers, 110
  bug fixes, 90–91
  business case, 91–96
  cost, 91–92, 93
  debugging, 90–91
  description, 87
  diagram, 88
  distribution vendors, 92
  freedom in choice, 94
  in-house development, 92
  information resources, 109
  migration, 95–96
  mixed platforms, 95
  platform-agnostic architecture, 94
  project developers, 92
  release, 90–91
  return on investment (ROI), 280
  system design, 89–90
  Windows operating system, 94–95
Open source licenses, 82
Open source tools, 172
Operating systems
  password control policy, 130
  security policy, 130, 132
Operations
  management, 184–185
  workflows, 210–214

Opportunities, 33–34
Oracle accounts and passwords, 129, 131
Oracle change request, 166–168
Organization, IT, 116–117
Organization for COBIT, 37
Origin of Sarbanes-Oxley Act, 32
Overimplementation, 172

P

PAM authentication mechanism, 69
Panda ActiveScan antivirus scanner, 202
Passwords
   construction guidelines, 74–75
   control policy, 131
   FastTrack CD, 18, 127
   policies, Oracle, 129, 131
   policies, Windows, 130
   policy enforcement, 204–205
   protection standards, 72, 75
Patton, George, 112
PDCA (plan, do, check, and act)
   COBIT description, 76
   Deming cycle, 225–226
"Pending" Wiki page state, 133
Performance assessment, 226
Performance management, 179
Personal processes, 71
Physical building access and badging
   policy, 129, 131
Planning
   for COBIT, 37, 114–115
   strategic IT planning, 115
Planning committee, 39, 47, 116, 120
Platform-agnostic architecture, 94
Policy approval workflow, 133–136
Policy management

corporate policy documents, 128–132
description, 127
policies, defining, 132
policy approval workflow, 133–136
Portals, 16–24
Power supply, uninterruptible, 184
Pregnancy analogy, 5
Problems and incidents, 183
Process flow, 267–268
Processes, personal, 71
Project management, 118–119, 153–154, 172
Projects application, 21

Q

Quality control process cycle, 77
Quality management, 119

R

Reference application, 18
Regression testing, 86
Relationships, IT, 116–117
Release, application
   closed source, 86
   open source, 90–91
Repairing faults, 191
Reporting viruses and spyware, 213–214
Requirements, external, 118
Resistance, 69–70
Resources, human, 118
Resources, information. see
   Information resources
Responsibilities of officers, 7
Return on investment (ROI), 275–277
Review in COBIT, 72

Risk assessment, 118

ROI (return on investment), 275–277

Round-robin domain name service, 194–195

Running the Live CD, 9

S

Samba NTLM encrypted security, 68

Sample configurations, 214–215

Sarbanes-Oxley (SOX) Act

　COBIT, distinction from, 113, 120, 153

　origin (history), 32

　responsibilities of officers, 7

　statistics, 4–5

Satisfaction, customer, 226–227

Scheduling, 258

Scope

　of audit, 113–114

　in COBIT, 72

Section 404, 3, 60–61, 95–96, 265, 275

Security

　account management, 203

　administrator roles, 206

　authentication, 198–201

　control objectives, 63

　data and storage, 201–202

　delivery and support domain, 180–181

　enterprise identity management, 198–201

　monitoring and controls policy, 129, 131

　network, 197–198

　password policy enforcement, 204–205

　permissions, 201

　policy, operating system, 130, 132

　server room policy, 132

　systems and applications, 203–206

　workflows, 210–214

Sentinel fast file scanner, 66

Server migration, 155–156, 160–161

Server room

　access policy, 129, 132

　environmental policy, 130, 132

　security policy, 132

Service level agreements (SLAs)

　delivery and support, 37

　description, 186–187

　elements, 187–188

　FastTrack CD, 208–209

　internal, 188–189

　managing, 178

　need for, 220–221

setfacl utility, 201–202

Shared storage, 193

Shoot the Other Node in the Head (STONITH) device, 194

Shorewall firewall, 64–65, 198

SiteManager, 17–18, 23

Six Sigma, 34

SLAs. *see* Service level agreements (SLAs)

Small and medium-sized companies, 226

Smoothwall firewall, 65, 198

Snort intrusion detection system, 65–66, 161–163

SOX. *see* Sarbanes-Oxley (SOX) Act

Spybot-SandD malware and spyware remover, 202

Spyware removers, 202

Spyware reporting, 213–214

Statistics, 4–5

Steering committee, 39, 47, 116, 120

STONITH (Shoot the Other Node in the Head) device, 194

Storage, shared, 193
Storage security, 201–202
Strategic IT planning, 115
Support cycle, 86–87
Support for COBIT, 37, 177–178
Sustainability, 50–52
Switches, 256
`syslog, 236–237
System design
  closed source, 85–86
  open source, 89–90
System security policy, 130, 132

T

Technological infrastructure, 116
Test environment, 162–163
Test plan, 272–275
Third-party services, 42–44, 49–50,
  149, 178–179, 209–210
Tools and applications, 62–69, 79–80
Training, 181–182
Tripwire system integrity checker, 66
Turcotte, Stewart, 112

U

Ultra Monkey Load Balancing and
  High-Availability project, 197
Uninterruptible power supply, 184

V

Vendors, 92
Virtual IP addresses, 192
Virtual Private Networks (VPNs),
  214
Virus reporting, 213–214
VPNs (Virtual Private Networks),
  214

W

Web server migration, 155–156,
  160–161
Web sites. *see* Information resources
Webmin interface, 209–210
Wiki
  application, 21, 127, 132–133
  collaboration, 140
  integration with workflows, 258
  page header and footer, 22–23
Wikipedia, 93
Windows operating system, 94–95
Workflow application, 24
Workflows
  change management approval,
    157–160
  compliance, 237–243
  configuration, 245
  developing, 244–245
  example, 245–255
  file uploading, 257
  operations, 210–214
  policy approval, 133–136
  security, 210–214
  security and operations, 210–214
  switches, 256
  testing, 255
  Wiki integration, 258
Working the list, 120–121, 153, 185,
  227–228

X

XYZ Sprockets example
  acquisition and implementation, 48
  control objectives, 47
  delivery and support, 48–49
  infrastructure, 45–46
  monitoring and evaluation, 49–50
  planning and organization, 47–48

Syngress: *The Definition of a Serious Security Library*

Syn·gress (sin-gres): *noun, sing.* Freedom from risk or danger; safety. See *security*.

How to Cheat at IT Project Management
Susan Snedaker

Most IT projects fail to deliver – on average, all IT projects run over schedule by 82%, run over cost by 43% and deliver only 52% of the desired functionality. Pretty dismal statistics. Using the proven methods in this book, every IT project you work on from here on out will have a much higher likelihood of being on time, on budget and higher quality. This book provides clear, concise, information and hands-on training to give you immediate results. And, the companion Web site provides dozens of templates for managing IT projects.

ISBN: 1-59749-037-7
Price: $44.95 US $62.95 CAN

Windows to Linux Migration Toolkit
David Allen

Linux to Windows Migration Toolkit is a unique book that offers a complete solution for IT managers and sysadmins to migrate from Windows to Linux. It provides migration process planning, automated migration scripts, anti-virus / anti-spam solutions, and specific migration and deployment details for all relevant technologies. The CD includes valuable automated scripts for migrating any flavor of Windows to Linux.

ISBN: 1-931836-39-6
Price: $49.95 US $72.95 CAN

Network Security Evaluation Using the NSA IEM
Russ Rogers, Ed Fuller, Greg Miles, Matthew Hoagberg, Travis Schack, Chuck Little, Ted Dykstra, Bryan Cunningham

Finally, a book that gives you everything you need to provide the most comprehensive technical security posture evaluation for any organization! The NSA's recommended methodology is described in depth, leading you through each step in providing customers with analysis customized to their organization. From setting scope and legal coordination to the final report and trending metrics, this book has it all.

ISBN: 1-59749-035-0
Price: $59.95 U.S. $83.95 CAN